History in Blue

160 Years of Women Police, Sheriffs, Detectives, and State Troopers

Allan T. Duffin

KAPLAN

PUBLISHING

New York

© 2010 by Allan T. Duffin

Published by Kaplan Publishing, a division of Kaplan, Inc.
1 Liberty Plaza, 24th Floor
New York, NY 10006

Grateful acknowledgment is made to the following for permission to use the following:
Photograph on page 185 reprinted by permission of Lucille Burrascano.
Photo on page 204 reprinted by permission of Lynda R. Castro.
Photograph on page 218 reprinted by permission of Julia P. Grimes.

Library of Congress Cataloging-in-Publication Data

Duffin, Allan T.
    History in blue: 160 years of women police, sheriffs, detectives, and state troopers / Allan Duffin.
        p. cm.
    Includes bibliographical references and index.
    ISBN 978-1-60714-626-1
    1. Policewomen--United States--History. I. Title.
    HV8023.D84 2009
    363.20973--dc22
                                            2009023220

Printed in the United States of America

10 9 8 7 6 5 4 3 2 1

ISBN: 978-1-60714-626-1

Kaplan Publishing books are available at special quantity discounts to use for sales promotions, employee premiums, or educational purposes. For more information or to purchase books, please call the Simon & Schuster special sales department at 866-506-1949.

DEDICATION

For Michele

and also for Max, Pollie, and Honeymoon

CONTENTS

INTRODUCTION

I<small>T'S</small> <small>BRIGHT AND EARLY</small>—five o'clock in the morning. A police officer pulls his car into the parking lot behind the station house. The sun is beginning to peek over the city. He wishes he'd gotten a few more hours of sleep. He heads into the building, waving at several other officers who are also reporting for their shift.

The metal door creaks on its hinges as he steps inside. His shoes click on the floor—linoleum as far as the eye can see, white and black with a slight yellow tinge, burnished to a scruffy shine. The smell of coffee wafts down the hallway. He grabs himself a cup from the rattling coffeemaker. Takes a sip. At least it doesn't taste like shale oil today.

A bit later, dressed in a crisp uniform, gun belt buckled low over his hips, he heads into the briefing room for roll call. His supervisor stands in front, glancing at his notes on the podium. He grabs a chair at a table next to his partner, pulls out his notepad and pen, perches his coffee in front of him.

There's a low murmur going through the room. He looks around. His fellow cops are talking to one another in hushed tones, occasionally glancing toward the front corner of the room. He looks over, but several officers block his view. Just what is so damn interesting? Finally, the officers move away and he can see what the fuss is about.

Sitting alone at a table in the front is a new officer. The uniform's the same, the hair is short—but there's something he hasn't seen before.

The new officer is a woman.

Over the years this became a familiar scene as female police officers showed up in squad rooms across the country. Women in previously all-male police departments. Women working a patrol beat. Women partnered with male officers.

How long has it taken for women to become equal players in police departments across the United States? The answer is short and revealing: It hasn't quite happened yet. But as each decade rolls by, female officers make a little more progress in their quest for acceptance and respect in a job that is unique in its challenges, both inside and outside the office. By signing on the dotted line and taking an oath, police officers promise to sacrifice many of their own needs for the greater good. Over time the idea of women wearing police badges has been hotly debated, joked about, deflected outright—and eventually, reluctantly, given its due.

While I was writing the book you're now reading, I was often asked, "Where did you get the idea to do a book about policewomen?" As with a lot of neat ideas, this one popped into my head while I was in the middle of something else. I had co-produced a television documentary about the military police, and one of the segments dealt with the first women who broke into the previously all-male ranks of the Army's MP corps. I wondered about policewomen in the civilian world—had anyone documented *their* stories?

Curious, I looked for books on the subject and found that a small group of authors had done great work detailing the basic history of female cops and chiefs in the United States, delving into various published studies, gathering oral histories of officers past and present. Most of the existing texts leaned toward the academic rather than the cultural—not necessarily the kind of books for a general readership. *More people need to read about this,* I thought.

So why was there so little information available about such a riveting subject? Social historian Janis Appier had one possible answer: "Historical scholarship on policewomen is generally sparse and limited in scope, largely because, until 1970, women composed only about 1 percent of all sworn personnel in the United States."

It made sense: less activity, less to tell.

Although women were involved, however peripherally, in law enforcement as far back as the mid-1800s, they remained a novelty in the career field for many years. At first they were restricted to what was then defined as "women's work"—caring for female prisoners, helping runaway children and delinquents, patrolling department stores and dance halls. The attitude of the public and the media reinforced existing social roles and blocked women officers from moving up the ranks.

But once the 1970s kicked into gear, changes in federal law helped boost the number of female police officers across the country. Since then the number of women in law enforcement has crept upward slowly, to its current level of about 13 percent.[2] It is still a small number—and it took a century and a half to get there. Along with the increase in numbers came wider-ranging publicity, an expanded scope of responsibility on the job, and an increasing number of sexual discrimination lawsuits.

Many newspaper reports made light of policewomen's achievements. This attitude was prevalent even as late as the 1980s. *Look, they wear pants instead of skirts! They can drive! They carry guns! Isn't that interesting?* Complementing such affected swooning were the questions that had haunted women in the workforce for ages: Were women too emotional for the job? Could they handle the physical requirements? Wouldn't it be awkward if they worked side by side with men? How would the public react? As a consequence, many police

departments road-blocked female candidates by establishing requirements that were difficult or impossible for them to meet: a minimum
height of five foot nine, a minimum weight more suitable to a man, a
requirement for a college degree when men didn't need one.

Even as male-dominated law enforcement organizations stacked
bricks in front of them, many women remained undeterred. They
put on pounds to meet the minimum weight, filed equal opportunity lawsuits, and applied for jobs over and over again, confident
that things would change. And each woman who passed an entrance
examination and navigated her way through the police academy
knocked down some of those bricks—and paved the way for more
women to do the same.

I wanted to celebrate this courage. But while documenting
changes in social attitudes, I also wanted to examine the dark side
of the story: deaths on duty, rocky relationships among coworkers,
women who tried but couldn't make it for one reason or another. So
for *History in Blue: 160 Years of Women Police, Sheriffs, Detectives,
and State Troopers*, I decided to construct a history by using personal
stories as the building blocks. The book is written from a decidedly
cultural perspective, told in the voices of the women who battled
their way into a traditionally male career field, making sacrifices in
order to do the job they loved.

To find the most interesting stories to tell, I interviewed active
and retired law enforcement officers and combed through archival
information and thousands of newspapers large and small. Sometimes the most interesting stories were buried in tiny type in the corner of a back page of a local newspaper. With regard to stories whose
principals are no longer with us, I took some light artistic license to
help bring the women's voices to life.

Because it would be impossible to cover every city, county, and state law enforcement organization in the United States, this book focuses primarily on municipal police forces—the cops who patrol the nation's cities and towns. Here and there we'll also meet members of the highway patrol, county sheriff's departments, and subject-specific groups like the transit police and park patrol.

While I'm talking about different types of law enforcement organizations, a word too about job titles: Although the word *policewoman* has officially gone out of style in municipal departments—which have adopted the unisex term *police officer*—I use it in this book as a general word. This and other antiquated terms such as *patrolman*—which some departments labeled female officers until a better designation was established—all signify the standard beat cop who watches over an assigned area in his or her city or town. Broadening our reach, *sheriff's deputies* might cover a county and other areas that a municipal police force does not. On the state level, *highway patrol officers* and *troopers*—different states use different naming systems—guard the highways and areas not covered by local and county cops. Regardless of the title, however, the responsibilities are similar.

My goal in this book is to tell stories that resonate strongly with the reader, and to place those stories in perspective along a historical time line. I explore a variety of themes and issues. From a psychological perspective, I investigate the notion that female officers were supposedly better than male officers at dealing with female suspects, wayward girls, and children—and therefore became "keepers of morality" within their communities. How did the assumption that women possess such qualities as empathy and intuition help define the job responsibilities of female officers?

In addition, I discuss key events in history with regard to how they helped or hindered the progress of the policewoman. From the time suffragists worked to secure the vote for women, to the time the federal government pushed to guarantee equal employment opportunities in police departments across the nation, policewomen were the subject of many a debate. Many key factors—the proliferation of bootleg liquor during Prohibition, the scarcity of men on the home front during the two World Wars, antiprostitution efforts, the growth of gang violence and the drug trade—helped expand the role of the policewoman and made her existence all the more important. The civil rights movement, the sexual revolution, and equal rights legislation all chipped away at the prejudices and stereotypes that had held policewomen back for decades.

I also note that, even with such progress, female officers still faced an uphill battle for recognition from male officers, members of the media, and the public at large, many of whom weren't quite sure how to deal with a woman in uniform. Federal laws designed to protect female officers on the job were difficult to enforce because they relied on individual departments that often had male supervisors who fought to keep the "boys' club" atmosphere intact. Differences in race, class, and sexual orientation often added fuel to the fire. While female officers struggled to convince the public to take them seriously on the streets, within the station houses they had to deal with male officers who saw them as second-class employees, harrassment in the form of rude comments and practical jokes, and few opportunities for promotion—if there were any at all. Angry dissenters felt that female officers were unfit for the job and were physically incapable of performing the duties of a cop, and even accused the officers of cowardice while on duty. One male supervisor went so far as to say that women should be barred from becoming police officers simply *because* of the discrimination they would face on the job.

The stereotypes lasted a long time: Female officers were assigned to administrative roles, jail duty, and other types of so-called "women's work." Basic things that male cops took for granted—the power to arrest a suspect, the authority to patrol a beat, the ability to drive a squad car while on duty—were not a part of the female officer's original repertoire.

Finally, this book examines the tools and technology of the job, including uniforms, firearms training, bulletproof vests and other protective gear, and methods of transportation such as squad cars and motorcycles. None of these items—each one critical to an officer's survival and effectiveness—were originally provided to female officers.

The police organizations of the early 21st century—which comprise some 650,000 officers across more than 13,000 municipalities, counties, and states—still grapple with issues that have interfered with women's maneuverability in the law enforcement field since the idea of hiring local policewomen first took flight in the late 1800s. I hope that this book is a good partner to other publications about female police officers and that it effectively adds to our body of knowledge about the courageous pioneers in uniform who continue to make history, day after day.

*Put a woman in a station house under salary and she'll be
trying to run [the] precinct inside of three months.*
>   —The New York Doorman's Association, upon the
>   announcement that women would be hired as
>   police matrons[1]

CHAPTER I

Limited Duties, Little Respect (1845–1900)

How LONG DOES it take to make significant progress in a career
field—to be given more responsibility, to be promoted for good performance, to be entrusted with the same duties as others in the same
job? For female police officers, who had to battle their way toward
some semblance of equality with their male counterparts in uniform,
it was a long wait—well over a hundred years. As early as the 1840s,
when six prison matrons were appointed in New York City to watch
over women inmates at the city prison and on Blackwell's Island
(later known as Roosevelt Island), in the East River, women in law
enforcement were only grudgingly allowed to serve in cities across
the nation. They had to fight repeatedly for the right to patrol the
streets. Their early responsibilities were limited to enforcing laws in
dance halls, skating rinks, pool halls, movie theaters, and other places
of amusement frequented by women and children. Debate raged in

city governments, in police departments, and among the public over whether female officers should be allowed to wear uniforms, carry weapons, be given arrest authority, or earn promotion to higher rank.

Much of the resistance to handing women law enforcement powers arose from the traditional understanding of the female role in American society. Historian Nell Irvin Painter has noted that, during the mid-1800s and beyond, "women were said to be the weaker, gentler sex whose especial duty was the creation of an orderly and harmonious private sphere for husbands and children. Respectable women, 'true women,' did not participate in debates on public issues and did not attract attention to themselves."[2] Although a growing number of women were entering the workforce—by 1900, some 21 percent of women over 16 years of age had jobs—they usually became teachers, salesclerks, millworkers, and domestic servants.

Nevertheless, women across the United States—whether casual observers or determined feminists—found strength in numbers as they questioned the status quo. Early efforts crystallized at a convention in Seneca Falls, New York, in 1848, where a slim majority of the women (and men) in attendance approved the Declaration of Sentiments, which denounced the "absolute tyranny" of men in such areas as voting, marriage and divorce, property rights, employment, religion, and moral behavior. Armed with a fresh outlook on their future, women's rights activists set out to rewrite the rules, both literally and figuratively, for women in American society.

The concept of the policewoman evolved very slowly, beginning with early efforts to provide care and direction to female convicts in the prison system. During the 19th century, people convicted of crimes—male and female alike—were piled into facilities of varying quality whose all-male staffs supervised their daily lives. Rather than being mixed with the male prisoners, the female prisoners were usually placed in separate quarters, ranging from common areas to individual cells to inconvenient cubbyholes that barely resembled cells at all. Some female convicts endured strip searches, rapes, and other types of abuse at the hands of the men running the prisons—and at the hands of the male inmates as well.

Citizen advocacy went a long way toward improving the lives of female prisoners. Aghast at the horrible conditions, reformers from organizations such as churches and women's clubs arrived in the jails to provide guidance and training to women who were serving time. The appointment of prison matrons—sometimes funded by private groups until city supervisors could be convinced to include matrons in their budget—was a natural outgrowth of the reformers' work.

One such reform organization was the Women's Christian Temperance Union (WCTU), which had been established in November 1874 to protest the negative effects of alcohol on American communities. "The liquor traffic is increasing, and so are its victims," wrote one WCTU member. "Our state institutions are filled to overflowing, and there are few homes in our state and nation that are not suffering from the blighting influence of this monster."[3] Frances Willard, president of the WCTU, argued that since male leaders were reluctant to push for temperance laws, women would need to do it—but first the women needed the right to vote. So the WCTU expanded its mission to include woman suffrage.

Along the way, other problems that affected women were brought under the organization's umbrella. Well aware of the sometimes horrifying treatment that female convicts suffered in prison, the WCTU campaigned for the addition of matrons—some of the earliest predecessors of female law enforcement officers—to police departments and the correctional system. Prison matrons provided assistance and direction to female prisoners and conducted bodily searches while shielding the women from possible abuse at the hands of male officers and inmates. In addition, prison matrons were considered to be better equipped than men in dealing with the specific needs of women. This concept—that a woman's capacity for understanding and nurturing made her well suited for dealing with other women—would drive much of the early development of the matron concept and, later, the initial duties of the policewoman.

"HER WORD IS LAW"

Increasing numbers of female prisoners led to the hiring of additional prison matrons, and by the late 1800s women's reformatories were built to provide female convicts with living quarters completely separate from regular prisons, which housed mostly men. With such heavy responsibilities, some matrons garnered a great amount of authority within the prison walls. Prison matron Annie Welshe was, according to one reporter, "the real head" of the penitentiary at Auburn, New York: "She has a force of women keepers under her, and she directs the entire management of the unruly inmates. Her word is law, and the system of discipline inaugurated by her works like a piece of machinery."[4]

Early experiments with the position of prison matron produced encouraging results. Prison matrons sometimes developed strong relationships with inmates, who often had much to gain from such interactions. In fact, some prison matrons formed lasting bonds with their female charges—many of whom were repeat offenders. Mary Campbell spent 17 years as a matron in the Essex Market Prison in New York. According to the *New York Times*, Campbell "had come to know all the women regulars, who remain in the same territory and drift into the same courts and prisons from year to year, until finally they drift beyond the reach of policemen and magistrates."[5]

Visits by friends and families of the prisoners provided matrons with a window into lives battered and broken. In the late 1800s, Flora Foster served as a matron in the prison commonly known as the Tombs, located in lower Manhattan. An observer wrote: "In Mrs. Foster's little reception room I have witnessed scenes of dramatic intensity—husbands bringing letters and refreshments to imprisoned wives, mothers weeping over daughters, lovers mute in the presence of a lover's grief, sharp lawyers counseling with sharper clients, scrub women, foul without and fouler within, young girls jeering at women older than their mothers, condemned women waiting to be sent for life to a prison cell, but among them all Matron Foster was as serene as a May morning."[6]

Sometimes love blossomed between matrons and prisoners. Matron Mattie Peebles met her future husband, Prescitiana Corpio, in the Kansas State Penitentiary. Corpio, who couldn't speak English, had been unable to mount an effective case during his murder trial— he insisted that he had acted in self-defense—and was sentenced to 30 years in prison. Peebles felt that he was innocent and spent three years working to get him pardoned. By the time the governor freed Corpio, the matron had left the prison and was living in the town of Dispatch, nearly 300 miles away. At Corpio's invitation, Peebles came to Kansas City to visit him, and their relationship progressed in a romantic vein. The two were married in February 1898.

Prison matrons also had didactic responsibilities. In keeping with the social mores of the day, the women who supervised the reformatories sought to train female convicts in the domestic arts. "To accommodate these goals," noted sociologist Joanne Belknap, "the reformatory cottages were usually designed with kitchens, living rooms, and even some nurseries for prisoners with infants."[7] A description of an 1883 visit to the Kings County Penitentiary in Brooklyn provides a glimpse into the life of women convicts, who resided in a separate building located in the center of the prison quadrangle: "In the female prison," reported the *New York Times*, "some of the prisoners were at work in a laundry, and others were making garments in a bright, airy corridor, which was enlivened by flourishing geraniums and other pot plants and creepers, tenderly cared for."[8]

While working in such tightly controlled environments, sometimes prison matrons could take their responsibilities a bit too far. In Concord, Massachusetts, two former female prisoners accused the warden of the state prison of allowing the matron to strip off their clothes and whip them. To avoid an embarrassing trial, the state settled the case by paying $150 to each of the women. At the Indiana Womens' Prison the matron was accused of flogging prisoners, along with other reports of cruel treatment. In March 1898, government inspectors in Trenton, New Jersey, requested the resignation of a night matron at the prison. One week later, they fired two more matrons. Although the matrons professed ignorance of any wrongdoing, their dismissals were apparently triggered by discipline problems in the women's department of the prison.

Despite such setbacks, however, the installation of matrons inside prisons was a gigantic leap forward in the caretaking and rehabilitation of female convicts. Now the stage was set for making reforms outside the prison walls.

POLICE MATRONS

In what other ways could women assist with law enforcement? Reformers focused their efforts on the place that served as the first stop for captured suspects: the police station itself. There, arrestees both male and female were searched by male officers and placed in holding cells. This approach created potentially awkward situations, triggered much tut-tutting among the citizenry and advocacy groups, and eventually gave way to the hiring of police matrons to work with female suspects.

In her travels across the United States, Susan Barney, the WCTU's national prison representative, saw firsthand the wretched conditions that many female prisoners suffered. WCTU members felt that the appointment of police matrons could go a long way toward improving the situation. After all, they argued, a woman's natural intuition and empathetic nature made her ideally suited to dealing with women and children in particularly delicate situations. Proponents felt that matrons and other female officers could defuse high-pressure situations more effectively than male officers could.

As an example, Barney told the story of how she had proved this point in a local police department she knew well. Barney had argued that the police would be well served by adding a police matron to their ranks. The police department wasn't convinced, but agreed to a challenge: If Barney could move a screaming female suspect from a holding cell into court, then the department would consider Barney's proposal. Barney accepted the terms. The police generously offered to send two male officers to the cell with her—it had taken four of them to place the struggling woman inside—but Barney said no. She walked to the cell, unlocked it, and walked in. The suspect, a woman named Sally, was crouched on the bed, her hair and clothes a mess.

"Who are you?" Sally cried out.

"I am your friend," said Barney.

"It's a lie! I haven't got any friends."

"But I *am* your friend."

Sally laughed bitterly. "Who are you, anyway?"

"I am a police woman."

Barney pulled a pin from her hair and started to rearrange the unruly mop on Sally's head. As the two women talked, Barney learned that Sally had first been arrested when she was barely 16 years old. She was now over 60 and had spent a lot of time in and out of jail. Barney asked if things would have been different had someone sat down and talked to Sally after her first arrest. What if someone had taken care of her? Helped her with her problems?

"Oh," replied Sally, "I would never have gone back again. But nobody ever cared."

At the end of their conversation, Barney asked Sally to accompany her to court. Sally agreed and went quietly. When the two women appeared before the judge that day, "the policemen said they would have cheered us if it had been proper," recounted Barney.[9]

A drunken woman sits in a police station cell in New York's seedy Tenderloin neighborhood in Manhattan, 1909. *(Library of Congress)*

Barney's story was a typical one. Women in law enforcement—as matrons in the prisons, then as matrons in station houses, and eventually as police officers in their own right—spent most of their duty hours taking care of women and children who had run afoul of the law. The duties deemed appropriate to women also had the benefit of freeing male officers to take care of more pressing matters.

However, not everyone thought that hiring police matrons was a good idea. In February 1883, the *New York Times* railed against a sum of $33,000 in the governor's budget "which is saddled upon the city of New York by the creation of the office of Police Matron, an extravagance which is loudly protested against by the taxpayers of that city."[10] When the the city council in Springfield, Ohio, approved a 41-cent-a-day salary for a police matron, the local newspaper scoffed at the decision: "Her duties require her to answer a summons at any hour on every day of the week. This absurdly inadequate allowance looks like an attempt to put an end to the matron experiment."[11]

Nevertheless, communities across the country did begin to hire police matrons. In New York, state law provided for matrons but at first police commissioners failed to bring anyone aboard. Then, in 1890, an alleged assault by a male officer of a 15-year-old girl inside a station house triggered a fresh round of lobbying from women's advocacy groups and provided added impetus to the matron program. In March of the following year the police commissioner finally appointed the first four sanctioned police matrons to serve inside New York station houses, taking care of female arrestees. To get the job, applicants had to obtain 20 written recommendations from women "of good standing" and were required to pass the civil service exam.

Many other cities soon followed suit. In Davenport, Iowa, a police matron was to be provided an office at the station house once the current occupants vacated the premises. "Davenport is large enough to have a police matron," said the police chief in 1889, "and there would be plenty for her to do if there was any fit place for her." The chief was anxious to crack down on delinquents in his city. "There are a number of girls who would be arrested," he said, "were there any proper place to put them."[12] Two years later the city's house of detention, run by matron Annie Davis, was well established. In one year Davis housed 274 women and children from ages 5 to 82. "The welfare of this department appeals to all right-minded people," noted a newspaper editorial, "and is deserving of the support and encouragement of all good citizens."[13]

Members of the women's club of Decatur, Illinois, were adamant about establishing a police matron in their city. In September 1890, they scheduled a meeting to discuss the issue. What would their matron do? Primarily, they said, she "would look after these half-grown girls who are on the streets apparently with no one to care for them and keep them out of wickedness." Police at the time were keeping an eye on a "disreputable" family that had taken in two girls, ages 10 and 14; the concern was that the girls would be raised to become prostitutes. A matron, said the women's club members, could take the girls away and place them in the local industrial home, from where they would be placed in good foster homes. The assumption was that, by acting as a safeguard against prostitution and other social problems, the police matron would prove effective as a moral backstop in local communities, putting youngsters on course to a solid future.[14]

Aside from women hired specifically as police matrons, widows of slain police officers were sometimes given honorary positions within the departments. Because pension plans for police officers were nonexistent, the paychecks that accompanied honorary titles allowed the widows to support their families. Chicago's police force had brought Marie Owens on board as a "patrolman" with arrest authority after her husband died in 1893. The titles given to widows meant little at the time; they were, however, the first whispers of what would eventually lead to official positions for sworn policewomen.

"NO PURE-MINDED, RESPECTABLE WOMAN"

Even with their limited duties, police matrons in the late 1800s suffered a barrage of negative publicity. Most of the commentary scoffed at the women's infiltration of the station house, whose officers had all been male until recently. "Put a woman in a station house under salary and she'll be trying to run [the] precinct inside of three months," complained the New York Doorman's Association.[15] The press approached stories about police matrons and other female officers with a condescending attitude, often portraying the women as confused or cute rather than as useful additions to the law enforcement community. "[Matrons] will be awarded immediate leave of absence whenever a mouse is known to be on the beat," crowed one of the local papers.[16]

Just as the police matron program was getting off the ground, the New York police force was rocked by a major scandal. Although beginning in 1892 the state assembly had enacted a series of laws to prohibit wiretapping, the police department continued to eavesdrop on suspects as it saw fit. This problem extended to the city's newspapers, which screamed at each other for stealing each other's hot stories by tapping telegraph lines. Something needed to be done. Enter the pugnacious future president Theodore Roosevelt, fresh from six years on the U.S. Civil Service Commission. Roosevelt joined the New York police board as its president in May 1895 and served for two years.

During a sweeping reorganization of the department, Roosevelt appointed two police matrons to high-level positions at police head-quarters. Minnie Gertrude Kelly joined the department in 1896 as secretary to the police board, directly assisting Roosevelt. Isabella Goodwin, a mother of four who had recently lost her police officer husband, was the second police matron Roosevelt hired. "As soon as I was appointed I threw myself body and soul into the work," Good-win said. "I grew to like it and, although it has its ups and downs and furnishes about as much hard labor as any other profession, it has its compensations also, and the excitement always keeps one's interest at the fever point."[17] Goodwin stayed with the police department for 30 years, serving as an undercover agent and, beginning in 1912, as an "acting detective sergeant"—in fact, the first female detective in the United States.

Indianapolis hired its first police matron, Annie Buchanan, in April 1891 after much lobbying by the WCTU. In a second-floor room at the city's police headquarters, Buchanan spent her duty hours counseling women, girls, and young boys. Like many other police matrons, she was on call at all hours of the day and night. This prompted the police chief to ask the city to provide some help for the overworked matron. In his annual report for 1894, the chief wrote: "I sincerely hope you may see your way clear to appoint for her an assistant, as provided for in the annual appropriation, that she may be relieved of the necessity of being on duty day and night, and thus prevent that impairment of health certain to follow the course of duty now incumbent on her."[18] Buchanan was rewarded for her efforts in 1913, when she earned a promotion that made her the first policewoman in Indianapolis.

A habitual truant appears in juvenile court in St. Louis, Missouri, May 1910. Police matrons and policewomen worked to steer young boys like this one away from a life of delinquency. *(Library of Congress)*

The WCTU was also successful at establishing a police matron billet (i.e., position) in Pawtucket, Rhode Island. Though Pawtucket's mayor supported the effort, the police chief worried about what would happen to the woman who volunteered for the assignment. According to the president of the local WCTU chapter, "[the chief] said the work for these unfortunate women was so degrading and revolting that no pure-minded, respectable woman would take it; and if they should see and hear these vile outcasts, not one woman in a hundred would accept the office, for it was not a fit place for a woman."[19] The WCTU persevered and, after the police force made room for the new matron at the station house, set out to find someone to fill the role. Eventually Mary Jenks was selected to wear the silver badge designating her as a police matron.

Jenks began her duties promptly at 8:00 A.M. on August 15, 1893. She found that the 45 male officers of the Pawtucket police force were quite happy to see her—they needed the help. "Lost children are always brought to the police station and here placed in the matron's care until claimed by some reliable person," said Jenks. "Insane men and women are also cared for pending commitment to a hospital or asylum. Many times the women who are brought in intoxicated, have young children, mere babies, with them. Stupid and helpless themselves, they cannot take care of the child but the matron must."[20] Jenks noted that the public was probably unaware of the variety of duties in the police matron's job description. "The inebriate, lewd, wanton, deserted, neglected and abandoned, friendless, penniless and abused, appeal to our sympathies, and in various ways receive attention," she said.[21]

As Jenks headed from the station house to breakfast one morning, a young girl who couldn't have been more than seven years old stopped her outside the front door.

"Mrs. Matron, is my mamma locked up?" asked the girl.

Jenks shook her head. She had not seen the girl's mother.

"Oh, I am so glad!" said the girl. "When I woke up this morning Mamma was gone and you did have her once, so I thought she might be here now. She had some beer in last night, and Papa did not come home either. Baby is sleeping—and I am so cold."

The girl needed help. Jenks had turned to head back into the station house with her when the little girl saw her mother stumble out of a nearby saloon. The girl ran up to her mother and trotted alongside her as the inebriated woman wandered down the street.

"Mamma, where were you?" said the little girl. "Where were you, Mamma?"

Jenks, following closely behind, was heartbroken to see yet another example of a neglected child. "There is a shadow on that little life," she later wrote, "a cloud over her heart that time itself will not wholly lift. There is a miasma in the atmosphere of that child's home that is more to be dreaded than any malignant contagion."[22] Indeed, matrons were quite concerned about the home lives of their charges. In the coming years they would become more and more involved in meting out discipline and working with parents to ensure a proper upbringing for the children in their communities.

Toward the end of the 19th century, with an increasing number of women in the United States entering the workforce, traditionally male-dominated government and social institutions struggled to deal with women's expanded roles in society. Gradually, the police matron, like the prison matron, became a regular part of the cultural landscape. The next step was to give law enforcement powers to female officers along with their badges, and bestow on them the title *policewoman*. The idea sounded simple and straightforward, but female pioneers in law enforcement faced a bloody, uphill battle before they could gain greater authority and acceptance among both male officers and the public.

I may suffer some annoyance from unthinking young men, who may not take my position as seriously as they should. However, I won't permit them to cause me much trouble.
             —Pearl Kray, police officer in Cleveland, Ohio[23]

CHAPTER 2

The First Policewomen (1900–1920)

BECAUSE THE APPOINTMENTS of prison and police matrons had proved so useful to law enforcement and correctional agencies across the country, forward-thinking social activists asked the logical follow-up question: Why not appoint women to the police force, with powers equivalent to those of the male police officer?

In March 1880, a Mrs. Blake had mailed a prescient letter to the *New York Times* about the need for policewomen to patrol her community. "When a drunken woman is arrested," she wrote, "she is arrested by a man; dragged to a police station, where she is confronted by a sergeant who is also a man; and finally locked up by a man in a cell which is frequently in close proximity to other cells occupied by men. From the moment that the policeman lays his hand, except in kindness, on the intoxicated woman to the moment when a masculine jailer thrusts her into a cell, the sacredness of her womanhood is outraged."[24] Nearly three decades later the idea was still being discussed, with the *Times* recommending in jest that male and female officers be partnered together, since the woman would "purify and refine" the man's masculine nature while the woman would gain "strength and firmness of character" from her male partner.[25]

As they had done with police matron positions, women's organizations across the United States encouraged their local police departments to create billets for female officers—essentially boosting the matron's responsibilities and giving her a more authoritative name. Society women used their extensive financial, political, and social resources to campaign for the establishment of female police officers in their cities. In New York, such well-known activists as socialite Alva (Vanderbilt) Belmont, suffragist leader Inez Milholland, and social worker Lillian Wald pushed the city hard for the establishment of a female police force. Their argument: Women officers would be especially helpful in cases where plainclothes male officers needed to collect evidence against female suspects.

In March 1913, Milholland testified before the city's joint committee on remedial police legislation. She was one of four women in a room packed with men. Setting the scene, the *New York Times* reported that Milholland "wore a navy blue tailored suit, and pointed fox furs, set off by a navy blue beaver hat with a yellow velvet bow. She carried a bright leather portfolio."[26] Milholland told the committee that male and female police officers should be able to work side by side. Asked about how to deal with women criminals, she answered, "If you really want to get them back and rehabilitate them . . . it seems to me that a woman, because she is a woman, and understands another woman's point of view, can be more efficient than a man, no matter how well-intentioned he is."[27]

To prove that the idea of a female police officer was valid, a number of society activists volunteered for law enforcement duties in their communities. For example, Helen Wilder, heiress to a sugar fortune, became the Hawaii territory's first policewoman in 1899. Like other early policewomen, Wilder was given the title but wasn't considered a member of the regular police force. She did have some experience in law enforcement, having served two years as a "humane officer." The press celebrated her efforts in saving animals from cruel punishment by human hands. In July 1897, Wilder had compelled the arrest of a local man whom she thought was trying to correct his horse too harshly. The man paid a fine in police court for abusing an animal.

Since the territorial government in Hawaii hadn't made provisions for a female officer, Wilder had to design her own uniform. "She wears a soft felt hat, on which glitters the silver star that shows she is a policewoman," noted one journalist. "She carries a revolver and is not afraid to use it."[28] The 23-year-old also packed a set of handcuffs that she wasn't afraid to use either. She once booked a streetcar driver on charges of abusing his mule. During another case, when a steamship captain locked his misbehaving children in a stateroom and fed them only bread and water for several days, Wilder boarded the ship and arrested the captain.

On the mainland, the city of Los Angeles bestowed a badge on one of California's richest heiresses. Fannie Bixby, daughter of a millionaire rancher, took the oath of office in January 1909. A Wellesley College graduate, Bixby had tried her hand at being an artist before deciding to dedicate her life to helping young women in trouble. In addition to her title as a "special policewoman" in Long Beach, Bixby was also a probation officer and served on the juvenile court commission in Los Angeles. "I was appointed by the police commission at the request of the chief of police to assist him in all cases of women and children that might come before the police," she said. "I work without pay, because I am interested in the work, and have a private income. My definite work has been to investigate cases reported at the police station of immorality among girls, delinquent boys, cruelty to children, et cetera."[29]

California state law required cases involving children to be reviewed by the juvenile court in Los Angeles. Delinquents from Long Beach who were put on probation in Los Angeles would get Bixby as their probation officer. "Sometimes boys are brought into court several times over for stealing and put on probation each time," Bixby noted, "till at last they come out all right." Tougher cases were remanded to a reform school. Bixby didn't believe in punishing the youngsters; instead she regarded her work as "nearly all preventive and corrective." Each child, she said, should be "dealt with according to his temperament—influenced, taught, cared for with love and patience till he wakes up to his own moral responsibility."[30]

Nettie Podell, a former probation officer herself, echoed Bixby's sentiments. Podell arrived in New York City in 1910 to run a settlement house in the neighborhood of Harlem, which was just beginning its demographic shift toward becoming a center of African American culture. Noticing that policemen usually ignored the "chewing gum brigade"—children selling gum at subway entrances and street corners until late in the evening—Podell declared that female cops would do a better job of tackling the problem. "When I was in Philadelphia," she said, "I patrolled the streets at all hours of the night, and after a long, hard fight I succeeded in keeping the children in their homes. . . . It is a mistake to have men trying to do probation work. They don't know how and never will learn."[31]

In Cincinnati, Ohio, a suffragist poses in a simulated police uniform to illustrate the newfangled concept of the policewoman, c. 1908. *(Library of Congress)*

So the policewoman—a mother figure with a badge—was conceived as someone who would provide gentle guidance and mete out discipline to misbehaving women and children in their communities. A 1907 appeal by Julia Goldzier of Bayonne, New Jersey, insisted that policewomen could stop boys from smoking and keep women out of saloons. Goldzier, who obtained 1,000 signatures on her petition to Bayonne's city council, noted that female officers could wear a practical uniform including a divided skirt, a dark blue blouse, boots, and a blue military hat edged with gold braid. The female police officer, said Goldzier, would inherit the police matron's traditional responsibilities and serve as an extension of parental authority. "First and foremost," said Goldzier, "the object of having policewomen is to protect the children who play upon the streets and whose mothers are too busy in their kitchens to look after their offspring and make pies and cakes at the same time." If men had policemen to look after them, said Goldzier, then why shouldn't women have police-women to do the same? Goldzier pointed to the example set by the city of Ghent, Belgium, which created its own police force of a dozen women between the ages of 40 and 50—old enough to know about life and trained to maintain the peace.[32]

Unfortunately, the mayor of Bayonne wasn't impressed with Goldzier's enthusiasm. "I guess the scheme's all right," he mused, "but if we ever get that force and if it's put up to me to see that the female police force of Bayonne runs along smoothly and without factional dissensions, *I quit!*"[33]

Undaunted, Goldzier kept up the pressure. In February 1909, she arrived in Albany, New York, the state capital, to argue for the hir-ing of policewomen to help neglected children. The city of Cleve-land, Ohio, had already green-lighted such a plan. Why not Bayonne? Nothing came of Goldzier's efforts in February, so in April she moved ahead anyway, gathering nine women volunteers to serve as "guardian mothers" in Bayonne. They would pull shifts in the afternoons. They would not wear uniforms. Someone suggested that instead of carry-ing clubs like male officers, each of the policewomen could wield a slipper to discipline any misbehaving children. "I shall teach the little boys to be polite," said one guardian mother.[34] Goldzier admitted that while the mayor hadn't officially sanctioned the experiment, he had given it his tacit support. After all, he figured, the women weren't *real* police officers, so how much damage could they do?

Five years later, Bayonne would finally hire its first official police-woman—by accident.

The city's playground commission asked Mayor Albert Daly to provide them with police powers to keep the swings and sandlots free of delinquents. Daly, assuming that everyone on the commission was male, approved the petition. But the secretary of the playground commission, who had signed the petition as "R. McAdie," turned out to be 23-year-old Ruth McAdie, who was quite surprised about her new job. "Now that she is appointed, however," said the *New York Times*, "the Mayor says she may remain, and he has confessed that the idea of having a policewoman is rather attractive to him."[35]

McAdie jumped into the job enthusiastically. She saw to it that electric lights were installed in dark areas of local parks to ward off lovers who spent their time on park benches engaged in the "horrible act" of spooning. Next she decided to clear the benches of lovebirds altogether, forbidding them to canoodle in the city's playgrounds as well. But the responsibility of supervising public morals took its toll on McAdie, who lasted only six weeks as a policewoman. She resigned after deciding that the notoriety was too much for her and that chasing spooners was less than dignified. After mulling things over, McAdie decided that she didn't really have anything against spooning in the first place. "My daughter is tired of the whole business," said McAdie's mother. "She was not brought up to be a policeman or a policewoman, whichever you prefer."[36]

Meanwhile, the traditional police matrons coexisted with the new policewomen, the former often complementing and sometimes augmenting the work of the latter. During a two-month period in 1911, for example, Kansas City's police matrons worked cases in hospitals and boardinghouses, assisted travelers, helped women find dresses to wear, and cared for 87 children. A newspaper report noted that "the very nature of this work shows that in the nature of things men could not have performed these kindly duties nearly so well as the matrons, if at all, and this fact shows that a useful work has been neglected in the past."[37]

GUARDIANS OF RETAIL

Although police matrons and policewomen might have outperformed policemen under certain circumstances in the early 20th century, the women did so within strict societal parameters. Major cities like New York and Chicago tentatively rolled out experimental programs that put female officers on the streets but tightly controlled their duties. By limiting female officers to enforcing moral standards and keeping an eye on women and children, police departments acknowledged the expansion of the female role in society while ensuring that policewomen continued to perform "women's work." Most policewomen were indistinguishable from other nicely dressed women walking around in public. Whether she was called a policewoman, a patrolwoman, or something else entirely, the female officer was often issued a badge and nothing else—no blackjack, no sidearm, not even a uniform.

The public, unaccustomed to seeing women wield any law enforcement authority, found the newfangled policewoman an interesting curiosity. In October 1902, the Professional Women's League, an arts organization, hosted several thousand visitors at its exhibition in Madison Square Garden in New York City. During the event, policewoman Grace Lyons, badge number 10, had to restrain an angry young boy who was making a fuss. She charged him with disorderly conduct. The struggle drew a large crowd of onlookers, many of whom had never seen a female law enforcement officer at work. The next day, the *New York Times* reported the story with the headline "Arrest by Policeman: Exhibition in Madison Square Garden Enlivened by Bluecoat in Skirts."[38]

In keeping with public attitudes about gender roles, many of the early policewomen's duties resembled window dressing rather than actual law enforcement. "My only weapon is a lace handkerchief. I don't carry any club," Dorothy Stewart told a journalist in December 1907. She was new to the job, hired by the Chicago police to patrol the foyer and lobby of the Auditorium Theater, home to political speeches, symphony concerts, and theatrical performances. In this case the policewoman was dressed for the occasion. The city outfitted Stewart in white gloves, a blue jacket, a "braided blue skirt," and a helmet. Stewart's role: to watch over women and children who came to enjoy the show. "Women, you know, don't like to stand in line before a box office, and this often angers a policeman," Stewart explained. "Some hot-headed ones are liable to take a woman by the arm perhaps more roughly than they think." Flirty and persistent men could also be a problem, but Stewart wasn't worried. "Should one by any chance appear he would find me after him in a jiffy," she said. "It wouldn't take me long to hustle him out, I assure you."[39]

Two years later the city hired Josephine Sullivan to patrol its popular State Street shopping district. Sullivan came to the job with solid credentials: she was a private detective for the McGuire & White Agency with four years of service under her belt. The city issued her a badge, a whistle, and a patrol box key so that she could call the station house. "She is said by prominent police officials to be one of the cleverest women detectives in the business," reported one newspaper, "and is often engaged by the foremost lawyers of Chicago to seduce evidence in important cases."

Sullivan's first day on the job—May 11, 1909—was marred by an unfortunate incident: she was robbed. Sullivan took her oath of office at city hall around noon, then reported for work on State Street. After a day of hunting for thieves, shoplifters, and pickpockets, she went home, kicked off her shoes—and realized that her pocketbook was missing. Sullivan retraced her steps and figured that a "well-dressed young man" who had sat next to her on the streetcar ride home was probably a pickpocket. "It certainly is a good joke on me to have had my purse stolen from me on my first day as a special policewoman," she remarked, quickly adding, "but then, it is possible that I simply lost it."[40]

Sullivan's appointment raised some questions regarding the employment of women in government positions. Anticipating complaints about discrimination in the city's hiring practices, Chief George Shippy asked Edward Brundage, an attorney for an investment firm known as the Chicago Corporation and a man long involved in city politics, for a legal opinion. Brundage responded that local laws could be applied to men and women on an equal basis. "No person shall be precluded or debarred from any occupation, profession or employment (except military), on account of sex," he said. "Women have been declared eligible to the office of superintendent of public instruction, master in chancery, attorney at law and others."[41] While these words were helpful to women who wanted entrance into male-dominated career fields, it would take another six decades before the federal government stepped in to give equal opportunity employment a push and establish it as the law of the land. In the meantime, enforcement was left to local municipalities, which had varying if not conflicting rules about the hiring and treatment of policewomen—often at the whim of police chiefs and city councils.

Gradually, however, test programs and titles like *special policewoman* were replaced by attempts to create a real career field for the female officer. American communities established official positions for policewomen on the city payroll, and female candidates took the civil service exam to see if they could qualify for the job. In 1913, after women like Dorothy Stewart and Josephine Sullivan had demonstrated the usefulness of female law enforcement officers, the city of Chicago advertised for more female candidates for its police force.

This didn't happen without some prodding, of course: activists like Gertrude Britton, of the Juvenile Protective League, had nudged the mayor to take the police matron program one step further and appoint female police officers. "[They] should make their way with women's weapons," said Britton, "the chief of which is common sense." The activists provided the city with a recommended list of additional qualifications: a "husky" build, nerve, ideals, experience in social service, and an understanding of young people.[42]

Initially, however, Chicago's policewomen had a more passive role. When the first 10 women joined the department, the chief ordered them to "instruct and persuade" rather than make arrests. But the edict didn't stick. On August 7, 1913, two policewomen grabbed a 23-year-old female on a disorderly conduct charge. A crowd gathered as the officers phoned their station from a nearby call box. "Three cheers for the women cops and their first arrest!" someone shouted. Policewomen had reached another milestone.[43]

Sometimes Chicago's female police officers were a little too effective. In the spring of 1914 a group of women picketed Henrici's Restaurant in support of waitresses who were attempting to unionize the popular eatery. Policemen soon arrived on the scene and arrested the crowd. But the women accused the policemen of being rough with them, which prompted a call for policewomen to take care of the problem instead. When female officers arrived to make the arrests, a crowd gathered to watch. As the mood on the street became increasingly tense, the women police handled the protesters at least as roughly as the male officers had. Following the incident, the chief of police temporarily pulled the policewomen off such arrests.

Despite the incident in Chicago—and a resulting editorial in the *Examiner* that quickly labeled the female police experiment a failure—women officers were gaining recognition. "They are evidently an institution that has come to stay," noted one newspaper. "As they actually demonstrate their worth in these cities where they have been employed, it is to be expected every city will approach the proposition seriously. 'Policewoman' seems destined to become a familiar term."[44]

Several early policewomen brought unique talents to their their new jobs. In Los Angeles, Lillie Williams applied to be the first female motorcycle cop in the country. It was 1912. Williams had a good pedigree: she regularly competed in bicycle and motorcycle events and had seven medals to her credit. She also fenced, swam, and rode horses. "Just set a speeder out in front of me and give me a chance at him on my motorcycle," she said. "All I want is a chance to prove this." To sweeten the pot she offered to pay for her own gasoline.[45] Two years later, Pearl Kray became the first woman to join Cleveland, Ohio's mounted park police. Kray was outfitted with a khaki split skirt, a hat, and riding boots. "I may suffer some annoyance from unthinking young men, who may not take my position as seriously as they should," she said. "However, I won't permit them to cause me much trouble." Kray covered a 25-mile beat on the 2:00–9:00 P.M. shift. "My duties are to see to it that the park rules are obeyed," she explained. "That covers a multitude of sins."[46]

THE FIRST SWORN POLICEWOMEN

To help spread the word, well-known policewomen traveled the country on lecture tours, speaking to government leaders and civic groups about how female officers could be an effective addition to local police departments. In 1908, the Portland, Oregon, city council gave the crusade a shot in the arm when a serious, bespectacled social worker named Aurora Matilda "Lola" Baldwin was given command of the city's new Women's Protective Division. The 48-year-old New

York native supervised antivice activities within Portland's city limits, hunting for houses of prostitution and keeping young women on the straight and narrow.

How did Baldwin rise to become superintendent of a city's female police force? While living in Nebraska, she got involved in social work, helping prisoners and unwed mothers find opportunities for better lives. After relocating to Portland, she took over the local Traveler's Aid Society, which helped find homes and jobs for more than 1,600 women during the Lewis and Clark Centennial Exposition in 1905. Fresh from that success, Baldwin asked the city council to allow her to continue helping young women, this time under the auspices of the municipal government. When the city finally agreed, Baldwin had to pass the civil service exam in order to qualify for a government paycheck. She completed the test successfully and received her badge on April 1, 1908, making her the first sworn female police officer in the United States.

Baldwin operated out of the local YWCA and favored a simple approach to the job. She refused to allow her officers to wear badges or uniforms. "The effectiveness of the protective work is due to its quietness, lack of show or publicity and its sincerity and sympathetic approach," she said. "The women deal with every condition imaginable. . . . They dress in ordinary civilian clothes, and their autos bear no marks to embarrass or alarm. They are friends in time of trouble."[47] Baldwin used her notoriety to good effect, traveling the country on speaking tours and helping other police departments create their own women's divisions. In Seattle, for example, the city council mulled over a bill that would provide salary and expenses—at $175 a month (nearly $4,000 in today's dollars)—to the city's first female police officer. The job was only part-time and had just one responsibility: counsel women who arrived in town for the Alaska-

Yukon-Pacific Exposition in June 1909. It would be another three years before the Seattle Police Department hired its first official policewoman for full-time duty. But it was a start.

Another celebrity policewoman who worked hard to promote the cause was Alice Stebbins Wells of the Los Angeles Police Department. She toured the country, visiting cities large and small to talk about her pioneering work as the first policewoman in the United States with the authority to arrest suspects. In May 1915, she delivered a speech at the National Conference of Charities and Corrections. Wells had worn her badge—star number 105—for five years. "For a long time past," she told the crowd, "the woman policeman has been a figment of the imagination, held up to ridicule as the acme of the absurd and impossible. But though the last echo of derision still reverberates, there has grown a policewoman movement as great in strength and size as any recent humanitarian movement has attained in equal time." Wells then listed cities that had added full-time female officers to their ranks, including Dayton, Denver, Colorado Springs, Minneapolis, Phoenix, San Francisco, St. Paul, and Topeka.[48]

Years later Wells would vividly recall the day she took her oath on September 10, 1910: "It was a man's world. There were no women employed in the department as telephone girls, record bureau clerks or secretaries. Male clerks, stenographers or officers performed the limited amount of such duties." Backed by 35 prominent citizens of Los Angeles, Wells petitioned the city for a position as a police officer. "I don't want to make arrests," she said. "I want to keep people from needing to be arrested, especially young people." It took three months of politicking with commissioners and councilmen—all of whom quizzed the five-foot-two former minister about her intentions—before the city passed an ordinance establishing one position for a female police officer in a department of 300 men.[49]

Wells's duties echoed those of the police matrons who came before her. "My field of work will be chiefly wherever young people gather for entertainment in parks, penny arcades, moving pictures shows and dance halls," she said. "I will deal chiefly with the proprietors of such places, seeing that all laws are obeyed and that the places are kept clean and moral." Wells added that in dance halls, she might be required to have stern chats with any young people who misbehaved.[50]

Unfortunately, the press continued to see female officers in a less than serious light. "Many journalists presented a caricature of a policewoman as a bony, muscular, masculine person grasping a revolver," note historian Peter Horne.[51] The *Los Angeles Times*, Wells's hometown newspaper, couldn't figure out what to call her. Officer? Officeress? The "first woman 'policeman'?" The *Times* finally compromised and labeled her "Officerette Wells."[52] However, Wells's growing popularity brought the career field some much-needed respect. "Many civic groups and police forces could see beyond the stereotype of the policewoman, and they deluged Mrs. Wells with questions and requests for her help in introducing policewomen into police agencies in their communities," writes Horne.[53]

To augment female officers and matrons, women leaders in certain cities gathered volunteers to patrol the streets in an unofficial capacity. "We are not organized to criticize or to interfere with the department, but to help," wrote Anna Kalhofer, who created New York's Mother Police force. Noticing how some young girls needed "a little talking to" and that some men could be "sneak-faced," Kalhofer signed up 500 unpaid female volunteers in her experimental program. Each volunteer patrolled one city block in an early version of a neighborhood watch. Variations of the "Mother Police" appeared in cities across the nation.[54] A thousand miles to the west, each of the five school districts in Rochester, Minnesota, had three volunteer "police mothers" who combed the streets at nine o'clock each evening—curfew time for children in the city. Any youngsters still loitering after the curfew were reported to the city's policewoman, Minnie Bowron, who would phone parents to let them know what their children were up to.

Little misbehavior went undetected under the watchful eyes of the Mother Police. In Salt Lake City, Jane Barrett reported that in one week she found more than 100 children under 18 years old who had violated the city's curfew. Barrett patrolled the business districts "from four or five o'clock in the afternoon until midnight or later," sending between 12 and 15 children home each night. The worst violators were minors who went to the movies by themselves. Some young men were on dates with young women "far under the age of legal responsibility."[55] By steering potential troublemakers to the local policewoman, members of the Mother Police helped draw attention to the increasing importance of the female police officer.

"STUPID OR MERELY OFFICIOUS"

Despite the progress of women in gaining employment rights during the first two decades of the 20th century, many men looked down on women of authority. A July 1910 editorial in the *Rochester Herald* warned of the dangers of hiring women who were too aggressive: "To give a stupid or merely officious woman that power and privilege would entail endless scandal, and not a little trouble. . . . A woman, too zealous in her efforts to preserve morals, would make many mistakes, and in this way do more harm than good."[56] For the time being, however, the duties of female cops dovetailed with the prevailing attitudes of American society. Women could be given a bit of authority—as long as they stayed within the prescribed boundaries of mothering and nurturing.

However, some men refused to accept women at all. When annoyed male supervisors were able to drive women out of the police force, they did so with relish. In February 1919, the Aurora, Illinois, police commissioner fired Mary Phillips for—supposedly— not accomplishing enough work during her tenure. The city then deleted the position entirely. Alma Longgale, a former vaudeville performer who became a policewoman in Racine, Wisconsin, was driven out of her job after a series of messages and phone calls from anonymous sources accused her of "making her home a rendezvous for businessmen." Longgale's tormentors also distributed pictures of her from her vaudeville days, when she worked as a "strong woman" and wore a leopard-skin outfit during performances. For further shock effect, copies of the photos were sent to the local YMCA and WCTU, among other organizations.[57]

The *Rochester Herald*'s editorial staff, so concerned about "stupid or merely officious" women, was no doubt horrified by the news from Chicago that the 3,000 members of the city's police force spent a week under the supervision of a woman while their chief was on vacation. The truth, however, wasn't quite so scandalous: Kate Adams, the chief's secretary, didn't actually have the title of acting chief—the assistant chief filled that role while Adams continued to manage the office. Nevertheless, newspapers delighted in reporting that Adams "took the helm and directed smoothly the routine of the busiest police department in the world."[58]

Bureaucratic inertia and male supervisors' tendency to treat female cops with disdain made the policewoman's job even more difficult. San Antonio, Texas, hired six policewomen—including one African American—in early 1919. After one month, the city commission grumbled that the women were harassing people instead of helping them, were filing incomplete case reports, and had made only two arrests, both of drunken men. "I cannot see that they have been of any value whatever to the police force in keeping down crime or vice," complained one of the commissioners.[59]

Adding fuel to the fire, a group of local women presented the commission with a petition to appoint a female officer to supervise the city's policewomen. The city stalled on the petition. "[The police-women] have ... been the source of a great deal of annoyance," said one of the commissioners. "They are costing us about $15 a day and I think we could use that to greater advantage in some other direction."[60]

Eventually the commission revoked the policewomen's appoint-ments and told each of them to surrender her badge, manual, and passbook (which provided her with free streetcar rides while on duty). One of the six women was demoted and retained as a night police matron. Two of the women refused to surrender their issue equip-ment at first, requesting that the commission explain why they were being dismissed from their jobs.

Denver, Colorado's first female officer, Josephine Roche, lost her badge in 1913 after a short time with the local police department. The Vassar graduate and settlement house worker found large holes in the city's policing of places and events termed "amusements." Denver's policemen turned a blind eye to dance halls serving booze after the city's midnight curfew, while cafés found ways to avoid paying the municipal liquor tax. "Many of these places were nothing more than wine rooms," Roche said, "where young girls were allowed to come without escort. That is against the law in Denver."[61] One night Roche rescued a policeman from a rioting crowd at a dance hall, batting people away with her baton.

Despite Roche's hard work, the city's police board took no action on her reports and even began to hide newly issued dance permits so that she wouldn't know when social events were being held. Meanwhile the local newspaper uncovered payroll graft among city employees, triggering a grand jury investigation. Roche was called to testify, which made her even less popular among the politicians of Denver. Undaunted, Roche kept doing her job until the police board finally fired her. The public howled in protest. The civil service board ruled that the police commission had acted illegally and announced a hearing into the matter. In the meantime, the sheriff of Denver hired Roche as a temporary deputy so that she could continue her work as a law enforcement officer. Then Roche's career took an interesting turn: she inherited her father's share of a coal-mining firm called the Rocky Mountain Fuel Company and became its president in 1929. She later served as Franklin Delano Roosevelt's assistant secretary of the treasury—a far cry from her humble beginnings chasing drunks out of dance halls.

Sometimes the reasons for firing a policewoman had little to do with performance. In Portsmouth, New Hampshire, the police commission ejected Vera Bash after just six months on the job. The reason? The 28-year-old was deemed too young and attractive to be an effective policewoman. "Her beauty interfered with her work," wrote the *Portsmouth Herald*. "Just how it interfered is not made plain. . . . The presumption is that no one had the hardness of heart to tell the young woman that beauty is not an asset to the police department."[62]

Fed up with substandard treatment from the men in charge of the town in which she lived, one woman took the concept of female authority a step further by attempting to establish a nearly all-female municipal government there—with a police force comprised entirely of women. In September 1911, Ella Wilson became the new mayor of the former oil town of Hunnewell, Kansas. She immediately announced her intention to fill key positions in the town with women. "I am going to have a city administration composed of women from mayor to dogcatcher," she said. "If no manner is developed by which we can raise lawful revenue I am going to ask public spirited women to take charge of the city offices."[63] Wilson was ready to replace the city clerk, treasurer, marshal, and street commissioner with female appointees. Meanwhile, Hunnewell's policewomen would wear regulation belts, carry nightsticks, and conceal revolvers in their dresses.

Wilson had spent six difficult months on the road to the mayor's office. She was elected on a write-in vote in April 1911, but the four men on the city council wouldn't acknowledge her new authority. When Wilson refused to meet with the council in a hotel bedroom, the men moved the meeting to a more appropriate venue but then failed to show up. Wilson appealed to the state attorney general, who filed a petition to fire the council. "When I quit the office of mayor," Wilson said, "there won't be any men crowing around about what they 'put over' on me."[64] The attorney general reminded the councilmen that failure to conduct the city's business would lead to a year in prison, a $1,000 fine, or possibly both. The council finally met with Wilson but opposed every one of her proposed appointments.

Then the governor of Kansas intervened, and the city council suddenly acceded to Wilson's requests. For town marshal, however, Wilson decided to appoint a man. "It has been rumored that I desired Mrs. Rose Osborn appointed Marshal," said Wilson. "This is untrue. An office that requires physical strength is not a woman's position."[65] Osborn would become the police judge for the city.

Despite her intention to appoint women to key offices, Wilson denied that her goal was to make Hunnewell a woman-run town. She did recommend that several men continue in municipal positions.

But in her view, men had failed in running the town government—the former mayor had spent much of his time drinking and allowed bootlegging and gambling to flourish in the city. Wilson's efforts to prove that men weren't superior to women when carrying out the duties of an executive office indicate that the increasing number of women in the American workforce—and in police departments across the nation—was having far-reaching effects.

"UNSEEMLY CONTORTIONS"

Many American communities in the early part of the 20th century felt that policewomen were sorely needed to keep people from moral ruin. In Poughkeepsie, New York, the Women's Civic League secretly sent one of their own deep into the bowels of the city to investigate the after-hours activities of the local citizenry. "I have made a study of the moving-picture theatres, the dance halls, and other places of amusement," the league member reported back. "What I have found satisfied me that there was a need of a stricter censor of the patrons of those places rather than the places themselves."[66] Likewise, Katherine Drummy, an Omaha, Nebraska, policewoman, spent two months inspecting the dance halls of her city and warned of the inappropriate behavior therein. "There is not a virile young girl in Omaha who isn't tempted to jingle her feet and twist her form into unseemly contortions when the orchestra strikes up a strain like 'Waitin' for *the Robert E. Lee*,'" Drummy reported. "It is part of the vivaciousness of youth."[67]

Concerned female officers did their best to control that vivaciousness. The matrons of Indianapolis reported the following statistics in August 1912: 93 violations of curfew, 11 cases of immorality, 8 minors removed from dance halls, and 20 girls "admonished and corrected." In Minneapolis, police matron Emile Glorieux helped close five dance halls during her first six months of duty.

Sometimes the suspects ran away to avoid being scolded for their inappropriate behavior. On a chilly night in December 1917, policewoman Anna O'Shea chased a young girl and several soldiers through Ossining, New York. O'Shea had caught the girl flirting before, and the young woman had promised to improve her behavior. She had apparently changed her mind. Stumbling through a snowfall two feet deep, O'Shea couldn't keep up, and the girl and her suitors disappeared into the night.

O'Shea had come to the village of Ossining, alongside the Hudson River and home of the Sing Sing Correctional Facility, by invitation. The civic league, comprised of prominent Westchester County women, championed O'Shea and asked her to join them. When she arrived, the local government gave her police powers. The aggressive O'Shea set about enforcing morals, chasing "flirts," and crusading against spooning. But when O'Shea's term expired, the village board decided not to renew her contract. Noted the *New York Times*: "She raised such a political storm by her many activities, which included pursuit of illegal liquor sellers, that after six months she was ousted by the village trustees."[68]

In March 1918, O'Shea spent two days stumping for candidates in the local election—coincidentally the first one in which the village women were allowed to vote. Unfortunately, O'Shea's losing streak continued: several of the candidates had voted against her reappointment as the town's policewoman; all of them were reelected. Two weeks later the civic league pushed to have O'Shea hired as a truant officer in the public school system. The school board said no, refused to recognize the civic league, and filed the petition away. However, O'Shea didn't give up. Three years later she asked the

Ossining police chief to recommend her for a position with the New York City police department.

Elsewhere, female officers continued to pursue miscreants who ignored the social mores of the day. In January 1914, Chicago declared war on the tango. Major M.L.C. Funkhouser, second deputy chief, instructed the ten policewomen patrolling dance halls to keep hot-to-trot couples at least six inches apart. "The tango can be danced decently and is a graceful dance," sniffed Funkhouser. "The way it is being done in Chicago is killing it."[69] Funkhouser said that dancers who broke the six-inch gap wouldn't have the courtesy of being notified; the policewomen would simply throw them into a patrol wagon.

Like many other municipalities, the oil-producing city of Olean, New York, struggled to police the young boys and girls who frequented its saloons, theaters, bowling alleys, and dance halls. In early 1919, the police chief assigned the local policewoman, Bertha Crane, to verify that businesses were following the child labor law, which prohibited boys under 16 years of age from working in amusement places after 7:00 P.M.

Crane was passing by a saloon on a Friday evening when she saw several young boys lingering outside the front door. It was nearly midnight, so Crane headed toward them. The boys fled into the saloon, dashing past John Dailey, the proprietor. "Stop them!" shouted Crane, but Dailey did nothing and, she said, gave her a "horse laugh" in response. The boys rushed out the back and escaped. Crane arrested Dailey for violation of child labor laws. Hauled in front of the judge, Dailey was mournful and pleaded guilty. A patrolman had instructed him to fire his underage employees the previous week, which Dailey said he had done. "I was in no way disrespectful to Mrs. Crane," said Dailey. He didn't recall anyone making a "horse laugh" toward her, and the boys had run through the saloon too fast for him to stop them. The judge fined Dailey $10 (about $120 in contemporary dollars) and sent him on his way.[70]

"Mashers"—men who accosted women, even lightly or mistakenly—were a frequent target of police officers charged with maintaining proper behavior in public. In St. Louis, Missouri, a man approached Alice Buckley while she was browsing in a ten-cent store. He gave her a friendly wink. Buckley ignored him, but the man sidled up to her and pinched her on the arm. Buckley then announced she was a police officer and promptly arrested him.[71]

Philadelphia policewoman Mary Diehl, dressed in a sharp blue uniform, rescued young women from mashers in one of the city's train stations. On one occasion Diehl sat quietly, observing the waiting room, and noticed a young man approach a woman who had just arrived at the station. A newspaper account related what happened next: "Convinced from the girl's actions that the man was forcing his attentions on the girl, policewoman Diehl stepped in and, after questioning the two, flashed her badge and said to the young man, 'Come with me.'" Diehl escorted the man outside. He promised to curtail his flirting, and the policewoman let him go. He was just one of many mashers who were shown the door every day: "If you don't believe she has the authority or the nerve to eject or arrest obnoxious or disorderly persons, just start something," said a station attendant to a curious traveler who saw Diehl at work. "She throws 'em out in bunches every day."[72]

The policewoman's moral purview included public beaches as well. Requirements for "acceptable" swimwear were gradually becoming less conservative, but bathers were still expected to cover up properly. "The girls don't need to wear winter flannels when they go to swim," Chicago police chief John Garrity said at a meeting of the city's committee on small parks and bathing beaches in August 1919.

"I can't see that stockings are a protection against immodest displays." Policewoman Agnes Walsh agreed. During the meeting she outlined the "ideal" bathing costume for women, which included a cap and a skirt that crept up no more than four inches above the knee. The suit would have small armholes and be cut conservatively at the neck. Shoes and stockings were not required.[73]

In New York, however, the rules were slightly different for public beaches. Bare legs were a no-no: stockings were required, and socks were not an acceptable substitute. One-piece suits, V-necks, and clingy or transparent fabrics were also banned for women. (Men, on the other hand, were allowed to wear one-piece suits and to dispense with socks.) If a female bather broke one of the rules, a plainclothes policewoman could escort her off the beach with a warning. Over 50 members of the women police reserves patrolled the beaches of New York, along with 150 male officers.[74]

The city of Newark, New Jersey, faced a different kind of problem: citizens wearing makeup at too early an age. Forbidden by their parents to paint their faces at home, young women on a night out were disappearing into restrooms at local train terminals and emerging with rouged cheeks. The city's police inspector launched a campaign to stop such clandestine activity. "I get my authority from the common law," he declared, "and I feel also that I am acting in the place of the parents of these girls, who would want me to do what I am doing, if they knew what was going on." On the first night of the antimakeup crusade, policewomen kept close watch over the city's train stations. "Now go right back and wash your face," one of the policewomen told a rosy-cheeked 16-year-old coming out of a restroom. All told, the officers flashed their badges at six young girls, telling them to wipe off their makeup. The girls complied, then fled the stations.[75]

In Appleton, Wisconsin, 30-year-old policewoman Mildred Gardner pursued a different type of minor criminal: delinquent library patrons. During June 1922, Gardner visited homes in the city to recover nine overdue books. Her annual report for the following year detailed seven arrests and supervision of 53 public dances. Gardner also helped arrange two adoptions, placed two girls in state institutions, returned four "delinquent girls" to their hometowns, and secured employment for 39 women in the city. And, of course, she chased those pesky overdue borrowers, rescuing 26 books that year and returning them to the library.[76]

Early policewomen also dealt with some bizarre cases mixed in with the routine ones. One officer had a curse placed on her. When Francis Schlatter, a self-proclaimed religious healer from California, was indicted for mail fraud in New York City in 1916, he denied he had done anything wrong. On the front page of Schlatter's self-published newspaper, his editor blasted policewoman Adele Preiss, who had arrested Schlatter for practicing medicine without a license. "The curse of the 109th Psalm shall be upon Miss Adele D. Preiss," read the editorial. "She shall get lame, blind, deaf and dumb, and the demons of hell will not give her any rest neither night or day; that every step of her life shall be but a curse for having caused the arrest of the Reverend Francis Schlatter."[77]

Policewoman Preiss was no stranger to weird happenings. Three years before the Schlatter case, she and Isabella Goodwin had, along with two male detectives, raided a séance. They arrested the medium, Helen Moore, and her 17-year-old daughter for fleecing the two dozen people attending the event. According to the daughter, Preiss and Goodwin guarded the doors to the house during the arrest and later accompanied the suspects to the West 17th Street station. The daughter was named as an accessory to the crime. But because the admission fee to the séance had been voluntary, the mother and daughter were eventually released after being charged with disorderly conduct.

A more normal case for Goodwin and Preiss involved the arrests of 11 young men in a New York City department store in November 1913. The aggressive lotharios were hassling women who passed through the store's waiting room. One of the men hung around for an hour and a half, then chatted up a salesgirl as she sat down nearby. "New York is a dangerous place for a young girl to go around alone," he chided. Another of the men asked one of the salesgirls for a date. On the testimony of five store employees, Goodwin and Preiss, along with a squad of male detectives and the store detective, hauled the 11 men down to the station. Despite their inability to post the $1,000 bail, the men weren't too worried about what they had done. But after the judge sent three of them to the workhouse for several weeks, the remaining eight suddenly became much more cooperative.[78]

Community leaders were also concerned about criminals who attempted to lure innocent children into criminal activity. On a pleasant afternoon in Des Moines, Iowa, 16-year-old Hazel Walker was heading home from school. From around a corner, a 19-year-old woman—"pretty, well-dressed and fascinating"—approached. She offered Walker her friendship, showed her some beautiful clothes, and invited her to the comfortable apartment in which she lived. Over time, the two became friends, went shopping together, and drove around town in a brand-new automobile.

The fun was short-lived. Soon a variety of men began to visit the woman's apartment. They were there to see Walker. The woman who had befriended the teenager turned out to be a scam artist. In the white slave trade she was known as a "decoy girl."

"I spent several nights with her and used to have a good time," Walker told policewoman Margaret Goddard, who arrested the teenager in the decoy girl's apartment in April 1916. "Then one night she left me alone in her room with a young man." After Walker had spent some intimate time with the man, the decoy girl urged her to move into the apartment permanently. Walker, ashamed of what she had just done, agreed. Thereafter, she was encouraged to take money from the men, surrendering a cut to the decoy girl each time. "I never found out whether she kept it all, or whether someone also got part of it," Walker told Goddard.[79]

Unfortunately, Hazel Walker's story was not unique. That year in Des Moines alone, the police ran across six other young women, all under 18, who had been roped in by the decoy girl. For social activists, the case highlighted the importance of having women keep an eye on the younger population in their cities.

CAPABILITY AND PRESENTATION

With more and more women joining the ranks of law enforcement officers, it was time for policewomen to have their own national membership organization. Backed by the International Association of Chiefs of Police, the International Policewomen's Association opened its doors in 1915. Four years later, more than 60 police departments in the United States had female officers on the payroll. Los Angeles policewoman Alice Stebbins Wells served as the association's first president and remained in the post for 17 years, until the financial difficulties of the Great Depression put a temporary halt to the organization's efforts. (The association would stand silent until 1956, when it was resurrected under a different name, the International Association of Police Women.)

As policewomen's duties expanded during the early 20th century, questions began to arise regarding their physical fitness for the job. Were they strong enough? Young enough? Able to deal with rough suspects? Should they be allowed to wear uniforms and carry weapons? Hot debate over these issues would continue for decades, eventually crystallizing in a number of discrimination and harassment suits that would be battled out in the courts. Until then, factors such as age and physical strength could block or delay a woman's entrance into a law enforcement career.

Police departments typically had physical requirements for their police candidates that specified both minimum and maximum weights. Sometimes women would go to great lengths to meet the specified numbers. During the summer of 1914, one Chicago applicant found herself 45 pounds over the 180-pound maximum, so she decided to go on a diet: "I don't eat or drink except a little water to keep my throat from parching," she told reporters. "For dinner last night I had a piece of ice the size of a walnut, half a slice of lemon peel and a swallow of water." By coupling her starvation diet with lots of exercise, the candidate dropped 25 pounds in five days. She asked the city for five more days to drop another 20 pounds. Her request was granted, with the caveat that she would be monitored carefully.[80]

Age limits were another area of difficulty for female applicants to police departments. Several women who signed up for the Chicago police exam in late November 1913 decided to lie about their ages. One said she was 27 and was then told that the allowable age range was 30 to 45. The applicant recanted, stating she was actually 31. Another candidate, admitting she had also lied about her age, left the exam, saying that "she preferred being young to getting on the force."[81]

The questions regarding physical traits were framed in terms of practicality. Could women perform the physical requirements of the job? "It's a question of present-day discussion whether or not physical force is the prime requisite of a cop," wrote James Walter Smith in the *Boston Evening Transcript*. "Some say there is a moral requisite of equal value with physique—brains and conscience as well as the power to swing a billy or subdue a burglar."[82]

Meanwhile, some female officers proved that women were more than capable of keeping criminals in line. In New York, Mary Boyd broke up a fight between a streetcar conductor and a "powerfully built" man. Noticing the two men struggling, Boyd boarded the streetcar, flashed her badge, and placed the passenger under arrest. The man refused to cooperate with her, but Boyd—"not a large woman, but . . . muscular"—yanked him off the streetcar and held him against a nearby post until the patrol wagon arrived.[83]

A number of years later, policewoman Alice Clement Faubel arrived in New York from the Windy City to extradite Laura Reed, a 27-year-old who had stolen a bolt of cloth from a Chicago department store and fled east. Reed was caught during a drug raid in New York, and the police connected her with criminal activity in Chicago. During extradition proceedings, the assistant district attorney looked Faubel up and down, noting her purple turban, black cape, large earrings, and multiple bracelets.

"Aren't you afraid you'll have trouble taking this woman all the way to Chicago without assistance, with the record she has?" he asked her.

Faubel was used to questions like that. "You may think so," she replied. "I'm a grandmother, and proud to be able to say so. But I'm also a first grade detective of the Chicago police department, and I pack a gun. Just rest easy about me."[84]

Faubel died four years later, in December 1926, at the age of 48, but not before she took down a succession of "mashers" and other criminals.

On one night in particular, Faubel was enjoying a movie when a man in the theater began flirting with her. When he refused to leave her alone, Faubel told him he was under arrest. He thought she was joking. "Quit your kidding," he said. Faubel then pulled out her blackjack and clocked the man over the head, yanked him out of the theater, and dragged him down the street. He appeared in morals court soon thereafter, admitting that he had been thoroughly cured of flirting.[85]

One female officer would never have to worry about whether she was tall or strong enough to be a cop. "This Female Sampson [sic] to Guard Visitors at the Panama Expo," trumpeted a newspaper headline in February 1915. Blanche Payson, 21 years old and six foot four, was the niece of the police chief in her hometown of Santa Barbara, California. She was hired as a special policewoman for San Francisco's Panama-Pacific International Exposition, assigned to patrol the Toyland exhibition and help women and children who were wandering th grounds. The newspaper focused on her appearance and bearing: "If Amazons were fashionable today, Miss Payson would be a general in the Army. She is of a vigorous type and carries herself like a—no, no, no! Not like a policeman, even though she is one, but like a soldier."[86]

Payson made such an impression guarding the Toyland exhibit that filmmaker Mack Sennett soon came calling, asking her to come to Hollywood. Sennett's Triangle-Keystone Company featured the untrained actress in a comedy film called *Wife and Auto Trouble* in 1916. For Payson it was the start of a long career in the entertainment industry. She went on to appear in more than 100 films before retiring from acting in 1946.[87]

Because their jobs could be dangerous, was it necessary for policewomen to carry weapons or wear uniforms? Many community leaders—and some policewomen as well—saw no need, preferring that female officers simply pin the official badge to their civilian clothes while carrying out their duties. However, a number of uniform styles and weapons were discussed and sometimes tested on duty. A proposed uniform for Chicago's female cops, for example, featured a long jacket and a skirt with a pistol pocket sewn into the right side in the event that the policewoman carried a sidearm.

Discussions regarding uniforms for policewomen would continue for years to come. At a conference of the recently founded International Policewomen's Association, held in Indianapolis in May 1916, members debated whether uniforms were useful or necessary. Alice Stebbins Wells, president of the association, thought that women should wear simple costumes and keep the accoutrements to a minimum. A Colorado delegate piped up with a contrasting opinion: "I think it is absurd to suggest a uniform. I'm sure I wouldn't wear one. I want to be just an ordinary normal woman and wear what I please, even high heels and white dresses when I feel like it."[88] Because America's policewomen were still primarily engaged in social work, some delegates to the convention felt that plain clothes worked better on the job—the less ostentatious the look, the better for dealing one-on-one with women and children.

Weapons were another matter entirely. Some policewomen carried clubs or blackjacks as they went about their duties. Certainly those devices were less of a worry to male supervisors than firearms were. Here again, some policewomen argued that carrying a gun ran counter to the policewoman's primary role of helping women and children. Others didn't want to carry a weapon because it was inconvenient. "In the first place, I don't need one," said Florence Schimke, a policewoman in Lakewood, Ohio, next door to Cleveland. "In the second place, they are too heavy to lug around."[89]

Other policewomen disagreed—sometimes out of necessity. In Butte, Montana, Amanda Pfeiffer's assigned shift required her to work after dark in the city's Chinatown section, where she roamed back alleys, dance halls, and noodle parlors. Pfeiffer petitioned the mayor for permission to carry a weapon for possible emergencies, and the mayor agreed. But this was a special case. For the time being, few female cops wore blue, and even fewer carried a gun.[90]

"THERE IS NO BAR"

For all of the growing pains associated with the transition from police matron to policewoman, female officers were making a big difference in their communities, and male supervisors were forced to admit that the experiment was proving its worth. For example, the city council in Warren, Pennsylvania, declared that their policewoman had cut down significantly on "street loafing" by young girls, bringing them home to their parents when appropriate.[91]

Another proponent of the female police force, Chief Henry Baker of Racine, Wisconsin, hired his first policewoman in May 1914. Baker noted that the value of female police officers was no longer a subject of debate. In juvenile cases, said Baker, policewomen were better able to gain the confidence of their younger sisters and brothers in battling "social evil." Because of this, the new female officer would help the police department run more efficiently. "[Policewomen] are the best aids to prevent young fellows interfering with girls and inducing them to take joy rides with them," said Chicago's chief of police. "They are also very effective in preventing boys and girls from using the cigarette and the sale of cigarettes to minors. They are valuable in the parks because girls who would not talk to policemen will confide in these women."[92]

In Missouri the Women's Christian Temperance Union created a policewoman's division during its 1915 convention and elected social worker Suzanne Frances Napton as the "WCTU policewoman" for the state. Although larger cities in Missouri had or were making provisions to appoint policewomen, Napton was charged with visiting smaller towns that hadn't gotten there yet. In an interview, she said that WCTU policewomen should be "attractive women of strong bodies and presence of mind who will inspire the youth to do better things."[93] To that end, the WCTU policewoman would battle social ills such as loafing in public and breaking curfew, while promoting such "wholesome amusements" as playgrounds and club homes for young people. "It is not true that country boys and girls are corrupted in the cities," Napton said. "These young persons begin their misdemeanors in the small towns and later drift to the cities. We must attack the trouble at its source."[94]

The city of Washington, D.C., which had six police matrons on its payroll in 1914, announced during the summer that it would begin taking applications for two newly created policewoman slots. Unlike the matrons, the policewomen would have arrest authority. No uniform would be issued, but the women would wear badges on their civilian clothes. More than 40 women applied to take the civil service examination for the two open positions. A prerequisite was that each candidate had to have ten "reputable women" vouch for her qualifications for the job.[95]

With enough policewomen in its ranks, the city needed a proper bureaucracy to train and manage them. In 1918, the D.C. police took another big step and formed a separate women's bureau to oversee its growing group of female officers. City commissioner Louis Brownlow helped create the bureau after he could find no laws that created a "sex barrier" on the police force. D.C. policewomen would have the official title of *patrolman* and the same promotion opportunities as male officers did. "There is no bar," said Brownlow. "She, regardless of color, may become sergeant, lieutenant, captain, inspector and assistant superintendent, and in the day that is shortly due a uniformed member of the force will be in charge of the police."[96]

The mission of the women's bureau was preventive: to save wayward girls before they went too far off course. Newspaper columnist Frederic Haskin described the duties of the women's bureau as follows: "To discover conditions needing correction, to supervise amusement places, to aid in locating runaway girls, to follow and warn girls in danger, to assist in enforcement of the law, to befriend girls whose home life does not give protection of the right sort, and to do personal work with women and girls."[97] The D.C. chief of police, Raymond Pullman, required that applicants to the women's bureau have "a social conscience and a desire to serve humanity."[98] He didn't want women who were just looking for a paycheck.

The chief of the women's bureau was Lieutenant Mina Van Winkle, a former suffragist and the wealthy widow of a New Jersey chemical manufacturer. Appointed in February 1919, she set the bar high for her employees, requiring better educational credentials for them than were required for the male officers in the department. Van Winkle's staff was trained in the use of firearms, although not all of them carried a weapon on the job. The ideal candidate for her bureau, she said, was a trained nurse. She made it clear that her policewomen were not matrons. "The police matron . . . attends merely to the physical wants of the women in her care," said Van Winkle. Policewomen, by contrast, focused on "the future social status" of people they arrested.[99]

A journalist described meeting Van Winkle in her headquarters on the top floor of a municipal building: "There is a long, narrow office filled with the clatter of typewriters, the rustle of papers, the low murmur of voices. At a large desk sits a full, handsome woman, from whom all the activities of the room seem to radiate. There is a certain delicate hauteur about her features, a fascinating stressing of consonants when she speaks, which make her personality unforgettable. She wears a smart dark taffeta dress, with soft lace collar and vest and trim kid walking pumps."[100]

In 1920 the women's bureau took charge of an old four-story hospital that would become its new headquarters. The first floor was comprised of offices, interview rooms, a kitchen, showers, and receiving rooms. Upper floors featured classrooms, clinics, wards for dependent children, and a house of detention for women over 17 years old. The expansion was necessary in light of the growing problem of delinquency in the city. "The American home is disintegrating," explained Van Winkle. "Homes are not made the center of interest. Amusements are found in commercialized places instead of in the family circle. The average family does not read anymore. People buy magazines and throw them away."[101]

When they weren't trying to reform young delinquents, Van Winkle and her officers worked a variety of other cases. On a spring day in 1918, a Russian countess checked into the upscale Willard Hotel, just a few blocks from the White House. Rumor had it that the countess was an enemy spy. The Justice Department dispatched a young J. Edgar Hoover—later to become the director of the Federal Bureau of Investigation—to work surveillance on the countess. Joining him was a 24-year-old D.C. policewoman named Imra Buwalda, who was quickly trained to pose as a maid in the hotel. Buwalda carefully observed the alleged spy's movements while cleaning the rooms on the countess's hallway. "To this day I can make the most beautiful bed," Buwalda recalled years later. "The countess? She wasn't a spy at all, but we did find out that she had a most interesting sex life."[102] Buwalda didn't elaborate.

Buwalda had started working for the women's bureau at a salary of a dollar a day. Dressed in civilian clothes, she and a partner drove around the city, keeping their eyes peeled for trouble. "One time we brought in a fifteen-year-old who had been so badly beaten up by the gang that 'owned' her that I had to turn to the wall and cry," recalled Buwalda. "My boss, Mrs. Van Winkle, told me sternly that she'd have to let me go if I became emotionally involved with every case, which would make me lose my effectiveness."[103]

A year after its creation, the D.C. women's bureau—which had eight members—announced that it would hire the city's first "colored" policewomen. But would the newly hired women be allowed to arrest white suspects in addition to African Americans? "Of course they will be assigned to operate among the members of their own race," said Van Winkle, "but if infractions of the law should come under their personal observation, they must fulfill their sworn duty and make arrests."[104] Van Winkle noted that southern cities—Washington included—needed to put a priority on their sociological work. She hoped that the hiring of African American policewomen would help educate people on the subject of race relations.

In addition to helping runaways, enforcing curfews, and finding missing persons, the women's bureau had to handle people whom Van Winkle labeled "the cranks who come to Washington to talk over their private troubles with the President."[105] One woman wanted President Calvin Coolidge's help in publishing a song she wrote, while another announced she was a telepath and demanded to talk to President Woodrow Wilson about his idea for the League of Nations (the forerunner of the United Nations).

Among Van Winkle's many accomplishments was a ban on the hip flask from dining rooms in the city's hotels. "Cabaret life, cheap literature and business careers are unfitting American girls for homemaking,"

l. "The poor are still devoted to the home, but the rich

le classes are more interested in dancing and drinking."[106]

While dining at the Willard Hotel in October 1920—soon after Prohibition had begun—Van Winkle noticed a couple at a nearby table sipping from a silver flask. Van Winkle walked over. The flask was filled with liquor. "You're under arrest," she said, but allowed them to finish their last sip. The man, son-in-law of a former U.S. senator, offered to drive the trio to the police station, and Van Winkle agreed. After posting bail, the couple departed the station. The next day they failed to appear in court, and the case faded away. Mysteriously, the police—Van Winkle included—refused to discuss what had happened. Why? As it turned out, the woman dining with the senator's son-in-law was not the senator's daughter.

On the streets of D.C., policewomen had no uniforms or weapons, rendering it difficult for them to, for example, break up a fight at a dance hall. The highly publicized first African American recruit lasted just 24 hours on the job. She had joined the force over the loud protests of her parents. On her first duty day she was assigned to check out local dance halls. She poked her head inside one of them, saw the gigantic, rowdy crowd, and quickly turned in her badge. "It was a good thing for us that she resigned," sniffed one male officer. "Imagine a fight starting in that hall and that we should be called out to protect a fellow officer, a colored woman, not in uniform and unknown to any officer in the precinct. I'm glad it didn't happen."[107]

As she navigated the bureaucracy of the police department, Van Winkle ran into trouble of her own. After five years at the helm of the women's bureau, she was charged with insubordination and faced a trial board in April 1922. The commissioner reprimanded Van Winkle for refusing to release two runaway girls as ordered. Van Winkle felt that she hadn't done anything wrong. She fired back at the commissioner, accusing him of openly admiring a young girl for carrying a concealed revolver.[108]

Because of Van Winkle's status in the city's social circles, the press and public wondered whose politics would eventually win out. "Mrs. Van Winkle lunches and dines at the downtown hotels where the social and official of life of Washington centers," the press noted.[109] Eventually, a trial board exonerated Van Winkle but added a caveat, saying that she didn't seem to understand the concept of proper discipline in the police ranks.

In November 1918, the D.C. police posted the first female traffic cop in the country. Leola King, smartly dressed in a tailored overcoat, cap, and boots, stood at Seventh and K Streets in the northwest district. To direct traffic, King whirled a large umbrella that had a Stop/Go sign attached to it. She had been a policewoman for two months before her assignment to traffic duty. Over lunch one day—she had 15 minutes to wolf down a quick meal—King told a reporter, "I like the job. All there's to it, is to keep one's head, know the traffic rules, and stand up for hours at a time."[110]

Policewoman Leola King directs traffic near the Carnegie Library in Washington, D.C., c. 1918. King suffered minor injuries when a truck hit her not long after she assumed her duties. *(Library of Congress)*

One night King noticed a large truck, packed with furniture, traveling in the wrong direction on Seventh Street. She signaled to the driver to stop, but the truck swerved away from her. As the driver made his turn, the rear fender of the truck swung around and knocked King onto the pavement. The vehicle sped away as King blew her whistle repeatedly. The driver finally stopped and got out. King, dazed but still conscious, listened as the driver told her that he didn't realize he had hit anyone. King was admitted to George Washington Hospital with minor bruises and some damage to her scalp. She returned to duty soon afterward.

THE GREAT WAR, HOME DEFENSE, AND THE WOMEN'S RESERVES

The year before the founding of the International Policewomen's Association, war had broken out in Europe. Over the next few years the United States inched toward sending troops overseas, while members of the woman suffrage movement took their case directly to President Woodrow Wilson's doorstep. The debate over giving women the right to vote had been brewing since the mid-1800s. While some states allowed women at the ballot box, most had not. President Wilson preferred to leave the decision to the individual states, but the publicity surrounding the suffragists' efforts—everything from mass parades to jail time—were making the issue increasingly difficult to ignore.

Beginning in January 1917 suffragists picketed on the sidewalk outside the White House. They held gigantic banners emblazoned with messages like "Mister President, what will you do for woman suffrage?" The protesters drew the ire of crowds of passersby who were aghast that anyone would be protesting during wartime. On

June 23, 1917, suffragists Lucy Burns and Katherine Morey walked a block from the National Woman's Party headquarters to the White House. They positioned themselves, as they had done almost daily for the past six months, in front of the northeast gate, holding their banners high. Unfortunately, the metropolitan police had decided that the women were obstructing sidewalk traffic and would need to move. A female police officer named Farling walked up to Burns and Morey. "You will have to move on," said Farling. "You can't stand here."[111]

A policewoman arrests two suffragists as they picket with banners outside the east gate of the White House, August 1917. (*Library of Congress*)

Burns and Morey were unimpressed. "We won't, because our position is constitutional and logical, while your position is unconstitutional and illogical," they told the policewoman.[112]

Farling grabbed at the banner, and the women struggled. Two police cars and a patrol wagon later, the suffragists were hauled away. After that, a policewoman and three police matrons were dispatched to stand in front of the headquarters of the National Woman's Party—

just in case the suffragists decided to walk another banner over to the White House.

Although he originally wanted the states to decide the issue of the women's vote, President Wilson eventually capitulated and supported the suffragists, setting the stage for the ratification in August 1920 of the Nineteenth Amendment to the U.S. Constitution.

Meanwhile, America's entry into the Great War (World War I) in April 1917 meant that large groups of young men would be reporting for service at military bases around the country. But it also meant that rowdy crowds of servicemen would be roaming the streets during their off hours, looking for a good time—and possibly causing trouble. As the *Boston Evening Transcript* noted: "The almost daily reports of raids on cabarets, eating houses, hotels and other places of resort—especially after midnight—are rousing people in the great city to an understanding of the perils to which our youth—young men and women, particularly our soldiers—are being exposed."[113]

In New York, several police divisions were headed by successful businessmen, all of whom performed their duties without pay. Their influence, both social and financial, was thought to be a bonus for a municipal government straining under the weight of its responsibilities. Among the wealthy volunteers, Frederick Wallis of Fidelity Mutual Insurance Company headed the city's purchasing department, while Dr. John Harriss was assigned as a special deputy to regulate traffic flow.

The Home Defense League—a volunteer force of 8,500 part-time emergency policemen—was renamed the New York Reserve Police Force in 1918. That February, with little fanfare and no advance notice, Police Commissioner Richard Enright announced that Rodman Wanamaker would become the special deputy police commissioner, with authority over the police reserves. Notoriously publicity-shy, the 55-year-old Wanamaker came from the family that had founded the Wanamaker's department store chain. He was a fan of the newly budding aviation business and had planned to send a pilot on a flight across the Atlantic in an airplane named *America*. Wanamaker "considered it a step toward universal peace, in which cause he was deeply concerned."[114] In 1913, he had personally funded the construction of the National American Indian Memorial on Staten Island.

Prior to Wanamaker's arrival, Enright had tasked police inspector John Dwyer to take a close look at the condition of the Home Defense League. "Languishing," lamented Dwyer, noting that lack of leadership and direction left the organization with little purpose or energy. Reviewing his fledgling police reserve program, Wanamaker decided that the time had come to add women to the mix. He was inspired in part by England's female police, whose various duties included patrolling munitions factories. "Women of character and ability can be easily found to volunteer for this work," he said in 1918. "With a volunteer force of this kind, trained and efficiently controlled, kept free from sensational or advertising methods and held aloof from contaminating vice conditions, a police commissioner would be armed with an agency that would be of great use to him personally and to the police and to the city."[115]

The push to add part-time female policewomen was closely linked to the perceived nobility of the war effort. Wanamaker and Dwyer moved quickly to establish the women police reserves as a viable public agency. "We didn't talk much about it," Dwyer would recall later. "We just went ahead and did it. We got uniforms for them, drilled them, and then sent them out on public view."[116] Wanamaker launched two new organizations: the Woman's Police Reserve and the Women's Police Training Corps. As soon as they completed their time in the training corps, female candidates would move over to the reserve force.

Wanamaker's lofty goals for the police reserves triggered a firestorm of negative publicity. Cartoonists parodied the women, and the public debated their usefulness as police officers. The reserve policewomen lacked the powers of arrest, but they were issued snazzy uniforms: blue jacket and skirt, black shoes with white spats, police cap, and a bow tied around the neck. Large bright stripes and white piping completed the ensemble.

In May 1918 the Women's Police Reserve, 275 members strong, marched behind the male reservists through the streets of New York as several hundred thousand New Yorkers packed the sidewalks to watch. Someone in charge felt that the women wouldn't survive the entire parade, so they were ordered to join about halfway through, when the parade crossed Broadway and Ninth Avenue.

Journalists like James Walter Smith painted a happy picture of the march: "They were the 'hit' of the parade. . . . Nothing neater, nothing more efficient looking had been seen in many a long day. They were proud of themselves, proud of their uniforms, proud of the duties they were to be called on to perform."[117] Dwyer himself said of his new recruits: "They are enthusiastic, and cannot get enough of drilling and other things."[118]

Members of the New York Women's Police Reserve pose for the camera in June 1918. At far right is Edyth Totten, a stage actress who wore captain's rank when she was in uniform. *(Library of Congress)*

Now that they were trained and outfitted, what exactly would the female reserve officers do? Despite the public's curious enthusiasm for the new police unit, social mores still dictated that female officers would be restricted to "women's work." The reserves would supplement the full-time policewomen by performing war-related duties. "There is a certain kind of police work that women can do as well as, if not better than, men," Dwyer told the *New York Times.* "Every housewife knows all about ice, coal and wood, and groceries and markets." So the new women's police reserves would enforce the law of the kitchen: "Our women are going to look after food and fuel violations in their neighborhoods," continued Dwyer. "And when they find them they will lose no time in reporting them."[119]

In addition, the female reservists would keep male military personnel in line. "This is the day of the soldier," said Dwyer. "He must be protected from temptation. There are many ways here in which the policewoman can be of invaluable aid. Again, she will keep her eye on the young people of her neighborhood. She will try to help the wayward girl who is keeping bad company. She will prove herself a girl-saver. This is one direction in which, being a woman, she can do work that no policeman can do. Almost in the same manner, she will exert a moral effect upon the boys."[120]

Dwyer was quick to add that the women's roles could be expanded: "Eventually they will relieve the men of many smaller duties which they have to perform," he said. "The work of the police force, since the war began, has increased so much that it has become imperative to find relief and these women will be able to do a great deal"—so that male officers could handle "larger and more urgent" calls.[121]

One of the reservists' duties was to help ferret out German agents operating inside the United States—specifically, male agents posing as women. The spies were recognizable by a few idiosyncrasies: short, cropped hair of different color than the rest; lack of attention to the corsage; a masculine grip on the pocketbook; an unfeminine tendency to cross the knees. For New York policewomen during the Great War, all of these characteristics pointed to one thing: the woman they were looking at was actually a man. More important, the man might actually be an enemy spy.[122]

Key to the success of Commissioner Enright's "experiment" and the targeting of German undercover agents was the concept known popularly as women's intuition. "[It] is man's reasoning with much of the slower processes of the male brain eliminated," said Enright, "and is, as has been proven by psychological tests both at Columbia and Harvard, correct 20 percent oftener than man's slower logic."[123]

One member of the Women's Police Reserve caught a German spy on the subway. The uniformed woman boarded the train on a very hot day and took a seat next to a redheaded, well-dressed woman in white. But there were a few things about the woman that didn't click. She was "remarkably cool looking for such a temperature." Her nose was very shiny. Her ankles didn't quite look like a woman's. The rest of the women in the car periodically adjusted their bodices, but this woman never touched hers. And she gripped her pocketbook tightly. The reservist got up and moved to the rear platform of the car. Since she had no arrest authority, at the next stop she signaled to a nearby policeman and explained what she had seen. The policeman slid into the car, grabbed the suspect, and arrested her. The woman in white turned out to be a man who was working undercover for the Germans.[124]

As for the regular police force, by August 1918 Commissioner Enright had appointed his tenth full-time policewoman. Placed under the command of a female supervisor, the ten policewomen would then fan out across newly created patrol zones in the city. Like male officers before them, some policewomen were now assigned to a patrol beat of their own.

THE EVILS OF BROADWAY, THE DANGERS OF DRINK

After the war ended in 1918, New York's police reserves, like the Home Defense League before them, were relegated to the background. Social welfare work returned to the forefront as ten full-time policewomen joined Ellen O'Grady, a deputy police commissioner, in the caretaking of women and children in the city. By 1920, an additional ten policewomen joined the ranks. Civil service exams were required of all female applicants, but those chosen were not granted the same retirement plan that their male counterparts enjoyed. Moreover, the city created two divisions: patrolwomen (previously known as protective officers) and policewomen (previously police matrons), with different entrance tests and responsibilities. In 1937, the city would settle the confusion by merging the two titles into one: policewoman.

O'Grady caused a furor in December 1920 when she resigned, charging that the department had hounded her as she attempted to carry out her duties. "They said I was to continue my efforts to protect children, but I was to keep away from Broadway," she explained. "They didn't want me to keep the women off the streets in the white light district."[125] Threatening to uncover "a thousand and one things about the police department," O'Grady noted among her grievances that she wasn't allowed to arrest a pair of rich men who picked up two teenage girls and took them back to an apartment, where the girls were mistreated. "I was told that my work was 'too strenuous' in looking after the morals of girls in moving picture houses and was told to 'go slow,'" O'Grady said. "When my detectives went to enforce the law in moving picture houses, the managers showed them receipts stating that they had contributed to the police hospital fund and they had been promised that no police action would be taken against them."[126]

The police commissioner denied the charges, and O'Grady left the force with the matter unresolved. However, she wasn't bitter. "I know I made good," she said confidently. O'Grady noted that among her accomplishments during the previous year was that she had steered thousands of youngsters away from a life of delinquency.

In the Midwest another policewoman left the force after becoming disillusioned with the job. Mrs. F. T. Hart, an ardent teetotaler, had changed her mind about the evils of liquor. "I was the worst prohibition crank in the country when I started to study the problem," she said. "I wanted every saloon closed and every bit of liquor confiscated." But after watching leaders of the prohibition movement in her town of Muncie, Indiana, get drunk inside and outside of the home, Hart decided that "many of the prohibitionists are hypocrites."[127] Hart recounted that one woman had beer delivered to her front door, in full view of the neighbors. Another woman, a prohibitionist, had beer from the same wagon delivered to her back door. "The woman who slips her beer into the house is a hypocrite and will not speak to the woman whose beer comes in the front way," said a furious Hart.[128]

The battle over Prohibition—and police efforts to seek out and destroy not only stills and saloons but also the people running them— was just beginning. The scarcity of men in the workforce during the war had helped emphasize the efforts of female officers everywhere as more of them were added to police departments across the nation. However, traditional male and female roles still drove the assignment of job responsibilities. Although policewomen remained focused on "women's work," several upcoming challenges—including another world war—were about to expand the duties of the policewoman into new territory.

That's no job for a lady!

> —Mary Sullivan's supervisor, when Sullivan announced
> she wanted to be a New York policewoman[129]

CHAPTER 3

Social Enforcers (1920–1950)

As THE UNITED States headed into the Jazz Age, police matrons and policewomen had their hands full, setting confused women and children on the right path and ensuring that citizens were behaving in ways that were socially acceptable. During the Roaring Twenties, relaxed social mores and a seemingly celebratory atmosphere were exciting backdrops to larger events. The establishment of women's police bureaus and the ratification of the Nineteenth Amendment, giving women the right to vote, would have important consequences during Prohibition and in decades to come. Noted one journalist: "A woman performing the duties of a cop seemed as preposterous at that time as a woman smoking cigarettes or voting for President, or doing a hundred other things which she now does."[130]

County, state, and federal law enforcement agencies were often slower than municipal police departments to add women to their ranks. Sheriff's departments typically had jurisdiction over specific counties, whereas highway patrol units covered what municipal police departments couldn't, including unincorporated areas or cities without their own law enforcement agencies. There were exceptions, and sometimes the responsibilities overlapped.

But old-fashioned attitudes still kept many women out of law enforcement. In 1924 a young woman wrote a letter to the governor of Michigan. She asked a simple question: *How can I apply to become a state trooper?* The governor's executive secretary scratched his head, then talked to the commissioner of public safety. Then the secretary wrote back to the woman: "I am advised that the department of public safety does not hire women for the purpose of law enforcement,"[131] he stated matter-of-factly.

In April 1930, women finally joined the state-level law enforcement ranks when the Massachusetts State Police added its first two female troopers, Mary Ramsdell and Lotta Caldwell. The two new officers were forbidden to wear uniforms and were assigned to cover crimes dealing primarily with women. Each woman covered half of the 200-by-100-mile commonwelath. Ramsdell and Caldwell weren't always allowed to work autonomously: whenever one of them visited a crime scene, a male trooper had to be there too.

And what about the state of Michigan, where the governor's secretary told a curious woman that she wouldn't be allowed in law enforcement? It wasn't until 1967 that the state finally got its first duo of female troopers, and even then they were hired as part of an experimental program. At the end of their training period, the two women weren't given cars to drive or even patrol responsibilities. Instead they were placed in desk jobs. It wouldn't be until the state police signed a federal consent decree in the mid-1970s—similar to what was happening in many law enforcement agencies at the time— that women were allowed to perform duties as full-fledged troopers in Michigan.

Even when they were able to earn a badge, female officers in the 1920s through the 1940s still faced harassment and discrimination from male supervisors who wanted to turn back the clock. Policewomen had no fans in the Hagerstown, Maryland, police department, where Captain Max Rickard offered the circular argument that women shouldn't be cops *because* of the discrimination they would suffer. "A policewoman runs into more lack of cooperation and difficulties than a male policeman," he harrumphed. "And the duties of a police-woman, as such, can be as well performed by men with greater ease."[132] Rickard was responding to a recommendation by a local physician that employing a policewoman to battle delinquency could reduce sexual promiscuity and, by extension, curb the spread of venereal disease in the city. To back up his claim that female officers were fairly useless, Rickard noted that Hagerstown had actually hired a woman in 1932—a full 15 years before—and subsequently found that male officers could handle delinquency cases more effectively.

By 1928, more than 200 cities and towns in the United States had hired female law enforcement officers, who numbered more than 600 nationwide. Some women were serving as sheriffs or deputy sheriffs in their local counties. The New York women's bureau had 125 women in its ranks; Chicago and Washington, D.C., counted 30 and 23, respectively.[133] During that year the civil service commission announced that it would hold exams in about 600 cities for positions open on the Washington, D.C., force. Salaries started at $1,800 (about $21,600 in present-day terms) and would increase to $1,900 after a year of service.

But although more female cops were put on the payroll, old attitudes about them still prevailed. "All local amazons who have enough courage, strength and common sense may take civil service examinations at the federal building here and may become lady cops," chided West Virginia's *Charleston Gazette.*[134]

Progress for women in law enforcement was also hindered by the advent of the Great Depression: after the stock market crumbled in late 1929, law enforcement organizations across the United States suffered damage as well. Women's bureaus were consolidated into other police divisions, and fewer new policewomen came on board.

Policewoman Lulu Parks of Chicago, who took her oath of duty in August 1913. She carried two revolvers—her regulation firearm and another smaller weapon—hidden under her clothes. *(Library of Congress)*

But before the Great Depression put a crimp in hiring practices, more and more female candidates applied to take the civil service exam, the entranceway into a government career. Local civil service commissions hosted the periodic merit-based tests that were supposed to select the best-qualified applicants for the job. A public advertisement for a civil service examination in Benton Harbor, Michigan, was typical of the time. While the list of requirements for policemen consisted of three short paragraphs, the qualifications for policewomen took up two-thirds of the advertisement, with highly detailed explanations. Whereas men needed a high school diploma or equivalent, women needed a diploma plus "one or more years in college of work in social science including some study in psychology, criminology, law or sociology; and some experience in work of some investigation or social welfare nature, or an equivalent combination of education and experience."[135] Also crucial to the female applicant were the ability to carry out "complex directions, both oral and written," and the ability to prepare reports.

The civil service exam in Washington, D.C., was another good example of how female police candidates were boxed in by stringent requirements. A newspaper advertisement announcing an exam for female applicants scheduled for July 25, 1923, said that the test would consist of a thesis, practical questions, and a "rating on education, training, experience and fitness." Applicants had to be high school graduates with "either two years' experience in systematic social service or educational work, or not less than two years responsible commercial experience involving public contact and tending to qualify the applicant to perform the duties of the position." Alternately, applicants could be graduates from nursing schools with a two-year residency. The starting salary was $1,460 per year (about $17,500 in today's terms).[136]

Nevertheless, qualified candidates pressed ahead. Mary O'Neill took the New York civil service exam in the fall of 1924, scoring highest among the 100 women who applied to join the women's bureau. O'Neill had always wanted to join the police force, but her parents initially said no to the idea. "I don't know what to make of the girl," her mother moaned, shaking her head. "She has cops on the brain. When other girls are reading fairy stories or studying their lessons, she is eating up every word the newspapers print about murders and robberies and how this policeman shot a holdup man and how that one grabbed a mother and her baby from under the wheels of a motor truck." During the Great War, O'Neill had been designing dresses for society women when she noticed the female police reservists at work. The sight of the women in uniform rekindled O'Neill's childhood dream, and she signed up for the civil service exam right away.[137]

WOMEN'S BUREAUS

Once they had passed the exam and other local requirements, candidates like O'Neill were typically assigned to their city's policewomen's bureau. Though the women's bureaus had the effect of segregating women and men, they also reinforced the importance of female cops and their particular responsibilities. Experienced policewomen were assigned to lead these special units. In New York, police commissioner Grover Whalen created a crime prevention bureau and assigned 50 policewomen to its women's division. To lead the new organization he hired Virginia Murray, a former Traveler's Aid official who had helped launch the women's bureau in Detroit.

Unfortunately, Murray's experience in Detroit had not been a happy one. She and 12 other policewomen were handed a staggering number of responsibilities in a city of one million people: misbehaving children, missing adults, runaways, abandoned or neglected children, crimes against children, and sex crimes against adult females. "After a year, MacMurray threw up her hands and left," writes author Doris Scharfenberg.[138]

MacMurray had gained enough experience in Detroit to bring a sociological perspective to her new position: "I have had enough experience with young boys and girls to know that most of them become wayward and delinquent as the result of an effort to have a good time," she explained. "Misunderstanding at home, lack of opportunity to meet friends and a yearning for adventure—these obstacles and impulses, present among the rich as well as the poor, lead many young people into trouble before they realize what has happened to them."[139] After taking over the New York unit, Murray split her group of policewomen into caseworkers, undercover investigators, and patrolwomen, with the rest serving in administrative roles.

Back in Detroit, social services expert Eleonore Hutzel reluctantly took charge of the women's bureau that Murray had vacated. "I was stunned by the proposal," Hutzel said. "I had never been in a police station in my life, and wasn't particularly interested." But once she accepted the job she found the work important and fulfilling. "She interviewed suspects, writing with her left hand on a glass-topped desk," notes Scharfenberg. "Her head was down as she scribbled awkwardly on a piece of paper, but her attention was on the person whose reflection she was studying in the desk's shiny surface. The interviewee, who had nervously expected the stare of a tough cop, relaxed under this technique."[140] Hutzel supervised the department until her retirement in 1948.

Meanwhile the women's division of New York City's police department received more than 200 applications from candidates who wanted to attend its new training school. The leaders of the bureau, Mary Hamilton and Isabella Goodwin, supervised a staff of 26 women who looked after the welfare of young girls in the city. The policewomen even had their own precinct house, at 434 West 37th Street. It was the only police station in the country run by female officers. Though the separate women's precinct would last just two years—closing after disagreements with the police department over its operation—it set a precedent. In 1924, the group of female police officers officially became known as the "women's bureau"—which was soon renamed the "bureau of policewomen."

The school at the women's bureau offered a program packed with practical and theoretical education. "Every policewoman should have definite college training or its equivalent in physiology, psychology and medical law," explained Hamilton.[141] A journalist writing in 1924 described the school as follows: "Here the women are instructed just as if in a college or a school with problems to work out on the blackboards, tests to take, and home work to study. Such subjects as the use of firearms, the methods of arresting a person, and the art of jujitsu are received by the women with far more interest than ordinary school subjects are received by pupils, however."[142] Physical tests required the candidates to jump three feet over a rope and to grip a special machine, squeezing it with a force equal to 100 pounds.

Weapons training for female officers under the watchful eye of a male police inspector. Undated photo. *(Library of Congress)*

With jujitsu included as part of her classroom instruction, Hamilton encouraged women of all types to take self-defense classes. "Even the woman quietly at home is exposed to any ruffian who rings her door bell or enters through a window," she explained. "She dare not be dependent on a police whistle or a scream."[143] Her advice for women accosted by unruly men? "Scratch 'em," she said. "Scratch 'em hard. Always wear a long pin in your coat lapel. At the first sign of mashing, use it."[44]

Hamilton's rise to the top of the women's bureau had been swift: she had volunteered with the police department in 1917, landed a full-time job, and took over supervision of female officers just seven years later. One of her earliest assignments was to escort an elderly society woman home to Park Avenue. The catch: the woman was clearly unhinged and had been found wandering around the city. Hamilton and her charge boarded a subway train and sat down in a nearly empty car. The train lurched and began clicking down the tracks. Then Hamilton felt a gun being pressed into her side.

"I'm going to kill myself," said the old woman.

Hamilton gritted her teeth as the gun barrel dug into her ribs.

"But I don't like to go alone," the old woman continued. "So I've decided to take you with me. I'm going to shoot you when we reach the next stop. If you move or speak to anybody, I won't wait that long."

Hamilton kept her cool. "It's a good idea," she replied. "I've been planning on dying myself for a long time. But dying on the subway is hardly a fitting demise, isn't it?"

Hamilton went on to recommend that the old woman do the deed at a cemetery outside the city. After thinking about it, the old woman agreed.

The two women got off the subway at Grand Central Station. Hamilton headed toward a telephone. "I need to have my maid bring us some prussic acid," she said to the old woman. "It's a much better way to commit suicide than by shooting." (Prussic acid, a blend of hydrogen cyanide and water, serves as an effective method of suicide when swallowed.)

The old woman thought about Hamilton's offer, then nodded. Hamilton asked her to get some nickels for the phone call, and the old woman meandered off.

Hamilton stepped to the telephone and dialed the police department. Officers quickly arrived on the concourse. When the old woman saw them, she yanked out her gun, but the officers were able to subdue her before she got off a shot.[145]

Among her accomplishments as head of the women's bureau, Hamilton redesigned the interior of her building. "The lounging room for policewomen is decorated in cream and white," noted the *New York Times*, "with purple curtains and cushions around the seats. The reading tables are covered with current magazines. Upstairs is a dormitory with twenty beds, lockers, mirrors and showers. Flowers abound and boxes filled with geraniums are in the windows."[146] A city guest dormitory inside the building served as a rooming house for runaways. The new training school made use of the building's library, gymnasium, and classrooms.

Well aware of the value of publicity for her cause, Hamilton posed for a photograph that ran in newspapers during the 1924 Democratic National Convention, held at Madison Square Garden. In the photo, Hamilton perched on the roof of a skyscraper, clutching a large suitcase in one hand. On the side of the suitcase was a message pleading for good behavior on the part of the delegates: "Don't forget your wits and wife when packing," it said. During the convention Hamilton had an information bureau available for travelers, with a phone information hotline as well. She warned delegates against shady practices by city porters, taxicab drivers, and eavesdroppers. "Don't fall for beautiful and flirtatious women or suave men," she urged, "and don't buy tickets for Central Park."[147]

Savvy book publishers, aware of the policewoman's increasing visibility, knocked on Hamilton's door and asked if she was interested in becoming an author. The result was a volume titled *The Policewoman: Her Service and Ideals*, which appeared in 1924, the year that Hamilton took command of the women's bureau. In the book Hamilton wrote that criminals were sick people who required proper care in order to be rehabilitated. She also talked about the minimum salary of the policewoman: about $1,000 annually in small towns, increasing to $2,500 in larger cities (in contemporary terms, about $12,000 and $30,000, respectively).

New forensic technology also caught Hamilton's eye, and she was an early advocate of the use of fingerprinting in police work. During her rookie probationary period in the summer of 1918, her captain instructed her to fingerprint a middle-aged Jane Doe lying in the morgue. Hamilton had no idea what to do, but an attendant helped her complete her assignment—which turned out to be a hazing ritual. "But to me it was never a joke," Hamilton wrote. Undeterred, she attended a fingerprinting course at New York University and later taught the subject at schools, hospitals, and federal agencies. "I realized how easy it would be to identify a dead, injured or ill person if his or her fingerprints were only on file in a clearing house established for this purpose," she explained.[148]

To make her point, Hamilton decided to fingerprint a gorilla. It was a blatant promotional stunt that didn't go as planned. After Hamilton entered the gorilla's cage, jostling and noise from members of the press terrified the animal, which suddenly wrapped its arms around Hamilton, who left the cage unconscious with four broken ribs. But Hamilton's prescience regarding the usefulness of fingerprinting was dead-on, as over the years government agencies and police departments gradually adopted the practice as part of their investigative repertoire.

Surprisingly, Hamilton lasted just two years as chief of the New York women's bureau. She resigned in 1926, having decided that men were better in the field and that women, for the most part, should remain in their traditional caregiving roles. She served for three years as a special investigator for the police commissioner, then launched a private detective agency.

Hamilton's successor at the women's bureau, Mary Sullivan, was originally hired as a police matron in 1911 after a brief career as a traveling saleswoman. "That's no job for a lady!" grumbled her boss when Sullivan announced her intention to join the police force.[149] According to reporter Mary Elizabeth Plummer, the 27-year-old Sullivan reported for work at the police department "in appropriate daytime dress of that era—long green gown, picture hat trimmed with white flowers, and fluffy green parasol."[150] Hamilton would serve more than three decades with the police, publishing her autobiography, *My Double Life*, in 1938.

Sullivan's adventures made for great newspaper copy. "She lived for weeks with a gangster's opium smoking moll to collect information on the murder of Herman Rosenthal, shot down in front of a New York hotel," wrote journalist Adelaide Kerr. "Wearing mulatto makeup, decked in dime store jewelry and accompanied by a Negro 'boy friend,' she gave the signal that filled the house with detectives."[151] Sullivan's makeup was so effective that back at the station house even her captain didn't recognize her. *Time* magazine profiled Sullivan in 1938: "She has guarded women prisoners from the Tenderloin [a red-light district in Manhattan], kept arrested women from committing suicide, taken care of abandoned babies, investigated dance halls, abortionists, matrimonial agencies, posed as a brothel keeper to get evidence against white slavers. She finds detective stories exasperating, thinks girls who answer matrimonial advertisements are taking a chance of getting murdered, writes sensibly, bluntly, complacently about feminine police work."[152] The celebrity of top cops like Hamilton and Sullivan—and Aurora Matilda "Lola" Baldwin and

Alice Stebbins Wells before them—effectively promoted the growing importance of policewomen across the nation.

Unfortunately, women in the 1920s were unable to hoist a drink to celebrate their success in uniform—not without breaking the law, that is. The same temperance movement that had helped establish jobs for matrons and policewomen was also greatly responsible for America's national experiment with Prohibition. The Eighteenth Amendment, ratified in 1919, banned the manufacture, sale, and transportation of alcoholic beverages. Unintentionally, it also set the stage for myriad criminal activities centering on getting illegal hooch to a thirsty public. The resulting mixture of booze, guns, gangsters, and the newfangled automobile—which became standard police equipment as well as a rumrunner's best friend—proved a heady challenge for law enforcement officers.

Society leaders were concerned about the enticing nature of liquor and automobiles, which, when combined, could lead to a young woman's downfall. Mason City, Iowa, cop Anna Merrincourt bemoaned the loss of social drinking as Prohibition made illicit activity all the more appealing. Take a "naturally sociable" woman, Merrincourt said, place her in a flashy car with a man, add a dollop of "hooch," and the man might try to take advantage of his date. A repressive home life could exacerbate the problems, added Merrincourt, who advocated for wholesome entertainments to combat the problem of "fallen girls."

When not fulfilling their traditional role as caretakers of wayward females, policewomen found themselves involved in Prohibition investigations and raids. "Along Broadway the saying is that it takes a skirt to catch a bootlegger," noted a New York columnist.[53] During an undercover operation in November 1924, male and female officers got dressed to the nines in tuxedos and evening gowns, then fanned out across cafés in Times Square. Once inside the dining establishments, the undercover police officers surreptitiously ordered alcoholic beverages. The police effectively played their roles as happy partygoers. Waiters soon appeared with several varieties of wine, gin rickeys, and horse's necks—brandy or bourbon mixed with ginger ale. Once the drinks were placed in front of them, the police officers flashed their badges and escorted the waiters to patrol wagons waiting on the curb outside. The operation netted several dozen suspects.

Though the bootlegging population was overwhelmingly male, a small number of female liquor suppliers plied their trade during Prohibition. The Anti-Saloon League counted nine female bootleggers in its arrest records. Among them were Mabel Casares, whose sailing vessels transported illegal rum; Gertrude Lythgoe, "queen of the bootleggers," who ran liquor from the Bahamas; and 24-year-old Frances Cannistrael, who was making between $1,000 and $2,800 a day dealing in illicit booze. One female bootlegger got into the business for family reasons. During her court appearance she told the judge she needed to support her eight children and an invalid husband.[154]

Why weren't there more female bootleggers? New York policewoman Mary Sullivan had a simple answer: physical inability. "A woman can't load and unload a truck of liquor and that is the game unless you are among the high-ups," she explained in November 1926.[155]

NEW DANCES, NEW IMPROPRIETIES

Still pursuing social miscreants as they had done for four decades, policewomen of the Jazz Age faced some new members in their rogues' gallery. Case in point: the flapper, who caused female officers no end of grief. Clad in short skirts, faces caked with makeup, puffing on cigarettes, flappers symbolized a new brand of female independence of the 1920s. Drinking, sex, and swearing also served as the flapper's calling cards. How would local policewomen deal with this brash new arrival? In Oskaloosa, Iowa, policewoman Nellie Howe ran around the city trying to convince flappers to dress appropriately. Skirts needed to reach the knees and stockings should be worn up rather than rolled down, Howe told the girls. The ever-watchful Oskaloosa city council outlawed cigarettes and revoked the seller's licenses it had granted to 17 merchants. In a time of bootleg liquor, bootleg cigarettes joined the list of outlawed items that had to be purchased on the black market in Oskaloosa.

At dance halls and inside saloons, new fads like the Chicago drag and the camel's walk offered more opportunities for young people to strut, and to get in trouble. In Worcester, Massachusetts, policewomen Elizabeth Tracy and Jennie Rice instituted a set of rules that forbade people from trying out either dance within city limits. Dancers were also banned from performing moves with names like the pivot, the shimmy, and the tickle-toe. Jazz music was a no-no, and couples could not dance cheek to cheek lest they get all worked up.

To enforce such rules, policewomen sometimes had to fight with their fists. During one late evening, Salt Lake City, Utah, policewoman Gussie Friend found seven people drunk at a dance hall. One of them, a 27-year-old woman, got angry at Friend and insulted her, so the policewoman put her under arrest. Then the drunk woman punched Friend, who fell to the ground. The girl's date tried to come between the two women, but Friend popped up and hit him in the jaw. The man's head slammed into a chair on the way down, and he sprawled on the floor, unconscious. Friend dragged him outside, then returned and grabbed the woman. Then the trio, nursing their various bruises, waited for the patrol wagon.[156]

Did social and sexual behavior need to be so strictly patrolled? In the nation's capital, women's bureau chief Mina Van Winkle thought so. She warned the public that young people were enjoying wildly liberal social lives and that young women were taking the initiative where "sex affairs" were concerned. "The young girls of today have liberty such as young girls have never before enjoyed," said Van Winkle. "They are virtually unrestrained. At the same time, they are wholly uneducated regarding sex. As a result, their natural impulse is to exhibit their sex—parade it. They do this by their scanty costumes, by their actions, in a hundred ways."[157]

Van Winkle was also concerned about the "purely animal-like" behavior that she saw as she made her rounds. "Visit a roof garden or cabaret," she warned. "There you will see boys and girls drinking and dancing in a way to arouse thoroughly their sex impulses. By the time the dance is over, many of the girls, as well as the boys, are drunk."[158] New York's 700 dance halls—including "closed halls," in which women made money by dancing with male patrons—operated under the watchful eyes of the police and concerned social organizations. The women's city club sent member Maria Lambkin and several other undercover investigators into the dance halls to observe and document public behavior. Lambkin was horrified at activities like "moonlight dancing," in which only part of the dance floor was illuminated at any particular time. In the dark areas were women kissing men they had just met.

Worries over sexual behavior extended to the policing of agencies that advocated birth control. Debate continued to rage over whether the dissemination of contraceptive devices and information was an act of obscenity. In April 1929, policewoman Josephine McNamara went undercover to an organization called the Clinical Research Bureau, posing as a weary mother whose delicate health was in jeopardy after bearing three children to a drunkard husband. Doctors at the clinic examined her and provided some contraceptives. McNamara reported to her superiors that the clinic was providing "demoralizing information and advice." The incident triggered a police raid of the facility, the second in six weeks. The owner of the clinic, activist Margaret Sanger, was no stranger to such activity. Ten days after she opened the first birth control clinic in the United States in 1916, the police had shut it down.

It was now 13 years later, and it seemed that little had changed. "A patrol wagon growled up West 18th Street [in] Manhattan," reported *Time* magazine. "Police officers headed into the basement of a brownstone. Soon appeared a dozen agitated women. Some carried infants. Then six more women with strained, angry faces walked out of the door. Policemen, with wastepaper baskets full of surgical instruments, rubber devices and index cards in their arms, herded the six women into the patrol wagon."[59] Sanger, though herself not under arrest, accompanied the women, doctors, and nurses to the police station as an act of support.

Over 200 women attended the subsequent court hearing, shouting and jeering at the proceedings. At first the women were rushed out of the courtroom, but the judge later allowed them back inside. In the end, the police court ruled that municipal statutes granted doctors who were acting in good faith the right to provide birth control education. Mysteriously, the police commissioner demoted the undercover policewoman Josephine McNamara soon thereafter.[60]

Elsewhere, women had to protect themselves against persistent mashers who still caused no end of trouble. Chicago park policewoman Alice McCarty, who had spent two decades on the force, was walking in Grant Park late at night when 23-year-old Robert Secor said hello to her. McCarty did not respond, but Secor persisted, finally tripping her and knocking her down. Secor tripped too, falling on top of her. McCarty yanked a gun out of her purse and pulled the trigger. Secor punched her in the face, then ran away in a panic. McCarty fired again, this time hitting Secor. Dashing through the park, the injured Secor stumbled across two other park police officers and claimed he had been shot by a pair of thieves. Of course, later investigation revealed the truth. McCarty apparently wasn't afraid to use her weapon: she had previously shot three other people and had killed a purse-snatcher.[161]

Captain Edna Pitkin, one of New York's police reservists. In the fall of 1922, Pritkin helped test a new 12-pound bulletproof vest designed by Leo Krause, who fired a .38-caliber bullet at her. "Didn't even tickle," she remarked. (Library of Congress)

To keep mashers at bay, some policewomen taught self-defense classes in their local community. In Salt Lake City, Gussie Friend showed women how to subdue a male attacker: "Don't work against a man's larger muscle groups—work against his weaker points," she said. "Give him a blow on the side of his neck or across his Adam's apple —that will knock him speechless and will hurt worse than pounding his chest." Friend said that attending martial arts classes was unnecessary. Instead, she recommended wrestling-type moves, explaining that a woman should jab her fingers into the attacker's eyes or stomp her heel on the man's instep. "Or if you want to give him the complete treatment," she said, "pull his nostrils apart and push all your fingers in his eyes; sink your thumbs up under his jaw—but hard; kick him on the shins; use your knees, feet, elbows and teeth." Repeated screams would add to the effect, she said.[162]

Also under police scrutiny were performance artists who often skirted the fine line between artistic expression and indecent exposure as they gyrated onstage in front of enthusiastic audiences. In 1933, "fan dancer" Sally Rand appeared in court on an indecent exposure charge—one of many she would battle throughout her half-century-long career. Rand's pleas to the court were unsuccessful; she was sentenced to a year in prison and paid a $200 fine. In an ironic twist, Chicago policewoman Bessie McShane defended Rand's onstage appearance. Working undercover, McShane had watched Rand's careful preparation for her dances, noting that Rand covered her body with cream and spent $42 each week for the maline (mesh) pants that she wore to cover herself during performances. Still, it wasn't enough to keep the police at bay. "We haven't anything against Sally, but if we didn't control her, hundreds of imitators would burst into the spotlight," said McShane. "We have nine under our eyes already."[163]

Not everyone tried to put exotic dancers behind bars. The city of Madison, Wisconsin, approved the act of Rosita Carmen, who performed a fan dance similar to Sally Rand's. The mayor himself watched Carmen's act and approved, as did one of the city's police-women, Pearl Guynes. "I have seen far worse things—more nudity—on the beach and in the ballroom," Guynes said with a shrug.[164]

Back in Los Angeles, dancer Joyce Baker surprised a patrolman who entered the nightclub where she was performing. Baker was wearing so little—three strips of flesh-colored tape and a G-string—that the patrolman realized he needed help. "I couldn't arrest her the way she was," he explained, "so I called a policewoman." Had Baker violated vice laws? An all-male jury pondered the question. "Why, it was only an exhibition of art, same as you see in a museum," grumbled Baker. "At $2 a night—and that's all I was getting—it would have to be art. Anyone who would perform professionally for that little would be nuts."[165]

During his testimony in court, the flustered patrolman who had viewed her performance disagreed: "She was exhibiting a lot more than art," he said, grabbing Baker's red ostrich feathers and demonstrating how the dancer waved them above her head. "I've seen more than thirty fan dances in my time—professionally—and never before did I see a fan dancer swing fans over her head like she did," explained the patrolman. The judge asked Baker for a demonstration of her act, then thought better of it. "There was nothing vulgar about the dance until that policewoman arrived," said Baker, who said that a female officer yanked four fans away from Baker and broke them. The amused jury spent little time deliberating: they acquitted the fan dancer, and she returned to work.[166]

Sally Rand was back in the news during November 1946, arrested in a Los Angeles theater for "an immoral, indecent, obscene and impure exhibition" during a Halloween performance. The policeman who made the arrest noted that Rand was wearing something "flesh colored, about one-and-a-half by three-and-a-half inches." In court, Rand repeated her performance for the judge. At the end of the demonstration, Rand stripped completely nude just as a curtain swooshed down in front of her. Was it too easy to catch a hint of bare skin? The judge didn't think so. Rand left the courtroom victorious.[167]

But Rand's bumpy relationship with the law was far from over. When a policewoman and nine male members of the Milwaukee vice squad arrested Rand for indecency in July 1950, the 46-year-old performer informed the police that she was doing the same number she'd performed for the past 17 years in cities across the nation. Later, when Rand was nabbed at a carnival sponsored by the Milwaukee firefighters association, she came prepared: at the police station she whipped out photostatic copies of correspondence from other police departments that had determined her act was not indecent.[168]

Some of the more salacious cases in the entertainment industry centered on theater owners like vaudeville magnate Alexander Pantages. In October 1929, Pantages stood trial in Los Angeles to answer a horrifying question: Did he rape a 17-year-old dancer at his local theater? Pantages was the owner of 60 vaudeville theaters and movie houses in the western United States. Eunice Pringle accused him of attacking her in a broom closet next to his office after he asked her to audition privately for him. Policewoman Katherine Bellus testified that Pringle had bruises on her body and that her clothing had been torn. At the end of a circus-like trial, Pantages was sentenced to 50 years in prison. Upon appeal, the state supreme court ruled that women under 18 years of age who reported a sexual attack could be discredited via evidence of previous sexual activity. During a second trial, Pantages's attorneys spotlighted Pringle's sketchy personal life, and Pantages was eventually acquitted.[169]

Nine years later a beauty contest sponsored by a creative theater manager in Los Angeles would lead to a vagrancy charge. Boris Posner beefed up his theatrical programming by holding beauty competitions before showing movies. But after his latest series of auditions, nine women came forward to accuse him of trying to get a little too familiar with them. One of the women turned out to be an undercover police officer, Malvern Schirey, whom newspapers described as "a plain-looking young woman with heavily rouged cheeks."[170]

During auditions for his upcoming beauty contest, Posner was taking the candidates' measurements. He asked Schirey to remove her outer garments, leaving her standing in a chemise. In court, a jury of eight women and four men looked on as the defense attorney leaned on her.

"Did he take any liberties?" the attorney asked.

"He sure did," answered Schirey. "My chemise strap came loose and he massaged my breasts."

The other would-be contestants in the courtroom giggled. Schirey continued: "I remonstrated and he stopped further familiarity, but for the sake of the evidence, I let him complete his measurements. He measured my breasts, my waist, and my hips."

Other witnesses recounted how Posner ran a measuring tape around their breasts and hitched up their skirts to inspect their knees. "Mr. Posner let his hands wander indiscreetly," recalled one of the women. Posner, of course, vehemently denied any wrongdoing. A confused jury spent three hours pondering the evidence and emerged deadlocked. Posner soon retired from the theater business.[171]

Although they were instrumental in pursuing criminals, policewomen usually played a secondary or undercover role subordinate to the male officers who supervised each case. Women were rarely in charge, especially over men. Old-fashioned rules about male and female roles in society still influenced police departments to a great degree, and would continue to do so for the near future.

"ONLY A WOMAN CAN DO THAT"

In the meantime, law enforcement organizations believed that juveniles still needed someone to watch over them in public, and many women answered the call. Police matrons and policewomen continued to act as "city mothers" in communities across the United States. In January 1936, 18-year police veteran Genevieve Searls climbed up the stairs of a ratty building in Syracuse, New York. It was a chilly day during a bitter winter. Searls had received a phone call from someone in the neighborhood about a family named White. The neighbor said that the oldest of the four White children, seven-year-old Johnny, had been knocking on doors asking for food to feed himself and his three brothers.

Searls opened the door to the Whites' second-floor apartment. The air was frigid; there was no heat in the four dingy rooms. "There were two dirty beds, hardly fit to sleep in, a broken cot, a kitchen table, a kitchen chair and a stove in which there was no fire," Searls recounted. Three of the children—two, three, and five years old—sat in one of the rooms; the youngest boy's lips were blue with cold. "None of the children had shoes or stockings," said Searls. "The only food in the house consisted of a bottle a third-filled of sour milk and a quarter of a loaf of stale bread on the kitchen table."

Searls asked the boys, "Where is your mother?"

"We haven't seen her in two days," they answered. It had been more than 24 hours since they had eaten. Their father worked long hours in a nearby restaurant and came home only to sleep at night. Otherwise the children were left to fend for themselves.

Searls and a patrolman asked neighbors for blankets, which were immediately wrapped around the shivering children. Then the police officers scooped up the boys and slid them into a waiting squad car. A local maternity home took the children in, and the parents were notified to appear in children's court. Policewoman Searls, with tears in her eyes, called it the most pathetic case she had ever worked.[172]

Policewomen in the 1920s and 1930s inherited from their pre-decessors, the police matrons, the responsibility of chasing down runaway girls. As before, too many of the runaways ended up in prostitution, sometimes by choice and sometimes by force. In New York City, Mary Hamilton collected 19,000 reports of runaway children in 1923. Nearly 70 percent of them were girls—"almost two thousand a month coming and going," she lamented.[173] Once again, the debate over who—male or female officers—was better at deal-ing with wayward girls continued without a definite answer. Some policewomen needed no convincing: "A woman will trust a woman," mused policewoman Mildred Gardner in Appleton, Wisconsin. "The policewoman is the only means of really getting at female delinquents. If we are to remedy conditions by reform, we must do it by inspiring trust instead of fear. Only a woman can do that for a woman."[174]

Alberta O'Neal, a junior high school teacher turned police-woman in Corpus Christi, Texas, took care of so many lost and wayward women—the vice squad nabbed up to 125 of them every month—that they were referred to as "Mrs. O'Neal's girls." The policewoman did her best to provide assistance to all of them. "One girl who arrived in town with exactly two cents in her pocket came up to the station for help this week," said O'Neal. The woman's fiancé, a soldier, couldn't take leave until the next day. The local Girls Club took care of the woman for the night. "So many women and girls come here like that," lamented O'Neal. "And sometimes their fiancés don't marry them, they drift to the streets and we pick them up a few weeks later."[175]

The Los Angeles City Mothers Bureau, formed in 1914, was comprised of ten women appointed by the police chief. Only the head of the bureau received a salary. According to historian Gail Ryan, the bureau "was recognized by Scotland Yard as the first police department crime prevention bureau in the world."[176] To try to avoid sending first-time offenders to the courts, the city mothers would visit the youngsters' homes and work with their families to set things right. The bureau also worked to place wayward girls in private homes wherever possible, rather than making the girls wards of the state.

One of the City Mothers Bureau's targets were "pennant stands." Women staffed these street booths, which offered college, high school, and city pennants for sale. Men passing by could roll dice to try to win one of the pennants. Meanwhile the women in the booths—who were actually prostitutes—attempted to secure tricks with new clients. Pennant stands began to proliferate after the police cracked down on open prostitution and "the use of rooming houses for immoral purposes."[177]

On the opposite coast, San Francisco policewoman Katherine Sullivan chased down her share of runaways as well. In 1928, she tracked a white slave ring across three states, arresting 21 people in the process. A 19-year-old woman who had escaped from a hotel room in Pittsburgh and tried to flee to Stockton, California, told Sullivan that she had been forced into a "disorderly house." The young woman then introduced the police to a 36-year-old man whom she accused of being a pimp. "He's the man who put me in a house in Pismo Beach, and another at Stockton," said the woman. "We met in a San Francisco beer tavern. Later, he leased me out." The man denied the charge and said that yes, he had met the woman briefly in a tavern in San Francisco, but no, he had nothing to do with prostitution. The police charged him with pandering anyway.[178]

After handling hundreds of missing persons cases for the Pittsburgh Police Department, Mrs. W. C. Butterfield threw up her hands and blamed parents for causing their children to run away from home. In many homes in the 1920s and 1930s, children helped support their families by holding down jobs of their own—something that worried police and social reformers considerably. Fathers and mothers, said Butterfield, should not "send [their children] out into the economic world at an age when they should have no responsibilities of any kind." She added: "Many come from countries where women and children are beasts of burden. While the lordly male can loaf; and they attempt to carry on the same method here. . . . The daughters and sons, educated to American ways, find the bondage of the old world maddening." When those daughters and sons weren't allowed to spend any of the money they earned, they responded by running away. "It is the girl who is starved for pleasure, who 'goes wrong' when she gets her first taste of it," explained Butterfield. "It is the boy who never has been allowed to keep money he has earned, who 'goes wild' when he rebels and keeps it."[179]

In Chicago, policewoman Alice Clemons also noted that a miserable home life contributed directly to the delinquency of young women. "Parents should fix up their homes so that the daughter need not be ashamed of inviting her men friends to call," she said. "Unless this is done the girls will run away to some rooming house where company can be entertained." Clemons sadly recounted a toast made by a runaway girl in a local restaurant: "Here's to hell. May it be as pleasant as the road to it."[180]

Sometimes city mothers sacrificed much more than time and energy to the job. In March 1930, Pearl Lanham had been a cop for two weeks. She was assigned as a crossing guard in front of a grammar school in Gary, Indiana. After helping several youngsters across the street, she stepped off the curb to begin walking back to the other side. Nearby a car roared down the street. Lanham had her back to the vehicle and was unaware it was careening toward her. The driver slammed on his brakes. The car hit Lanham, throwing her eight feet and killing her instantly. More than a hundred screaming students witnessed the accident. The dead policewoman was just 33 years old.[181]

Although the constant influx of children needing help was stressful on local policewomen, the rewards of steering wayward boys and girls onto the right path ultimately made the efforts worthwhile. When Anna Brice, the only policewoman in Chester, Pennsylvania, wrapped up her career in the summer of 1945, she wrote about her experiences for the local newspaper: "As a policewoman I have patched up love affairs, helped to reconcile husbands and wives and to settle family quarrels." Helping to rehabilitate young girls was at the top of her list. "Many of the girls keep in touch with me," she wrote. "Their letters are among the things I treasure most. . . . Some of the letters are written from jail, some from Sleighton Farms [a reformatory school]. Others, from luckier girls who are back home again, tell all the homey details about washing, ironing, taking care of their children, knitting and crocheting."[182]

CAR TROUBLE

Another critical development of the 1920s was the greater mobility of the average citizen. As the widely available and relatively affordable automobile made its way onto American streets in greater numbers, incidents and accidents became commonplace. In July 1922, the Chicago Police Department declared war on "vamps"—flirty women—who caused trouble for men driving through the busy Michigan Boulevard district. The police were more concerned about auto accidents than about public morals. "[The vamps] insist on decoying some handsome man just as the traffic cop signals 'go,' " explained policewoman Mary Ready, who was assigned to shoo the women off the sidewalks. Ready's first sweep of the vamps resulted in six arrests of women who told her they were models and manicurists. Ready, unimpressed, charged them with disorderly conduct. "If they'd only vamp the guy on foot instead of the Adonis at the wheel it wouldn't be so bad," mused the policewoman.[183]

Elsewhere it was women drivers who were causing the traffic problems. Mattie Tipton, a policewoman in Jacksonville, Florida, believed that women's expectation of being given "courtesy" led to minor accidents. "The woman at the wheel feels that she is entitled to certain privileges, traffic laws or no traffic laws, and she is going to have them," Tipton explained. "She cuts corners, ignores traffic lights and makes pedestrians jump for their lives." Tipton also noted that 15 percent of fatal accidents involved women behind the wheel.[184]

In other cases involving automobiles, women were the victims. On a Saturday night in Ogden, Utah, a car full of men screeched past the corner of Harrison and Capitol Avenues. Suddenly a woman fell from the automobile and lay in a crumpled heap in the middle of the intersection. Sometime after 10:00 P.M. a passerby found the woman. Thinking her dead, the good Samaritan prepared to take her to the morgue. But upon closer inspection it turned out that the woman was conscious—if just barely. The passerby drove the woman to the hospital, where doctors took a look at her and immediately pumped out the contents of her stomach. Policewoman Addie Sanders was called to investigate the strange case. She arrived at the hospital and hurried into the emergency room. After chatting with the rescued woman, Sanders found out that her first name was Myrtle, that she was 21 years old, and that she was married. A group of men had invited her to take a ride in their car; she had accepted. Speeding down the road, they gave her a drink. Myrtle downed it and passed out soon afterward. Then the men tossed her out of the car. With the male carousers long gone, there was little else for the police to do but charge Myrtle with public drunkenness.[185]

Common criminals also found the automobile a handy tool for their activities. Alice McCarthy, a Chicago policewoman, snagged 40 automobile thieves during the summer of 1932. "Miss McCarthy is equal to any man on my force," said her supervisor. When asked how she was so successful, McCarthy answered flatly, "I put a gun on them and tell them to drive to the station, and they go."[186] McCarthy had a more difficult case two years later, when she shot a 20-year-old purse-snatcher. The policewoman was serving as a lure when two men followed her down the street. One of them hit her over the head and yanked her purse away. She steadied herself and saw the man dashing away from her. This time when she pulled her gun, she used it: she fired at the thief and killed him.

In 1941, reporter Mary Elizabeth Plummer introduced 29-year-old New York policewoman Kathryn Barry as someone who "looks like a well dressed secretary from the downtown business district." The daughter of a police sergeant who was killed in the line of duty,

Barry was described as typical of the new breed of female cop: "young, agile, alert, intelligent, versatile." Like other policewomen, Barry stayed on call for when she was needed rather than being assigned to a beat. "Her typical working garb is a blue silk dress, a tailored coat and a little fur-trimmed hat. Plain gold ear-clips for adornment," Plummer wrote.[187]

Nine years later, readers met up with Barry again. The policewoman jumped onto a Brooklyn drug dealer's car as it screamed down the street trying to escape from the police. "Out of the shadows shot Detective Barry—five feet two in dangling earrings and spike heels," wrote a reporter. "She clung to the running board as the car careened down the street and the driver beat her knuckles, punched her face and did his best to drive her off." Barry pulled out her pistol and aimed it at the driver, who finally screeched the car to a halt and gave himself up.[188]

It wasn't long before police departments began considering the use of cars in their day-to-day activities. Policewomen in Lowell, Massachusetts, proposed that pursuit cars could be used "to ferret out petting parties and send erring girls home." The local police department couldn't provide the requested cars but did have two motorcycles in its budget. "If the policewomen need speedy transportation, I can think of no better vehicle than a motorcycle," said the superintendent. "I have already asked the city government to provide two more cycles for the department, and if the policewomen would like to use them in their petting party crusade, they may have them."[189] Along with horses, bicycles, and motorcycles, the squad car would become a useful tool in the policewoman's arsenal.

SECOND WORLD WAR

What did the female officer look like in the 1940s? In April and May 1941, reporter Mary Elizabeth Plummer spent a day with the New York City Police Department, coming away with a picture of the average policewoman: "She may be fresh from college, and wear a bow on her pageboy bob . . . or she may be a young matron, a widow, or a white-haired woman in her fifties. She's likely to be slim, but strong and muscular, rather than Amazonian. This is particularly true of the newer girls, who are mainly size 14 or 16."[190] In a separate article, Plummer wrote: "Most of them are good sportswomen. All swim. Most of them drive a car. Some manage their own apartments. A number are interested in music, and go to concerts in their free time. Several are performers."[191]

Free time would be at a premium by that December, when the Japanese attack on the American naval base at Pearl Harbor, Hawaii, propelled the United States to enter World War II. Women on the home front stepped into jobs vacated by men who had entered military service—jobs like manufacturing, administration, and law enforcement. "Women are being inducted into all the usual women's jobs and also as junior executives, personnel officers, salesmen and sales executives, and into engineering and accounting," stated an annual survey by the Northwestern Life Insurance company. "All graduates who want jobs can have them," said bullish job placement officials at colleges across the country.[192]

Women also entered the military, primarily in support functions, freeing men for combat-related duties. At home, auxiliary and reserve police forces added female members to help patrol cities and military installations. Rosa Sessler was one of four roving patrol officers—and the only woman—who provided around-the-clock security to the

Army quartermaster's sub-storage base in Sparta, Illinois. Daughter of a policewoman and wife of an Army infantry soldier, Sessler wielded a .45-caliber pistol while making her rounds: "That automatic is fully loaded with seven bullets," she said, "and I'm not going to be afraid to use it if the occasion arises."[193] In Fresno, California, members of the Women's Army Corps worked as military policewomen (MPs) beginning in March 1944, watching over the main gate and helping visitors find their way. The new female MPs were, however, unarmed.

Meanwhile the nation's capital saw an influx of female war workers—labeled "$1,440 Girls" after their annual government salary—who arrived in the city during the war years. Nearly 40,000 women, averaging 20 years old, joined the wartime bureaucracy, and the policewomen's bureau tried to keep watch over them. Some of the new arrivals were unprepared for the rigors of working in often dreary government jobs and sleeping like sardines in the city's overcrowded buildings. Signs of mental strain usually popped up within three weeks of arrival, said policewoman Rhoda Milliken, chief of the women's bureau. Milliken noted that about a hundred women per month returned home, and the number of girls turned over to the local council on mental hygiene doubled to 32 per month after the war started. Many of those women ended up at St. Elizabeth's psychiatric hospital for treatment.

The ever-growing number of parents engaged in wartime employment triggered an increase in child delinquency as well. Milliken noted a 32 percent jump in the delinquency figures in Washington, D.C., between 1940 and 1942. "They may be reflecting home tension or merely seeking excitement and attention to keep up with defense- and war-occupied parents—mothers who wear uniforms, fathers who are air raid wardens, and brothers in the service," explained Milliken.[194]

Up north in New Castle, Pennsylvania, policewoman Catherine Dukes had her hands full with delinquency cases: "New Castle has its problem kids, plenty of them." But, she added, the reasons were understandable: "About 10 percent of them are the incorrigibles that have always been and always will be," she said. "The other 90 percent, however, are often 'swell kids' who have gone a little wild either because they are in the brief 'wild oats' stage, or for one of two more serious reasons—too little home life or too much of the wrong sort."[195]

But juvenile delinquency paled next to a more pressing problem brought on by the war: misbehavior by men and women in uniform. As in World War I, off-duty military personnel flowed into nearby communities looking to blow off steam. Policewoman Josephine Murphy suffered a black eye during a 1,200-person riot that erupted during a dance at the Elks hall in Cambridge, Massachusetts. A soldier landed on his head after being thrown from a balcony 15 feet above the dance floor. Bottles and fists flew, and the riot spilled into the street as police rushed into the melee.

Transient soldiers and sailors brought with them spouses, girlfriends, and prostitutes—along with "social [i.e., sexually transmitted] diseases." While prostitution in Chicago declined as a result of girlfriends and female war workers arriving in town, said policewoman Dorothy Tedell, "most of the offenses that occur in Chicago are committed by servicemen from out of the city and the girls who follow them here. These girls are crazy about a uniform. They have no regard for the serious matters involved, as long as the man is in uniform." Police were busy yanking young women out of taverns and away from loud parties. "It is hard for tavern operators to tell the age of a young girl nowadays because she can make up to look much older than she actually is," explained Tedell.[196]

Ogden, Utah, home of military installations such as the gigantic Ogden Ordnance Depot, a munitions plant, faced the problem of social diseases head-on. The U.S. Army and the city health board asked the local police department for help. When Army doctors treated soldiers for venereal disease, the soldiers were asked for the names of their sexual partners. Armed with that list of names, police-women like Addie Sanders tracked down women who were report-edly infected with venereal disease. In August 1942, Sanders nabbed two women, both in their early twenties, and charged them with vagrancy. The suspects denied they were prostitutes, insisting that they worked as taxi drivers in the city.

Meanwhile, residents of Fresno, California, could sleep easy at night: the police chief declared that the city had no organized pros-titution whatsoever. Army soldiers reporting back to their posts with venereal diseases were, the chief said, being infected by amateurs, not ladies of the night. "It's the bobby sock girls and lonely wives the Army needs to watch," said the chief.[197]

Sometimes what seemed practical was actually against the law. In 1945, a female hitchhiker, arrested in a local bar, stood in the El Paso, Texas, police court on a vagrancy charge. The judge asked what crime the woman had committed. "She had on a dress with no middle," explained policewoman Callie Fairley. After her arrest, the suspect asked Fairley for help. She needed money, she said. Fairley fired off three telegrams to different locations in California, but none of the addresses turned out to be real.

The judge peered at the suspect, whose outfit now definitely had a "middle" to it. Farley saw the curious look on his face.

"I got her another blouse to come to court in," explained Fairley.

The judge asked about the skimpy clothing that the suspect had been wearing. "That's the way women dress in California," insisted the woman. "It was a whole dress when I started out, but it got hot coming across the desert and I cut it into two pieces."[198]

Police officers in Washington, D.C., faced a similar case the next year—except this time the woman was completely nude. On a sunny September day, bookbinder Walter Linscott glanced out the window of his tiny shop in the Senate Law Library of the U.S. Capitol. What he saw amazed him: a beautiful 30-year-old brunette was preparing to sun herself on the fourth-floor ledge. She was taking off her clothes.

The bookbinder leaned out the window. "Hey, you can't do that out there!" he yelled at her.

"I'm just taking a sun bath," the woman answered, undeterred.

Linscott phoned the Capitol police. Two policewomen—one from above, one from below—moved toward the woman. When she saw them, she got up and started to run. The policewomen grabbed her. She struggled against them, dropping money and other items from her purse as they covered her up and escorted her off the ledge.

Meanwhile energetic military personnel continued to cause mayhem. In Madison, Wisconsin, a 20-year-old soldier on furlough led police on a wild chase through the city streets at two in the morning. Police had received a complaint call from a resident who told them that someone was driving recklessly, screeching his tires, and leaning on the horn. As officers chatted with the resident, the culprit screamed by in his car. The police jumped into their cruiser and gave chase, joined by two more squad cars along the way. Policewoman Jean Reese was riding in the back seat of one of the patrol cars. During the high-speed pursuit she was thrown back and forth, bruising her knees and elbows. Up ahead, the soldier jammed the wheel around a turn in the road and flipped his car, abruptly ending the chase. When he had gathered himself together, he told the police that he yearned to get behind the wheel of a jeep and was simply practicing his driving. When the Army got its soldier back, he was placed behind the wheel of a truck, where his race-driving compulsions would be kept in check.[199]

Three weeks later Reese requested permission to carry a blackjack as she went about her duties. Pearl Guynes, head of the Madison women's bureau, saw no need for her employees to carry weapons of any stripe. In fact, Guynes had already confiscated one blackjack from Reese. But the chief of police disagreed. He felt that women could be armed as long as they showed they were capable of handling their weapon of choice. So the chief recommended the .25- or .32-caliber pistol, since, he said, small-caliber guns were better suited to the female hand. Reese appreciated the chief's plan, saying she would train with her own .25-caliber pistol. Other police officers weren't so happy: the chief of detectives wondered out loud where policewomen could possibly conceal a pistol or blackjack since their purses were already stuffed with other items. Although she prevailed on the issue of carrying a weapon, Reese continued to butt heads with Guynes on other matters. Finally, Reese gave up and resigned in March 1944, at the end of her one-year probation period.[200]

Like Jean Reese, Callie Fairley, a policewoman in El Paso, Texas, apparently approached some of her duties with a little too much vigor. "[She] has become possibly overly energetic in connection with some arrests," admitted the El Paso police chief in 1944. A former nurse, Fairley was the city's first female detective. During World War II she worked three nights a week helping the military police comb the streets for soldiers in trouble. At a local tavern one evening, Fairley angered a Marine sergeant's wife by stepping between her and her husband during a long kiss. The wife accused Fairley of slapping her. The chief conducted an investigation but proposed to the city council that Fairley be left alone. "[The sergeant's wife] received a bloody nose and face bruises and lacerations on the same Friday afternoon that she was arrested by Mrs. Fairley," wrote the chief; however, he explained, the arrested woman "left the police station with her features intact and undamaged, and appeared at her hotel, one hour and a half later, with the bloody nose and other injuries." The police chief acknowledged that Fairley might have been a bit hasty in arresting the wife, especially since the city had no ordnance against kissing in public, but regarding the woman's injuries he was clear: "Mrs. Fairley didn't do it."[201]

In the interest of maintaining the peace, however, the chief considered pulling Fairley back to other, less volatile duties. "We want to cooperate in every way with the war effort but it may be necessary to make this change," he explained.[202] Fairley weathered the storm, staying with the police department until her retirement at the age of 70. In May 1963, the Junior Women's Club named her El Paso's "Mother of the Year."[203]

Some policewomen's problems happened while they were off duty. Newspapers called policewoman Louise Motz "New York's prettiest cop" and "the terror of all subway mashers." In 1930, however, a woman named Emma Jacobs accused Motz of petting, drinking, and husband stealing. Jacobs's husband was spending time in speakeasies with Motz, who apparently enjoyed sitting on the man's lap. The commissioner decided that it was conduct unbecoming an officer, but before he could request that she resign, Motz quit.

In March 1941, New York policewoman Mary Shanley, promoted to detective first grade, celebrated her success a bit too heartily. Famed for nabbing pickpockets by the dozen—"I can usually tell in twenty minutes whether a suspect is legitimate or not," she claimed[204]—Shanley was enjoying some off-duty time at a Queens bar and grill. At one point she pulled out her service revolver and fired it into the air. Witnesses said that Shanley was drunk, a charge she denied. She maintained that she had downed only a single drink. "I thought I was going to faint," she told the deputy police commissioner at her trial. "After the drink I felt very sick. I can't tell you what happened after that." Shanley was demoted back to policewoman and temporarily suspended from duty.

New York policewoman Mary Shanley, scourge of pickpockets everywhere, in June 1937. *(Library of Congress)*

Shanley's celebratory gunshot wasn't the first time the energetic policewoman had fired her weapon in public. She had earned the nickname Annie Oakley for her stance on the use of firearms: "You have the gun to use, and you may just as well use it," she said. One day she tracked a purse-snatcher out of St. Patrick's Cathedral, shooting twice into the air to draw his attention.[205]

"DON'T OVERDO EITHER ONE"

While women were entering the ranks of law enforcement in increasing numbers in the 1940s, the debate over the design of policewomen's uniforms continued in the background. In a move that would be repeated in departments across the country for decades, the New York Police Department issued its female officers a special piece of luggage: a combination gun holster and makeup kit. Introduced in 1943, this practical item had space to carry a .38-caliber service revolver and came with "a lipstick in medium red, a powder compact and a case of dry rouge." Mayor Fiorello La Guardia, blunt as always, encouraged women officers, "Use your gun as you would your lipstick. Use it only when you need it, and use it intelligently. Don't overdo either one."[206]

Detroit's police department introduced a similar type of purse in the fall of 1947, available in tan and black leather. Five years prior to that, the city's 55 policewomen had been issued an experimental uniform, which they had to purchase themselves. The costs, according to the *Detroit News,* were as follows: "a blue felt hat, cut on the lines of a police cap, but with feminine lines, $6; blue dress with short sleeves, $11.28; sharkskin collar for the dress, $1; blue gabardine topcoat, $46. The women also pay $12.85 for their oxfords, but these are not considered part of the uniform."[207]

The experiment proved highly unpopular, and the Detroit policewomen shunned the new uniforms. In 1948, the police commissioner, Harry Toy, resurrected the discussion, asking for feedback from the women who worked for him. They responded that they didn't want to wear uniforms full-time, nor were they interested in wearing the getups for special occasions like parades or inspections. The women didn't want the uniforms even if the city shouldered the cost. The new clothing, they said, would interfere with their job performance.

Commissioner Toy, undaunted, unveiled a new uniform the following year. "Word of his latest creation set women four floors away, screaming," noted the local press. Tightly fitted in blue with a necktie, and topped with a beret sporting a tiny gold wreath, the new outfit cost $150—for which, again, the policewomen would have to pay out of their own pockets. "It might be cheap for Toy but he doesn't live on salaries like ours," one policewoman grumbled. "And in these uniforms we'll wind up feeling we ought to tip our hats to women."[208]

Issues of fashion aside, as the responsibilities of policewomen grew, so too did the dangers of the job. Southward along the west coast, the city of San Diego was having its own problems with thieves. On a quiet night in April 1927, police officers Rena Wright and Charles Harris pulled their car to a stop in Balboa Park, a 1,400-acre area renowned for its lush landscaping. Both officers were dressed in civilian clothes. Both were armed. A holdup man had been robbing people passing through the park. Wright and Harris were there to stop him. Their plan was simple: When the thief approached the officers, Harris would pretend to be robbed while Wright subdued the man.

Suddenly a bright light flashed from the rear of the car, momentarily blinding the officers. It was the holdup man. He trained his flashlight on them and appeared to recognize Harris. The thief quickly fired three shots at Harris, who returned fire, blasting five times into the blinding light. But two of the robber's bullets had pierced Harris's heart. Meanwhile, a shocked Wright didn't have a chance to get off a shot. The holdup man fled into the night, leaving her alone with her dead partner. Wright drove back to the station with Harris's body beside her. The police were never able to capture the holdup man, and the case remains unsolved.

With American society moving along at a faster clip—heightened sexuality, cheap booze, speeding automobiles, wartime intrigue, and the rest—policewomen faced a growing number of responsibilities, even if their supervisors and the public at large still considered them to be a novelty useful for "women's work." But an investigation conducted by New York policewoman Winifred Hayes in 1948 showed that there were dangers even in situations that seemed ideally suited to the female officer. For two weeks Hayes subjected herself to multiple hair treatments, mudpacks, shampooing, and massages at a beauty parlor in Harlem. Hayes was posing as a customer in a shop that was rumored to be a front for a drug operation. Soon Hayes had the evidence she needed, and just before the sun came up the police raided the beauty parlor. In an apartment at the back of the shop, the police uncovered 1,000 marijuana cigarettes, a pound and a half of marijuana seed, and some cocaine. It was a small haul, to be sure, but one that foreshadowed the growing problem of illegal drug use—a problem that would increase steadily in the near future.

I have a gun in my purse. I have a blackjack, nightstick, handcuffs and some mace. And I know when and how to use them. I can protect myself and my partner if necessary.
— Mary Weinmumson,
New Orleans Police Department[209]

CHAPTER 4

The Long Uphill Battle (1950–1970)

ALTHOUGH POLICEWOMEN HAD already been on duty in their communities for several decades, police departments across the United States were still appointing their first female officers well into the 1950s and 1960s. Following tradition, however, policewomen's duties remained chiefly the same: take care of women, children, and—in a new wrinkle—parking meters. With more and more vehicles on the road—74 million by 1960—an increasing number of female cops were becoming enforcement officers (better known as meter maids), assigned to track parking and meter usage.

The 1950s were a period of perceived conformity, beneath which were brewing major cultural and political changes in American society —the sexual revolution and a sharp increase in the number of women in the workforce, to name just two. By the early 1960s, approximately 2,400 women were serving in municipal police departments across the United States.[211] The 1960s also saw the first highly publicized court cases brought by policewomen against their own departments for gender discrimination. But even with the progress represented by civil rights legislation and the establishment of federal equal opportunity laws, female police officers still had major hurdles to jump: The age-old perception of women as the "weaker sex," coupled with the entrenched dominance of men in the profession, made the journey ahead anything but smooth for policewomen.

Jefferson City, Missouri, was similar to numerous other American cities that were figuring out how to make the best use of female officers in the postwar decades. In 1953, the Jefferson City chief of police recommended that Mrs. Harry Baysinger, a secretary in the department, be appointed the city's first female officer. Her proposed duties? "[The chief] plans to use Mrs. Baysinger to counteract shoplifting," explained the local newspaper. "In addition, her services will be invaluable to cases in which women are involved."[212] Further, Baysinger would not be the only female officer; because the city was undergoing new construction for parking spaces, the chief considered using women as meter maids. The newspaper found this to be a "sound economical practice" because "meter maids do not necessitate the same salaries as policemen." And utilizing Baysinger and other female officers in this way, the chief reasoned, would give male officers time to handle more important issues.

In many cities the qualifying exam for female police candidates included a physical fitness test similar to the one given to male candidates. On a children's playground in the Bronx, more than a hundred candidates for the New York Police Department took part in lifting 30-pound weights and running an obstacle course, among other strenuous activities. One of the hopefuls, Margaret Maloney, was a 27-year-old mother of three who told a reporter that housework was ideal preparation for the rigors of police duty. "Lifting children and carrying washing to the roof are great exercises," said Maloney. "It is the girl who pushes a pencil around at a desk who amazes me when she passes the test." In addition to performing a standing broad jump, candidates had to complete an abdominal lifting exercise. "We had to raise up to a sitting position holding a fifteen-pound weight behind our heads with both hands," explained Maloney. "I couldn't do that at all at first, and I wasn't sure I could do it in the test. But I sat right up. It really develops your stomach muscles."[213]

Of the 132 women who took the test two years later, only ten failed to pass. The chairman of the civil service commission was impressed: "I must confess that you young ladies have put to shame the people who have labored under the illusion that a woman must be husky looking to become a policewoman," he said. "Some of you look more like Hollywood studio models than young ladies who might be tangling with violators of the law."[214]

Women take the qualifying exam for the New York City police force, 1947. (*Library of Congress*)

But behind the sunny pronouncements of community leaders lay an important truth: even with more women applying to be police officers, there were precious few jobs available for them—and the entrance qualifications could be extremely difficult to master. In Los Angeles, a 1959 civil service examination drew 3,000 applicants; of those, only nine were selected to join the police department. "The public just can't realize how much a woman goes through to get on the police force," noted policewoman Alice Elliott. "For a full year we took tests ranging from a two-and-a-half-hour written examination to the Rorschach personality test."[215]

Martha Schnabel knew how difficult it could be. She joined the San Antonio, Texas, police department in 1958, becoming the sixth woman on the force. She had always yearned to be a police officer, but her life as a military spouse meant that she and her husband had to pack up and move periodically, making it difficult for Schnabel to establish a career of her own. Finally, prior to her husband's retirement from the Air Force, Schnabel saw a newspaper advertisement for policewomen. She decided to apply.

First, however, Schnabel had to gain weight to qualify. She spent a week gnawing on bread and bananas and washing them down with milk, adding seven and a half pounds to her petite frame. Then she began a battery of qualifying exams. She recalled her written test as an unnerving experience: "I am five feet, four inches tall, and weighed 105 pounds. I walked into the basement of that auditorium. There was a huge policeman, with a big gun on, walking up and down the aisles, and sixty-two other women, who all looked like amazons to me. My first thought was, 'Dear Lord, what am I doing here?' "[216] Once she completed her training, Schnabel found that many male officers were still unwilling to accept a woman in uniform. When Schnabel graduated from the police academy in 1958, her boss decided to insult her:

"We had a beautiful ceremony, but the chief of police had to ruin the whole thing," she recalled. "He called my husband over and, right in front of me, told him that at home my badge didn't mean a thing."[217]

RISING CRIME

Although the United States had entered an era of stability and prosperity in the 1950s, problems of crime and drugs, especially among young people, began to bubble to the surface. Policewomen were positioned to focus on the problems of youth in many American cities.

After World War II the American teenager became a recognized demographic segment of society. Madison Avenue marketed a growing array of consumer products to teens, the older generation was concerned about their tastes in music and fashion, and parents worried that their children were growing up too fast, too soon. One phenomenon amid the concerns about teenagers was the increase of "girl gangs" in inner-city neighborhoods.

The arsenal of the girl gang featured a variety of effective tools. "The most common weapon is the jackknife, although the switchblade has its fans," noted *Parade* magazine in April 1955. "But some are partial to bicycle chains, honed-down nail files, razor blades, or rings with jagged points. A new favorite is the 'church key,' or beer-can opener."[218]

How bad was the problem? *Parade* was quick to assure its readers that towns across America weren't exactly being overrun by young girls sporting switchblade knives. "This does not mean every kid in blue jeans and bobby sox packs a knife in her windbreaker or goes around with her dukes cocked," wrote Sid Ross and Ed Kiester. Most American girls were normal, they reported. "The percentage that strays still is made up mostly of sex delinquents,

chronic truants or the plain unmanageable. But among the delinquents is a new and growing minority dedicated to violence."[219]

In Philadelphia the police imposed an 11:00 P.M. curfew on girls
under 18. Frustrated policewoman Norma Carson said that she did
not have enough officers to patrol the streets effectively—there were
just 24 policewomen on the payroll. A two-day sweep of the city
in November 1953 rounded up a thousand delinquents. "We have
received complaints of girls burglarizing homes and businesses, and
helping gangs of boys steal automobiles," said Carson. "We have cases
of girls stealing autos." Carson added that Philadelphia was "faced
with the problem of more serious offenses committed by girls than
ever before."[220]

In Bridgeport, Connecticut, shoppers found out that their city
was a dangerous place to buy clothes. During the 1956 holiday season
the town was terrorized by half a dozen girls, all 12 or 13 years old.
The gang swiped items from local stores and even ducked into dressing rooms to steal shoppers' wallets. Police nabbed one of the girls
as she attempted to lift a wallet from a store customer. Policewoman
Ella Brown sat down with the girl and talked for a while. The girl
eventually turned on her fellow gang members and told the police
where to find them. As the notorious gang headed to juvenile court,
the police recovered from their stash seven wallets, assorted items
of clothing, and several hundred dollars' worth of costume jewelry.

In addition to the rising visibility of the gang culture, illegal
drugs became a more prevalent social issue during the 1950s. Lois
Lundell, director of the Illinois Crime Prevention Bureau, noted in
March 1957 that the United States had between 50,000 and 60,000
addicts roaming its streets. Most were young people, and most had
become addicts within the past three years. Lundell expressed frustration about public apathy toward the problem. "Generally," she

explained, "while they are in the high school age bracket, comes the introduction to the marijuana cigarette through a friend or a bunch of the guys who already smoke them."[221] Using marijuana was more a matter of peer pressure than trying to escape reality, Lundell added.

The San Antonio Police Department put newly appointed officer Martha Schnabel to work in the local jail, where she oversaw the needs of women incarcerated there. "The most pitiful prisoners were the addicts who were booked into jail, usually for prostitution or theft, because they needed the money to supply their habit," recalled Schnabel. "After a few hours in jail, the withdrawal symptoms began. These girls were mainliners with heavy tracks on their arms, necks, and in some cases, the veins had just about collapsed all over."[222]

Young-looking female cops were sometimes placed undercover to rout out drug dealers. Women officers proved useful because they could get into places where men wouldn't have been admitted. "Among them you can see reminders of a Broadway showgirl, a bobby soxer, your grandmother, the most studious girl in your class, your favorite nurse and the girl you left behind you with the wistful heart-shaped face," noted an observer. "This comes in handy when they wish to pose as, say, a showgirl drug addict, or a night club hatcheck girl who wants to search certain suspected pockets."[223] In certain cases, a fresh-scrubbed policewoman dressed as a bobby soxer—resplendent in a poodle skirt and rolled-down socks—made a convincing high school student.

In 1959, the Seattle police investigated drug dealing at one of the high schools in the city. Key to the case was undercover work done by Maureen Sears, a 22-year-old rookie policewoman. Sears dressed for the part: "She donned a sweater, skirt, car coat and flat-heeled shoes so she could mingle unnoticed with other girls near the high school," noted a newspaper report. Inside a local café, Sears stood six feet away watching nonchalantly as Richard Mulron, an 18-year-old high school student, sold four marijuana cigarettes to a young boy. The boy flipped eight $1 bills into Mulron's hand. What Mulron didn't know was that the bills were marked and that the boy, who had admitted to purchasing drugs in the past, had promised the police he would help catch the dealer. Four detectives milled around nearby, observing the transaction. The police grabbed Mulron for dealing. Mulron—"who affects a shaggy haircut and long sideburns"—shrugged after his arrest and said he didn't know the cigarettes had marijuana in them, even though he was selling them for $2 each, a sky-high price for a regular cigarette. "I figured they weren't Bull Durhams [a brand of cigarette] either," he said. Mulron claimed that a stranger had approached him one day with a bunch of mystery cigarettes in his hand. "You want to float or get high?" said the stranger, who stuffed the joints in Mulron's pocket and then vanished. The Seattle police rolled their eyes. Aside from Mulron's rather unconvincing story, he was a repeat offender: the police had previously arrested him for dealing drugs.[224]

Sometimes a case called for a female officer to play the woman-in-distress role. On a rainy Sunday night in December 1959, Phoenix policewoman Dixie McCauley knocked on the door of a reputed drug house. The two men inside opened the door. "I'm having car trouble," McCauley said. "Can you help me?" As the two men chatted with her and stepped to her car, police officers arrested them and dashed into the house. In the bathroom they found a hidden stash of heroin worth $250. As the officers clicked the handcuffs onto his wrists, one of the two men complimented the female officer: "That was pretty smart," he said to her. "I really thought you did have car trouble."[225]

McCauley had worked for a newspaper before joining the Phoenix Police Department as one of its seven female officers. When asked about the dangers inherent in the job, she wasn't too worried. "Besides, a policewoman is never sent out alone," she said. "There are always several men around where they can keep a constant watch on her, and in some cases she carries a walkie-talkie in her purse. That way the men can tell the instant trouble arises."[226]

As undercover policewomen got more involved in ferreting out drugs and drug dealers, McCauley's case looked rather innocuous by comparison. In January 1967, the Los Angeles police used a female cop on an undercover narcotics case for the first time. Over a three-month period, seven rookie officers—including the 22-year-old policewoman—infiltrated the city's drug culture. The team made 200 drug buys, scoring $5,000 worth of marijuana, cocaine, heroin, LSD, and barbiturates. Meanwhile in Portland, Oregon, male and female officers went undercover as hippies, netting 40 drug arrests in one week. The police noted that youngsters were using an increasing amount of hard drugs like heroin and morphine.[227]

Drug users sometimes made for challenging—and bizarre—interactions with the police. One night in 1968, Chicago police-women Geraldine Perry and Joan Halloran, both brand new to the force, were working the midnight shift in a squad car. Heading north on Lake Shore Drive, parallel to Lake Michigan, the two officers saw a young man standing in the middle of the road, looking as if he needed help. Perry and Halloran pulled to a stop nearby. Suddenly the young man ran up to them and yanked the driver's door open. "I am going to God!" he screamed repeatedly, shoving Halloran over and taking the wheel.

The man's religious pronouncement caught the policewomen off guard. "We were quite concerned that he was going to take us with him," recalled Perry, "and we weren't ready to go!" Before Perry or Halloran could react, the young man, later identified as Bradimir Ilic, stepped on the accelerator and sent the patrol car careening down the road. "He repeatedly would jam the accelerator to the floor," said Perry, "causing the car to not only go at high speed, but in an erratic and dangerous manner." As Ilic took them on a screaming two-mile ride at 100 miles per hour, Perry and Halloran thought about reaching for their guns but decided it would only make the situation worse. Instead Perry grabbed the radio. "In those days we didn't have hand-held radios and our radio was attached to the dashboard," she said. Ilic was too busy driving to pay attention. "He didn't seem to notice or respond when I began radioing for help."

A mile and a half north of the car's position, police threw together a roadblock. Seeing officers ahead, Ilic jammed the steering wheel to turn the vehicle around. He lost control and the car ground to a halt. Perry and Halloran held him until other officers arrived. Later, when doctors took a look at Ilic, they said he had probably been taking LSD when he accosted the policewomen.[228]

Though the incident paled in comparison to cases that Perry and Halloran would tackle in the future, it remained a strong memory for the two policewomen because it happened at the beginning of their careers. "Interestingly enough, we caught some flak for not having used our weapons," said Perry, looking back on the incident years later. "However, since the suspect was driving at a high rate of speed and we were all together in the front seat, it didn't seem to Joan and me that drawing our weapons was the prudent thing to do, especially given the close quarters we were in."

At home, to avoid frightening her children, Perry decided not to tell them about what had happened. "I didn't want them to be worried about Mom when she went to work," explained Perry. But when the story made the local papers, Perry was stuck. Her children came home from school, asking, "Mom, is it true that you got kidnapped?"[229]

WIFE, MOTHER, POLICEWOMAN

Perry's story demonstrates an important point: many female officers were pulling double duty, donning the uniform for their shifts, then returning home to take care of their families. During the 1950s, in an era when a cultural emphasis on domesticity and family issues overshadowed women's ongoing efforts to gain equality with men, this dichotomy was not lost on the media. Policewomen often appeared in newspaper stories that spotlighted their ability to hold on to their femininity while simultaneously acting as cop, wife, and mother. Newspapers ran expanded stories on individual personalities, often with photo spreads depicting the female officer at work—driving a meter maid cart, shuffling paperwork at her desk, strolling down the sidewalk on her beat. Sometimes the photo essays showcased the policewoman in fashionable civilian garb.

Jeanne Bray, badge number 654 in Columbus, Ohio, appeared in side-by-side newspaper photos. One portrayed her in a police uniform, while the other photo showed her "as wife and mother" in a dress, gloves, and hat—"pretty and feminine." But Bray was hardly a delicate flower: hired as a police officer in 1960, she made the department's pistol team and took first place honors in five National Rifle Association pistol championships between 1962 and 1967. She later served on the NRA's board of directors.[230]

Dorothy McCracken, a traffic cop, was one of eight women on the police force in Fresno, California. She was featured in a July 1953 newspaper story that gave details about her job but led off with a quote from her that emphasized stereotypically feminine concerns: "This job certainly is rough on the hands and complexion!" Later in the article, McCracken described her duties as a mother of three children: "At nights and on my days off I wash, iron, clean the house and cook the meals for my family." McCracken's police job entailed meter maid and traffic control duties. Every now and then she had to deal with angry drivers. McCracken related a story about one of her fellow parking control officers, who was issuing a ticket when the driver yanked the ticket book away from the officer and tore it up. Then, while yelling at the top of her lungs, the woman scratched at the officer's face. "This same woman," recalled McCracken, "screamed something about the officer driving her to a nervous breakdown." But the truth was much simpler: the woman didn't have a driver's license and was desperate to escape the officer's suspicious gaze.[231]

Like McCracken, Mary Ambrosio, one of ten policewomen in Long Beach, California, was featured in a November 1959 newspaper photo essay that contrasted her work life and her personal life: "In her leotard, Mrs. Ambrosio learns ballet grace in gym class. . . . She must keep in prime shape for the nightly vigil at cells of city jail." The story featured a photograph of Ambrosio talking to a female prisoner and one of aiming her pistol, with a training officer's assistance, on the firing range. Then there was Ambrosio in a party dress, brushing her hair. "A policewoman finds time for feminine pleasures," read the caption, noting how she was "primping for an evening free from the strict regimen of her job."[232]

On-duty clothing for policewomen was still often makeshift. Female uniforms were not standard issue across most police departments during the 1960s. Some women made their own clothes; others adapted whatever they could for the job. When Jane Sadler became a policewoman in Olympia Fields, Illinois, in March 1965, the city was unable to issue her a proper outfit. Styles available for purchase, said Sadler, were "too masculine and too heavy," so she designed her own out of wool flannel. The town's chief of police gave her buttons and shoulder patches to sew on the jacket. "I think it's time policewomen started to look like women, and I find this type of uniform comfortable, practical and feminine," she said, adding that her two children liked the uniform so much that they wanted to use it to play dress-up.[233]

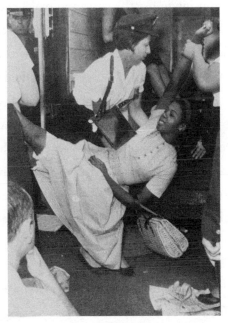

Female officers carry a civil rights demonstrator to a patrol wagon in Brooklyn, New York, 1963. *(Library of Congress)*

Behind all of the talk about styling their hair and maintaining clear complexions, policewomen were dealing with much more disheartening issues. They were considered secondary to male officers, were paid less, and often weren't taken seriously in their jobs. Even small children could give them grief. In April 1954 a precocious youngster named Andy Magill arrived in the Hyattsville, Maryland, police headquarters. He had been brought there as a lost child. When Thelma Baze sat down to talk with him, Andy said, "Lady, call the cops. I want to go home."

"I *am* a cop, Andy," Baze answered.

Andy shook his head. "Call the *men* cops, lady. I want to go home."[234]

The term *sexual discrimination* was still years away from becoming a recognized part of the workplace lexicon, but angry policewomen were beginning to use the courts to make their voices heard. Cora Wiley was a good example: at the end of her career she calculated that the San Antonio Police Department owed her $3,377.23 in back pay, plus 6 percent interest. Wiley had worked in the juvenile division from 1923 through 1951. She wasn't officially a policewoman, but she nevertheless had arrest authority. Wiley went to court, arguing that because the civil service commission established a police officer's pay scale in October 1947, she should receive equivalent pay from that period through her release date—five years' worth. The judge agreed, saying that Wiley's job responsibilities were technically those of a policewoman, even if she didn't carry the title.

One of the earliest reported harassment cases occurred in Anniston, Alabama, in the summer of 1953. Policewoman Florence Owens accused her chief, J. L. Peek, of pinching and patting her "on several occasions." Owens also said that her boss had invited her to spend a weekend with him at a nearby cabin. The 30-year-old divorced mother of two turned in her resignation. Peek, who had held his post as police chief for 15 years, charged that the town mayor had worked with Owens to entrap him. He filed a $250,000 lawsuit—but offered to rehire Owens once the court case was decided. Owens, for her part, filed an affidavit that confirmed Peek's accusations about the town's mayor: the situation had indeed been a trap. Peek's defense for his harassing behavior? "I won't bend my head the way the hinges work," he said.[235]

Policemen who couldn't or wouldn't adjust to having a woman working among them sometimes took extreme measures to make their point. In the tiny town of Athens, Texas, the entire police department—that is, Chief Joe McGee and his two policemen—resigned after the city decided to hire its first policewoman. The men walked off the job in November 1957 when Jessie Sweeten, a 23-year-old female, was brought on board. For his part, McGee trooped 30 miles south to the town of Van, which quickly hired him to be their chief instead.[236]

Bureaucratic red tape could also hinder a policewoman's progress. Also in 1957, the city council of Newark, California, reluctantly agreed to add a policewoman's position to its annual budget. Whether by mistake or by design, one of the requirements made it difficult, if not impossible, to apply for the position: the city required a degree from an "accredited policewoman's school." Meanwhile in St. Louis, policewoman Viola Messerli quit in August 1954. Her resignation cited "personal reasons," but the truth soon came out: the department wanted to move her from working juvenile cases to babysitting parking meters. "I have been suddenly informed it is of greater importance that parking meters be checked rather than juvenile delinquency be curbed," Messerli said. "These are not my convictions."[237]

Then there were supervisors who blatantly tried to run the women off. Mary Reilly, the lone policewoman for the town of Reno, Nevada, walked away from her job in April 1958. She was the last of three female officers to leave the department. The chief, T. R. Berrum, did everything he could to get the women to go. He informed Reilly that he was cutting her salary in half and moving her to a phone operator position. "The women never worked out here," grumbled Berrum.[238]

Incidents like these, which were periodically reported by the media, were early signs that something would need to be done about the harassment and discrimination that policewomen were experiencing on the job. Change was coming—and soon.

"IT WASN'T TRUE TO LIFE AT ALL"

Stories about crime and law enforcement continued to dominate newspaper pages as well as a new addition to the American home, the television set. Real-life criminals provided much of the raw material for such stories, proving time and again that truth is indeed stranger than fiction.

In one story reported in the newspapers, a bored milkman made life interesting for a Chicago policewoman in 1950. Tired of delivering milk, William Fritz wanted something to spice up his daily routine. One day he came up with an idea: "For a thrill," he said, he took a small hand drill with him on his route. After dropping off the milk bottles in front of an eighth-floor apartment, Fritz pulled out the drill and made a small hole in the door. He jammed his eye against it and looked inside the apartment, where he spied a housewife who was getting dressed. Fritz was beginning to enjoy his job a lot more.

Some two dozen peepholes later, Fritz's customers were entertaining him regularly as he went about his delivery route. But some of the residents had come across the holes drilled in their front doors and were furious about it. After filling in the holes, the residents called the cops. The police came up with a simple plan: lie in wait, then capture the culprit red-handed. Policewoman Beatrice Bresn and a male officer waited for Fritz behind the door of an apartment that still had a functioning peephole. Fritz set the milk on the ground and bent down to look through the peephole. He saw an eyeball staring back at him. Bresn threw the door open and aimed her pistol at Fritz. "I haven't got any money," cried Fritz, raising his hands. Bresn assured Fritz that he wasn't being robbed. Actually, he was under arrest.[239]

Then there were the criminals who thought that a makeover might help. In June 1953, a superintendent at Chicago's North Avenue

Beach noticed a suspicious-looking female loitering near the women's locker room. The superintendent called policewoman Josephine Conlon, who followed the suspect inside. Conlon decided that the loiterer needed to be looked at, so she called two park policemen to help her make an arrest. At the station the suspect was interviewed and fingerprinted. Finally "her" identity was revealed: "she" was Isaie Aldy Beausoleil, a male fugitive who had been listed on the FBI's Ten Most Wanted list for a year. The Feds wanted to talk to Beausoleil about the murder of a woman in the city of Monroe. Beausoleil had decided to masquerade as a woman while he was on the lam. Unfortunately for him, his disguise was less than effective: with a broken nose and coarse features, he made for a rather unconvincing-looking woman.[240]

If reading about real-life police work in newspapers and magazines wasn't interesting enough, the public could settle in at home or at the local cinema to watch policewomen—both factual and fictional—make their rounds. The growing popularity of television in American homes during the postwar period propelled the development of dozens of cop shows, many of them—*Dragnet,* for example—making the transition from radio. Mary Sullivan, former head of the New York women's bureau, inspired the 1946–1947 radio series *Police Woman.* The ABC program, broadcast each Monday at 9:45 A.M., dramatized cases from Sullivan's career. Written by Phillips Lord, who also penned the popular cop drama *Gangbusters,* the series brought in actors to dramatize Sullivan's cases, with Sullivan providing commentary. Actress Betty Garde starred in the 15-minute episodes, which cost $250 each to produce.[241]

In the movies, female police characters were often relegated to background roles. However, there were films that featured them more prominently, though not always to the best effect. Los Angeles policewoman Margaret Boyd noted one negative portrayal to newspaper columnist James Padgitt in July 1950. Referring to a police officer played by actress Lovyss Bradley in the RKO feature *Outrage*, Boyd said, "The character is tall and gaunt and unattractive and in questioning the [victim] she acted like a female monster. It wasn't true to life at all." Padgitt added that the police department "prides itself on the wholesomeness and the gal-next-door type of beauty. The Hollywood glamour variety is out."[42]

The burgeoning television industry made use of the policewoman's notoriety. At 7:00 P.M. on Wednesday, January 17, 1951, Los Angeles television station KECA (later KABC) premiered a docudrama that starred actress Jeanne Cagney. Titled *Policewoman U.S.A.*, after a half-hour radio pilot that had aired the preceding year, the program used live wraparounds for filmed reenactments and featured commentary by real-life policewoman Mary Ross, the first female member of the Los Angeles vice squad. According to reporter Terry Vernon, "One thousand, eight hundred feet of film [about an hour's worth] was shot against the actual L.A. backgrounds for the authentic documentary presentation of this show."[43] Unfortunately, *Policewoman U.S.A.* never became a series.

One TV series that did go into production was *Decoy*, which aired during the late 1950s. The low-budget program featured actress Beverly Garland as undercover New York policewoman Casey Jones. The opening titles proclaimed that the show was "presented as a tribute to the Bureau of Policewomen, Police Department, City of New York." Garland explained her approach to the lead character: "In some of the scripts, I'm supposed to be pretty scared with a 'why am I doing this crazy job?' feeling. I won't ever become hardened to the job." Filmed on location, the half-hour drama series appeared in syndication for 39 episodes. "I'm just surprised the daring young policewoman with a .32-caliber pistol beside the powder puff in her purse is so late in arriving on home screens," winked newspaper columnist Erskine Johnson. "Oh well, aren't the ladies always late?"[244]

One curious incident from 1950s television involved a policewoman maintaining her integrity during a potential case of game show rigging. In 1959, producers from *The $64,000 Question* approached New York policewoman Clare Faulhaber to see if the former college English instructor would like to appear on their program. Because Faulhaber's area of expertise—drama of the middle English period—was rather narrow, the producers asked her to cover all of English literature instead. They would, however, provide her with some guidance. "The questions might be narrowed down to a particular character, book or chapter," they told her.

"This isn't fair," she told the producers.

"The public won't know," they responded.

Faulhaber was shocked at the offer. The producers told her to go home and think about it. She never returned. "I let it drop because I wasn't interested," she said. "At no time did they say they would give me the questions," she explained. "But it was hinted that I might be asked, for example, about Jane Austen or, specifically, about chapter three of *Sense and Sensibility*. Then I would have six months or so to read it over and over. That's pretty much like giving you the questions." The offer died on the table, and with it the issue of whether the producers were attempting to convince an officer of the law to lie to the viewing public.[245]

MORE UNDERCOVER WORK

Back on the streets, policewomen in the 1950s and 1960s were playing an increasing variety of roles in undercover assignments. They posed as Communist sympathizers, baby buyers, flirty female lures, and drug addicts—their versatility demonstrating that female officers could be as effective at working dangerous cases as they were at policing parking meters and truant children. New York women's bureau director Theresa Melchionne noted that her officers investigated molesters, medical fakes scouring the city for "lonely older women," fortune-tellers scamming women for money, and "individuals who attempt to lure girls for illegal purposes." Undercover work required officers to have a certain amount of thespian talent. "Our women must be fine actresses," said Melchionne. "They are called upon to play all kinds of roles in civilian clothes. One policewoman who is twenty-three looks only fifteen. She is often called upon to operate as a teenager to trap criminals."[246]

In the aftermath of World War II, the Cold War between the United States and the Soviet Union led to a "red scare" that involved many law enforcement agencies in efforts to identify Communist sympathizers. In New York, the police department placed undercover officers inside Communist cells. One of those officers, Ruth Eagle, posed as a Communist Party member for two and a half years during the late 1940s. When the local cell realized that she was a cop, Eagle had to dodge gunshots to stay alive. She would later testify in front of a Senate committee investigating possible Communist infiltration of the U.S. Army.[247]

From 1943 through 1947, Detective Stephanie Horvath also went undercover in a local Communist Party cell. During one meeting, a public school English teacher was elected as the club's educational director. "Comrade Dave," as Horvath knew him, was one of eight teachers later suspended by the board of education for allegedly having ties to Communism. In June 1956, Horvath appeared before the House Committee on Un-American Activities in Washington, D.C.

She testified again in August 1957, this time in front of the Senate, regarding ongoing Communist activity. After the party expelled her in 1947, she had kept in touch and continued reporting its movements to the police department. Following World War II, she said, "publicly announced and advertised meetings and rallies were filled to overflowing, and collections taken up in the name of the Communist Party or its numerous front organizations were always responded to generously." During her testimony Horvath talked about the government's attempted dismantling of the party. "It was not until after the initial blow came—and that was in the form of the first trial of the eleven Communist leaders in Foley Square . . . that the Communist Party structure first began to weaken," she said. Federal prosecutors invoked the Smith Act, which made it a criminal offense to advocate the overthrow of the U.S. government, and the alleged Communists went on trial at the courthouse in Manhattan's Foley Square in 1949. After a nine-month trial, all of the defendants went to prison.[248]

Police officers were also caught in the net of anti-Communism. In 1954, after firing two male officers for participating in Communist Party activities, the New York Police Department dismissed policewoman Helen Bloch for allegedly being a member of the party back in the late 1930s. Bloch, a World War II veteran who had served stateside in the naval reserve and was later a WAVE, tried to resign in lieu of being fired, but the department refused her request. The bureaucracy wasn't interested in making exceptions.[249]

Outside the realm of politics, and despite the general prosperity of the postwar United States, some parents found themselves strapped for cash and turned to desperate measures: they attempted to sell their children. In such cases, policewomen were deemed particularly useful. In Los Angeles, a bizarre event at a gas station triggered an undercover assignment for a local policewoman. On a January day in 1951, a husband and wife pulled up in their car, pointed to their 11-year-old daughter, and engaged the station attendant in conversation.

"Would you like to buy her for $10?" they asked him.

Having fallen on hard times, the O'Briens—parents of five children and with a baby on the way—needed gas for their tired automobile. The gas station attendant thanked them but said he really didn't want to purchase their child. Then he gave them $5 and free gas. The O'Briens left their daughter, Shirley, behind anyway. They later sent the gas station attendant a postcard saying that they were hitchhiking to San Francisco because their car had died on the road in Bakersfield. They ended up at a local police station. Back in Los Angeles, policewoman Elizabeth Eggleston responded to the call from the gas station attendant. When she arrived on scene, she met the dejected little girl who had been abandoned. "My parents sold me for five dollars and a tankful of gasoline," Shirley sniffed.[250]

In Salt Lake City, a car salesman met a 30-year-old husband and his 19-year-old wife. They asked him if he'd like to make a unique trade: their six-month-old daughter for a used car. The husband was looking for work and needed transportation, so he thought that bartering with one of his three young children was a good idea. The auto dealer reported the incident to the police, and officer Fran Kari went undercover posing as the salesman's wife. On the day the young couple came back to the car lot, Kari listened to their pitch and replied, "It's worth it to me if it's worth it to you." When the couple got ready to give their child up, Kari made the arrest, charging them with a felony. Their three children ended up in the foster care system.[251]

Dedicated undercover officers sometimes suffered minor embarrassment to put down a case. Boston policewoman Mary Connolly helped win 11 convictions of exotic dancers and nightclub employees for hosting an immoral show at the Club Zara in 1960. To demonstrate what she had seen, Connolly threw a bra and G-string over her police uniform, then did a bump-and-grind across the courtroom during five hours of testimony. She said that the dancers—whose panties began a scandalous five inches underneath their navels—were able to take cash from customers and "work [it] into safer places without benefit of hands."[252]

Some undercover officers had the opportunity to be in close contact with Hollywood celebrities—but probably not in the way they had hoped. Witness the following exchange at the home of a world-famous entertainer.

"Frankie?" An attractive young woman stood at the front door of Frank Sinatra's house in Palm Springs, California. It was February 16, 1957, at about four in the morning. Sinatra was dozing in his bedroom. He didn't come to the door, so the woman tried again, in her best sultry voice: "Daddy?"

Still nothing.

"Darling?"

Silence.

"Lover boy!"

The woman waited a little longer, then gave up. She stepped away from the door and walked over to Jerry Holland and Dick Williams, two Los Angeles policemen who were waiting nearby. The woman, Glory Dawson, was also a police officer. Holland and Williams produced a key, unlocked Sinatra's front door, and stepped through the house into the bedroom, where Sinatra lay asleep. They shone a flashlight in his eyes, shook him awake, and served him with a subpoena. One of the officers read the subpoena out loud. Sinatra was ordered to testify in front of a state Senate committee that was investigating saucy celebrity magazines like *Confidential*. Sinatra had helped his buddy Joe DiMaggio track down DiMaggio's soon-to-be ex-wife, Marilyn Monroe, as she visited a friend's apartment. DiMaggio thought he'd catch Monroe in a compromising position, so with a group of private detectives he broke into the apartment that Monroe had supposedly entered—only to find out that she was actually next door.

Regardless of his involvement in the "wrong-door raid," Sinatra didn't appreciate the police intrusion into his home. During a deposition hearing, Sinatra's recollection of the story contrasted sharply with the police version. Sinatra claimed that Dawson was a "loud-mouthed" woman who broke into his house with the two policemen, violating his privacy. Holland verified that Dawson had been used as a lure, but told the court that he had apologized to the groggy Sinatra after the officers shook the singer awake, and that Sinatra cursed at them as the subpoena was read.

Confidential splashed the details of the wrong-door raid across the pages of its February 1957 issue. The tenant in the wrong apartment, Florence Kotz Ross, sued and was eventually awarded $7,500 (about $55,000 in today's dollars) in damages. The magazine, like so many others of its kind, eventually went out of business, a victim of the lawsuits and bad publicity brought about by its salacious content.

As more policewomen got out of the station house and patrolled their communities, they began to work the same types of issues that their male counterparts had dealt with for many years. The women's role however, were slightly different. In 1967, while chasing prostitution cases, Los Angeles policewoman Colleen Nielsen aided in the apprehension of a suspected pimp. "He promised me love, protection, medical care, an abortion if I never needed one," said Nielsen. "And I, of course, turned him in. I think the district attorney's office is now preparing the case against him."[53]

After a man raped six women in the North Hollywood area, Nielsen and her partner, Angela Cimino, participated in a sting operation to catch the suspect. On their second night of walking around, trying to attract the suspect's attention, the policewomen suddenly realized they were being stalked. "I knew that he was running across the railroad tracks, lying in wait for me," recalled Nielsen. "I was in communication with my backup men, and my bug was working fine. Suddenly I heard a figure rustling in the bushes—the very same bushes where he had attacked a woman before." Dashing across to cut Nielsen off, the suspect bumped into a police officer and was arrested.[254]

Often female officers posed as prostitutes during sting operations. An October 1967 sting operation in Grand Rapids, Michigan, netted 23 men who were charged with soliciting prostitution. Two female officers posed as hookers. Kathryn Visser—described by the local paper as "slightly chubby, gray-haired and in her forties"—worked a four-hour shift from 10:30 P.M. Monday through 2:30 A.M. Tuesday. She brought in ten men who had approached her on the street. Once a man gave her his pitch—offering money for sex—five vice squad cops, listening to the radio hidden in Visser's purse, appeared and made the arrest. "A few of the men are always angry," noted Visser. "Some of them try to argue but they know we've got them cold. None of them have ever tried to hurt me, though."[255] Visser added that in her three years of posing as a prostitute she had arrested hundreds of would-be johns.

On the opposite end of the morality scale, New York policewoman Margaret Powers posed as a woman of the cloth in 1969 to nab two shakedown artists. When a nun in Queens lost her wallet, a man stopped at the school where the nun worked as an instructor and told her how she could reclaim the missing item. When the nun and her mother superior showed up at a local home—holding a cake as a thank-you gift—they were told to cough up $15 to get the wallet back. So the nuns went to the police station, where they met with Powers.

"I told my detectives that anyone who would shake down a nun is no good," the policewoman noted. "I told them, you want another nun, you got one." Powers, wearing a habit, went back with the mother superior to talk to the thieves. Detectives made the arrest.[256]

RIGHT OF PROMOTION

In addition to the problems of pay inequality and harassment, police-women in the 1950s and 1960s found few opportunities to move up the chain of command. In 1961, New York police officer Felicia Shpritzer wanted to be promoted to sergeant. Shpritzer, who had a bachelor's degree and two master's degrees, had joined the depart-ment in 1942 and worked in the youth division for 17 years. When she asked about the sergeant's exam, she was told that she couldn't take it. Shpritzer was one of six women who had applied for the exam; all of them were turned away.

Shpritzer had had enough; she went to court, charging the city department of personnel with "discriminatory, archaic and illegal" practices. When asked her opinion about why she was barred from the exam, Shpritzer had a simple answer: "I am of the female sex," she said. Shpritzer noted that the city administrative code stated that officers in the juvenile aid bureau, where she was assigned, were eli-gible for promotion. But the police commissioner, Michael J. Murphy, threw the code back at her, citing a section that stated, "There shall only be one rank of policewomen within the police department."

But the New York court of appeals agreed with Shpritzer, and the police department held a make-up test in 1964. Instead of just the original six female applicants, a total of 127 women crowded into the testing area at Brooklyn Technical High School for the four-hour exam. "Pass or fail, I will never regret having made the opportunity available to women," Shpritzer said before taking the exam herself. Shpritzer and another policewoman, Gertrude Schimmel, were awarded sergeant's stripes and placed in charge of the approximately 160 officers in the women's bureau. The two sergeants would have to go to court again in 1967 in order to be allowed to take the lieutenant's exam, which they also both passed. Schimmel would continue making milestones for the department. Promoted to captain in 1971, she was awarded the title of deputy inspector the following year, and became a full inspector in 1974. Then, in 1978, Schimmel was promoted to deputy chief.[257]

A Philadelphia policewoman followed in Shpritzer and Schimmel's footsteps, filing a lawsuit against the city in 1967 after she was denied promotion three times in a row. Ruth Wells entered the police academy in 1955, a time when women were required to resign if they became pregnant, and single mothers weren't allowed to apply at all. Academy students "were not permitted, under any circumstances, to fraternize," Wells told journalist Adam Heilman in 1992, "not at lunch, never." The Philadelphia civil service commission required women to take an oral exam for promotion to sergeant—something not required of the male candidates. The commission's reasoning: since there were fewer female police officers, an oral rather than a written exam was satisfactory. Wells pointed out a conflict of interest: "The commanding officer of the juvenile aid division appointed the oral board, which called into question the board's evaluations. It would have been different if the oral board would have been completely separated from the command of the juvenile aid division." Once on duty, Philadelphia's female officers were loaned out wherever they were needed. "The curious thing was that whenever one of the male officers needed women for an assignment, we would be detailed to the narcotics unit, homicide unit, major crimes unit or any unit of the department without being given the title or the compensation for it," said Wells.[258]

Unfortunately, Wells was unsuccessful in her quest to set things right. The Pennsylvania supreme court dismissed her complaint, saying that "many of the tasks performed by the police force are of such a nature, physiologically speaking, that they cannot and should not be assigned to women."[259] After all of the legal wrangling, Wells was right back where she had started.

The police department in Baton Rouge, Louisiana, hired its first female officers on September 15, 1969. Pictured left to right: Bertha Martone, Patricia Millet, Patricia Bennett, and Sandra McGrew. *(Courtesy Baton Rouge Police Department)*

Sharp discrepancies between male and female officers' paychecks continued to cause problems. In 1967, when female officers accounted for at most 2 percent of the nation's police forces,[260] Marie Von Burgen and Alice Bardell went to the Michigan civil rights commission regarding their annual salaries, which were $700 less than what the department paid male officers—$9,350 versus $10,050. Von Burgen and Bardell argued that women should have equal pay, especially since the female officers faced the same "element of danger" that the male officers did. As evidence, Von Burgen pointed to bruises on her face. A teenage girl, drunk and disorderly, had given them to her. "I think it's a sad state of affairs if an individual's ability is judged by how much weight he can lift or how strong he is," said Bardell. The city disagreed, pointing to the job description for female officers, which didn't include such requirements.[261]

Bardell and Von Burgen were preceded in 1966 by Faith Barnes, a policewoman in Cohoes, New York, who had the audacity to ask about the $900 difference in pay she had discovered between male and female officers. For four months Barnes tried to get a clear answer from her superiors, to no avail. Finally, she filed a lawsuit. When her efforts made the news that December, the chief of police accused her of "abandonment of duty" and suspended her.

Compromising with the department, Barnes admitted to "poor judgment in publicly quarrelling with superiors" and spent ten days on suspension. After that she returned to the juvenile division but was placed on the night shift—"a complete waste of my time and the taxpayers' money," she fumed, noting that little was accomplished during those hours. "I've been told by [the police commissioner] that plans had been underway for the past two years to replace me with someone else," she added.[262]

Meanwhile, the state commission for human rights studied Barnes's case and agreed with her complaint. The commission cited New York's equal-pay law, which had been passed on September 1, 1965, and forbade different salary scales based on sex if the jobs were equivalent in effort, skill, and responsibility. The city had to make up the difference in pay to Barnes, who by then had resigned and moved to a civilian job as a secretary at the U.S. Army arsenal in the city of Watervliet. After being drummed out of law enforcement, Barnes was back doing a job traditionally considered "women's work"—an ironic turn of events for a policewoman who created a firestorm by asking a simple question about her paycheck.[263]

SOLO IN A PATROL CAR

While female officers battled their departments over administrative issues, another big debate was brewing: Should women be assigned their own patrol beats — and, if so, should they be given their own squad cars? As early as July 1965, the police department in Warren, Michigan, a suburb of Detroit, gave its only female officer a vehicle of her own. Unfortunately, Mary Conforti had to contend with people making jokes about the television series *Car 54, Where Are You?*, a sitcom featuring two bumbling policemen who drove a squad car together, since her real-life vehicle had the same number as its TV counterpart.

In the fall of 1969, Dade County, Florida, assigned its first female officer to a patrol car. "As far as I know," said Nicole Coffey, "I'm the only woman in the country riding in a routine patrol unit alone." Coffey, a graduate of the police administration school at Michigan State University, patrolled residential areas and primarily worked with breaking-and-entering complaints. The press noted that Coffey "wears a size 8 uniform which features a hat too large for her. . . . She supports five pounds of equipment on her twenty-three-inch waist, including a gun and handcuffs."[264]

After she graduated at the top of her academy class—ahead of seven other women and a dozen men—rookie Mary Ellen Morton took to the streets of Miami in her squad car. Her uniform, which featured a short skirt, included a .38-caliber service weapon belted to her waist. Miami's female cops rode alone. On the street, Morton suffered a fair amount of rubbernecking and whistling from men. "When people gawk and stare, at times I feel like saying, 'Want to take a picture?'" Morton said in a 1972 interview.[265] Nevertheless, she met many interesting people during her rounds. A man who was furious about receiving a parking ticket spouted off about Morton's purported sexual hang-ups. On another occasion, Morton was questioning a woman who suddenly slapped the policewoman across the face. When she needed assistance, Morton appreciated the backup she received from the male officers. "When a woman officer calls for help, everyone comes running," she noted.[266]

Some cities, like New Orleans, paired female officers with male partners in patrol units. The program wasn't as progressive as it sounded, however. Instituted in 1967, the New Orleans program was created with women in mind: the patrol experience would be helpful in training female officers before they took on "traditional" women's roles in the department. Not everyone in New Orleans was happy about the experiment. Fifteen angry policemen's wives stormed the superintendent's office, concerned about having male and female cops in an "intimate situation" for eight hours at a time. Moreover, what if their husbands attempted to protect a female partner while trying to defend themselves? But the furor died down quickly. "Actually, they were a totally disorganized group and even refused to identify themselves," a police spokesman said of the wives. "It appeared no two of them had similar views on the matter. They couldn't get together on what they felt."[267]

Policewoman Mary Weinmumson waved off the wives' concerns. "Good heavens, if a guy wants to play around, he can find other places than on his beat," she said. "That would be the last place." After four years on the New Orleans force, Weinmumson welcomed her new assignment to a patrol car. She felt that worried spouses were a result of the "echo chamber" nature of being at home all day: "The way I figure it—and being a woman, I know—the little woman sits home in her own little world populated by her husband and children. Because she has little else to think about, she worries that something dear to her, that husband, is in danger." Male police officers, she noted, had "neither the mood nor time for any hanky-panky business."[268]

The solution to the problem of pairing male and female officers—and the answer to the question of whether policewomen should patrol their own beats—came from Indianapolis. The two officers assigned to the city's Car 47 wore boots, tie tabs, and specially designed hats. Their runs were often restricted to minor calls. Nevertheless, Car 47 of the Indianapolis Police Department was unlike any other patrol vehicle in the country: in October 1968, Elizabeth Robinson and Betty Blankenship became the first female officers to team up and land their own regular vehicle patrol.

Robinson and Blankenship hatched the idea after they enrolled at the local police academy in 1967. Both women were looking for something more challenging in their careers. The Indianapolis Police Department hadn't brought any female employees on board for five years, but Robinson kept trying. Finally, she and three other women —including Blankenship—were accepted into the 13-week academy.

When Robinson told her uncle that she was going to become a police officer, he was aghast. "Why in the world would you want to join the police department?" he said. The environment at the police academy took some getting used to, since the factory that Robinson had just left employed mostly women. Now Robinson and her three female classmates were the minority in a class of men. But Robinson recalled that everyone "got along fine."

It was understood that, after they graduated, the women officers would not be going out on the street except as juvenile detectives. But one of the instructors at the academy, Winston Churchill (no relation), was open to suggestions. One day during a break in classroom instruction, Churchill was in the hallway chatting with Robinson and Blankenship. "He talked about how women could go out on the street and do a lot of the things the men were tied up with," remembered Robinson. Female officers could be used to respond to minor calls and allow male officers to focus on other duties. "He felt that it would free up the men to do the critical police work," said Robinson.

Robinson and Blankenship sensed an opportunity. "If you ever get in a position where you can do that," they told Churchill, "let us know, because we would certainly be interested in it."

After graduation the women reported for duty. Blankenship recalled that she was "mandated to wear a white blouse, a skirt that dropped to mid-knee and two-inch heels, no more, no less." The department also issued her a purse for her gun. "We were given assignments that were deemed appropriate for women," she told a reporter. "Nothing unladylike, mind you."[269]

The department assigned all of its female officers to the teletype office. Six months passed. Robinson and Blankenship were moved to the juvenile division, fulfilling what they had been told while at the academy. But then came word that Winston Churchill had been appointed as the city's new police chief. Robinson and Blankenship hadn't forgotten his conversation with them at the academy, so they made an appointment to see him. Churchill hadn't forgotten them either. In no time at all, with no additional training, Robinson and Blankenship were holding the keys to Patrol Car 47.

On their first day, in October 1968, the news media snapped pictures as the two policewomen started their shift. "The first day was about meeting people and having pictures taken," recalled Robinson. "We didn't get to do too much." Despite the novelty of the situation, Robinson said that the public attention was fairly subdued. However, she and her partner were well aware of the importance of the roles they had taken on.

Robinson and Blankenship had some radio car experience from their time in juvenile division, so they felt somewhat prepared for their new duties. "We'd take calls about dog bites and people who needed information, accidents and things like that," said Robinson. "We also did a lot of emergency runs. The fire department didn't go out on all of them like they do now." The partners learned to help each other out. Robinson wasn't too familiar with handling dead bodies, and Blankenship didn't like dogs. "So I'd take care of the dogs, and Betty would take care of the dead bodies," said Robinson.

As with so many other departments across the country, many Indianapolis policemen resisted the female officers' new authority. Sometimes the dispatcher, nudged by a supervisor, would bypass the women and route incoming calls to male officers instead. "We'd call into control and ask, 'Why didn't we get that call? What's going on?' Some of the dispatchers were told not to give us certain runs," noted Robinson. Nevertheless, she added, "We found plenty to do out there."

Having policewomen driving around in a radio car was something new for a conservative midwestern city like Indianapolis. Many suspects didn't take Robinson and Blankenship seriously—until the female officers locked them up, of course. On some calls, people waved the women off, asking for "real police" instead. Robinson and Blankenship patiently explained that they were indeed the real thing.

That first rotation in Car 47 lasted until August 1971—nearly three years. Throughout that time, Robinson and Blankenship pursued Chief Churchill about adding more women to the patrol. "There were so many runs, and we needed the women out there," said Robinson. Halfway through the rotation Chief Churchill added another female team.

Robinson and Blankenship's experience in a patrol car helped move the concept of the policewoman further into areas traditionally reserved for men. According to historian Dorothy Moses Schulz, "Although they eventually left patrol and returned to traditional policewomen's duties, they broke the link to the mothering concept that had been the basis of women's roles in policing. Once this link was severed, the stage was set for the modern women-on-patrol era to begin."[270]

CHANGING REQUIREMENTS

Women like Elizabeth Robinson and Betty Blankenship were still the exception rather than the rule in the 1960s. "We're stuck in an office when we could be of some help out on the street," complained a policewoman in Syracuse, New York. The city's four female cops worked in the youth division, covering the hours between 8:30 A.M. and midnight. When the police arrested women outside of those hours, county matrons in the local jail would take care of processing. "I'm a glorified secretary," said the female officer.[271]

Despite efforts to blur or destroy it, the dividing line between male and female officers remained fairly clear. When Gayleen Hays joined the Los Angeles police force in 1967, "the setup was simple and straightforward," she wrote. "The men wore pants and worked in the field; the women wore skirts and stayed in specialized areas: working the jail, handling the juvenile division, or doing desk work. Women weren't assigned regular patrol (except the J car, where juveniles were involved) or traffic. They couldn't rise above the rank of sergeant or work burglary, homicide or metro motors. Policewomen were totally separate from the men on the force."[272]

For female officers working in detention facilities, things could get pretty hairy. In February 1969, a 40-year-old woman who had been arrested at an Albuquerque bar for causing a public disturbance while drunk went on a rampage in the women's holding cell. Policewoman Maxine Aragon had brought the woman to the station at 10:20 on a Wednesday night. Aragon began to perform a search when the suspect kicked her, yanked her hair, and threw a punch. Aragon tried to steady the drunken woman. Another officer rushed over and, trying to help, accidentally sprayed Aragon with tear gas.

For some policewomen, dealing with female suspects was the biggest challenge of all. "Each woman [prisoner] is a separate case because women are much more difficult to deal with than men are, especially the drunks," explained Shirl Hovas in November 1968. Hovas, a former fashion model who had become a sergeant with the Los Angeles Police Department, was one of two female supervisors covering the 40-bed jail facility. She supervised 12 other policewomen. "[Female prisoners] just will not accept their situation," Hovas continued. "They must scream, run the gamut between tears and threats and go into general hysteria."[273]

What type of woman made the most effective police officer against such behavior? "She needs a calm personality coupled with a lot of nerve and a cool head," said the police chief in Long Beach, California. "Above all, she must be a well-adjusted person." In 1963, the Long Beach department employed 17 policewomen—seven in uniform and ten in plain clothes. The female officers began their careers as clerks, moved to the jail, and later might work with women, children, or shoplifters; they might also work undercover or in store security. When some were "slapped around" by suspects, the chief sponsored a course in self-defense for his employees.[274]

Regardless of where they were assigned and whether or not they liked their work, female officers were aware that things were changing. "I'm telling you, it's a dream job in a relatively new field for women,"

Los Angeles policewoman Colleen Nielsen told *Parade* magazine in March 1969. "I think in the whole country there are probably less than five or six thousand policewomen. We easily need double that number."[275] At the time Los Angeles had 151 women cops in its ranks. "In the early days, a woman on the police force was a jail matron or turnkey," Los Angeles sheriff's lieutenant Murle Hess told a training seminar sponsored by the Women Peace Officers Association in 1968. "That's not so today. Women are expanding into other fields, and into jobs with greater responsibility. The emphasis today is on brains, not just a big, husky woman with lots of brawn."[276]

But there was a long way to go. Despite promotion to lieutenant and assignment as a watch commander, Hess was still working at the county jail, which was supervised by a female captain. Gaining mainstream acceptance for female officers was an ongoing process. Some policewomen defended themselves by going public about hot-button issues such as sexual discrimination, harassment, and pay inequality. In doing so, women cops gained some valuable ground. However, such changes were not all-encompassing—different police departments implemented changes in different ways, and some did not change much at all. But a series of critical events during the early 1970s would give the cause a massive push forward.

*When I went into the profession women were allowed sheerly
through men's sufferance. Women cops were not allowed to take the
promotional exams. They were advanced only at the discretion of
their supervisors. That's how I made it from policewoman to officer
third grade. But when I took time off to have a family, I was demoted
to policewoman again.*
>   —Dorothy Uhnak, New York City Transit Police[277]

*When I was little, I always wanted to be a policewoman. I also
wanted to work with juveniles—but I never expected to end up here.*
>   —Saundra Brown, Oakland, California, police department[278]

CHAPTER 5

Forced Progress (1970–1980)

POLICEWOMEN ACROSS THE United States were still considered second-class public servants at the beginning of the 1970s.
Women had made small inroads into the male-dominated profession
of policing, but many policewomen still weren't taken seriously by
police and public alike. Sure, some carried guns now and made arrests,
but most faced discrimination in many forms, both subtle and overt.
The city of Indianapolis, for example, had 74 female officers, but more
than half of them were relegated to secretarial positions within the
department. Women in state and county positions faced the same
problem. "The sheriff told me I couldn't carry a gun because women
were emotional and any of the other women in the office would be
jealous," recalled Kim Zangar, who spent a year as a deputy sheriff in
Washington before switching to the state patrol in the late 1970s. "So

he sent me out in a car alone, without a gun. You can figure out why I left and went to the other agency."[79]

Yet clear changes were taking place. After years of working primarily behind the scenes, more and more policewomen were out in the community on a regular basis. Some won high-profile discrimination lawsuits and earned the right to their own beats. Female officers who had been stuck in an office or toiling in the prison system or on juvenile cases began to patrol the streets in larger numbers. "In at least seven cities," reported *Time* magazine in May 1972, "lady cops are driving squad cars, responding to radio calls and investigating crimes. Their experience to date indicates that their sex does not handicap them on the job."[80]

Although female officers still comprised about 2 percent of the nation's police force, their numbers were increasing across the board: 20 policewomen out of 2,600 police officers in Boston; 75 out of 1,503 in Atlanta; 66 out of 7,000 in Philadelphia; and 700 out of 30,000 in New York City. Of the 400,000 police officers in the United States in 1972, about 6,000 were women. In a sign of the times, New York City deleted the separate designations *policeman* and *policewoman* and began using the unisex term *police officer*.

The problem of having different educational requirements for male and female police candidates continued to cause friction between applicants and their local police departments. Constance Klein, a Detroit bartender who wanted to be a police officer, joined two other women in filing a lawsuit against the city's police department in 1974. The issue: male officers needed only a high school diploma, while women were required to have at least two years of college. Not everyone in Detroit thought that women belonged on the police force, however. "This is a rough town," grumbled a male police sergeant. "In the scout car area especially, force is sometimes necessary, and I don't think most women could handle it." But Klein wasn't deterred. "With the proper training, a woman could handle scout car assignments as well as a man," she said.[281] The judge at the U.S. district court agreed: pending trial, he instructed the Detroit police to hire one woman for every man brought aboard.

Still, many women didn't think that law enforcement was open to them as a career. "I thought he was nuts!" recalled Lori Fry of a male sergeant in San Bernardino, California, who urged her to apply for the police academy. Undaunted, the sergeant assigned Fry—who was working on the department's complaint desk—to periodic ride-alongs with various patrol officers during their shifts. The goal of the ride-alongs was to familiarize employees with life on the street. The sergeant also asked Fry to help take statements and write reports. Although she was confident she could do the job, Fry was still worried about the idea: "I had reservations because of my size—I was barely five foot four—and just could not imagine a fight or how I would handle a gory crime scene or accident."

As the ride-alongs continued, Fry would learn that she could handle them quite well. One day she was observing in a patrol car when a call came through to break up a bar fight nearby. With no one else available, Fry accompanied the male officer to the bar. The policeman grabbed one of the revelers and attempted to cuff him. Meanwhile a large man swiped a beer bottle, broke it, and started after the officer with the jagged glass exposed. Fry had to do something. She grabbed a chair, tripped the assailant, and yanked a pool cue off a nearby table.

"Stay facedown," she told him, aiming the pool cue at his head. "If you move, I'll take your head off." The man complied, believing that Fry was holding a gun behind his ear.

After the incident was over, the male officer told Fry that if she could think that quickly on her feet with no formal training, she would do fine on the streets. And for the first time, Fry could see herself as a police officer. The male officer became one of her chief advocates and cheerleaders, writing letters of recommendation for Fry as she began to seek a full-time position.[282]

Similarly, future Iowa state trooper Donna Bacus was unaware that law enforcement was a possible career choice. "As a young girl growing up in Iowa in the 1970s, I hadn't given much thought to pursuing a career in law enforcement," she said. "I didn't even know that was an option. I had grown up participating in athletics and thought my dream job would be to coach an athletic team." Bacus was working at a hardware store when one of her coworkers—the wife of a state trooper—asked her to consider a career in law enforcement. Like many other female officers, Bacus had to deal with the surprised reaction of her parents when she announced her career intentions. "It was a shock for them, especially my mother," said Bacus, whose younger sister also joined the state troopers. "Her daughters went to work at the local hardware store, and the next thing she knows, they're wearing badges and carrying guns!"[283]

Jill Rice was a teenager when a horrific incident in Indianapolis inspired her to become a cop. On October 26, 1965, police found the battered, malnourished body of 16-year-old Sylvia Likens lying on a mattress in Gertrude Baniszewski's house in the eastern section of the city. Baniszewski was supposedly taking care of Likens and her sister while the girls' parents were traveling with a carnival. For several months Baniszewski and various children from the neighborhood teased, tortured, and burned Likens. Eventually the girl's body could no longer withstand the constant torture, and she died alone in the dilapidated house.

The news of Likens's death horrified Indianapolis residents. Rice was sitting in a classroom when she heard what had happened. "When they announced in school that Sylvia had been killed, it left such an impression on me that I wanted then to become a police officer," she recalled. The murder hit Rice especially hard because she and Sylvia had been classmates. After she graduated from high school, Rice attended Indiana University and majored in police administration. While college programs in criminal justice were not exactly new, the idea of female students majoring in the subject was still a novelty in many cities: "There were almost no girls in any of my police classes," said Rice.

In 1978, Rice fulfilled the promise she made to herself as a teenager and applied for a position with the Indiana State Police. Unfortunately she was as hindered at home as she was at the academy. "My husband thought it was a joke, and didn't believe I wanted to be a police officer," she remembered sadly. "He did little to encourage me." At 31 years old, Rice found herself nearly alone at the academy, one of two women among a class of 72 men. "Almost every night I was told by the counselors and staff that I wasn't going to make it," she said. Rice would prove them wrong: on December 14, 1979, she became the 11th female trooper in the state.[284]

"LET'S SEE WHAT THE GIRL'S GOING TO DO"

Female candidates for police academies throughout the United States came from all walks of life. Norma Jean Almodovar, whose career switch from Los Angeles police officer to high-class prostitute triggered some raised eyebrows in the early 1980s, recalled applying to be a law enforcement officer back in 1972: "I felt lucky to be one of only six women considered worthy of hiring; these women were unlikely candidates for the job. Besides myself, a newly remodeled wallflower, complete with contact lenses and red hair, there was a tall, lean, tan, young blonde with a leathery outdoors face; a short, middle-aged Italian woman with a gap between her teeth and with a body that looked as though it had borne many children; two young black ladies who might have been lion tamers; and a Hispanic-looking woman about my age with long blondish hair."[285]

The police academies might have been opened to women—although the women's training regimen was slightly different from the men's—but the environment was often unwelcoming. Rookies like Barbara Hopkins sometimes found themselves alone among large groups of disgruntled male candidates. When Hopkins arrived at the Baltimore police academy in 1973, she was the only woman in a class of 120 students. Hopkins was a divorcée and recent college graduate who had never fired a gun in her life. Predictably, the men in her academy class were less than thrilled: "I was nervous enough, and everyone would look at me and say, 'Let's see what the girl's going to do,' " Hopkins told the *Baltimore Sun*.[286]

Some women, repeatedly told that they couldn't be cops, decided to prove the naysayers wrong by applying to the academy. In Seattle, Peggy Timm was a waitress at an around-the-clock coffee shop who dreamed of doing something else with her life. "I regularly waited on police officers," she recalled. "One night I said to them, 'I want to be what you are, a police officer,' and they all laughed so hard." Timm never forgot the slight. Two years later she was one of 2,000 applicants to the Seattle police academy—and one of 70 selected to begin training in the fall of 1975.[287]

But jumping the gender gap proved difficult for Timm and the other female candidates at the Seattle academy. The screening process included questions about sexual orientation and whether the women had previously undergone abortions. Like male candidates who were perceived as "weak" during training, the women faced a number of rough spots. "I was the youngest and, at five foot three and a half and 108 pounds, the smallest in the academy," Timm said. "They were always trying to get me to gain weight, and they were always unhappy that I was short. Every single morning for six months when we lined up for roll call someone would say to me, 'Timm, get out of that hole.' I suppose it was funny, but at the time I didn't feel that way."[288] Rumors about sex between trainers and trainees also put a damper on the women's progress. "There were only nine of us and 1,200 [men], so rumors were flying," recalled Debbie Allen, another Seattle officer who attended the academy with Timm. "All I know is that if I had had sex with every man that the rumors said I had, it would have been a physical miracle," she said.[289]

Minority female candidates for the police department were far more rare than white female candidates. In 1970, Oakland, California—where African Americans comprised more than a third of the population—had only seven policewomen, all white, on its force of 710 officers. Saundra Brown, an African American and former insurance claims representative, would change all that. On December 15, 1970, Brown took the last in a series of tests to become a police officer. The familiar roadblock regarding education requirements once again reared its ugly head: female candidates for the police force were required to have a four-year college degree or previous experience in a law enforcement job; male candidates needed only a high school diploma or the equivalent. Fortunately, Brown had a sociology degree from Fresno State College.

During the department's 15-week training academy Brown took courses in criminal law, report-writing, first aid, role-playing, traffic investigation, field interrogation, search and seizure, city ordinances, and self-defense. "Oh, I did all right, I guess," she told reporter Joan McKinney after completing her training. "I can throw the biggest guy in the class. And I have quite a bit more confidence in myself than I did before I started."[290]

Things got even tougher after graduation. Few female rookies at the academy meant few policewomen out on the streets. After she graduated, Brown wasn't issued a uniform but did receive a department shoulder bag in which to carry her handcuffs and service weapon. Oakland police chief Charles Gaines had Brown handling youth cases but planned to rotate all of his department's female officers to various divisions. "Maybe women's intuition combined with police knowledge and skills can give us some feedback on how to do things better, particularly in the areas of vice and intelligence," he explained.[291]

As the first African American policewoman in Oakland, Brown became a local celebrity. Newspapers featured a photograph of the 23-year-old rookie toting a shotgun in front of silhouette targets as a male range master stood next to her. Coincidentally, Brown became a cop just as the Oakland Police Officers' Association filed suit against the U.S. Civil Service Commission because women were not allowed to take the sergeant's promotion exam. "I figure this will have to change soon," commented Brown. "They can't ask a person to stay on one level for twenty years and expect them to do it."[292]

Still, old-fashioned attitudes about women were hard to shake. In Madison, Wisconsin, Pia Kinney-James sat silently in her patrol car, watching the road. Behind the wheel, her male training officer barely spoke to her. Sometimes hours would go by without a word between them. Finally he broke the silence.

"You took some man's job," he growled.

"Excuse me?" Kinney-James said.

"How's he supposed to support his family?"

Kinney-James gritted her teeth. "How am I supposed to support *my* family?" she answered.

As a rookie cop, Kinney-James felt that she had three strikes against her: she was black, she was a woman, and she wore her hair in the Afro style common at the time. Male officers looked down their noses at a divorced single mother. Her parents didn't want her to join the police force. "They were worried about my safety and how people would treat me," she said. "They tried to talk me out of it."[293]

On another day, responding to a backup call at a local bar, Kinney-James opened the door to see a male officer talking to an angry man wielding a knife. The male officer looked at Kinney-James. Then he looked past her at the open door.

"Oh my God, where's my backup?" he said.

"I'm it," she answered.

"This guy has a knife!"

"We'd better go take it away from him," she said matter-of-factly. And they did.

Kinney-James and other female officers in Madison's police department had a powerful ally: the police chief, David Couper, believed in equal opportunity hiring. "He took some guff from old-time officers," recalled Kinney James. "He was progressive in that he saw early on, before court orders, that women and people of color had to be brought on."[294]

Couper had visited a number of European police departments before joining the Madison police force. He saw how his overseas counterparts had integrated women into the ranks and was convinced that the United States needed to do a more effective job of bringing women into policing. "I had a supportive mayor and set about to 'equalize' the department, which had one black officer—a male—and no women on patrol," recalled Couper. At the time, six women officers worked in the juvenile division but were forbidden to carry weapons or apply for promotion. "I knew that women could make a great contribution to the department and help me make the kinds of changes that I knew needed to be made to the all-white 'boy's club,' but I had to do it in numbers," explained Couper. "It would not have worked if only one or two women were hired for each academy class. I needed to approach a majority of women and permit them to be truly women—not women who acted just like the men did."

While Kinney-James faced anger and confusion among male officers on her beat, Couper dealt with it at headquarters. The members of his department and the wives of the male officers—including Couper's own wife—responded negatively to what he was attempting to accomplish. Most people in the local community, however, welcomed the female officers with open arms.

One issue that women in the community discussed with Couper was what they saw as insensitivity on the part of male officers in handling rape cases. In response, Couper established a policy requiring that both a male and a female officer had to respond to calls involving suspected rapes. The policy demonstrated its worth fairly quickly. "After a few years," said Couper, "the women said that they didn't need to accompany the men in the department—many of whom were their contemporaries—because in their opinion the men did as well as they did with regard to compassion and sensitivity. In a few years, we were able to rescind the 'male-female' requirement to incidents of sexual assault."[295]

THE FEDERAL PUSH

In 1970, the Ford Foundation pledged $30 million to establish the Police Foundation, an independent, nonprofit research organization whose goal is to "assist a limited number of police departments in experiments and demonstrations aimed at improving operations, and to support special education and training projects."[296] One of the foundation's studies in the 1970s found that U.S. police departments were directly or indirectly keeping women from joining their ranks. "In many cities there is a total fear and real hostility to the idea of having women doing anything in policing other than secretarial duties and dealing with juveniles," noted Catherine Milton, the Police Foundation's assistant director.[297] Among other issues, women weren't allowed to take training courses that would make them eligible for other duties, were blocked from taking promotion exams, and were sometimes required to have more education than male candidates. Such barriers, however, were in the process of being eliminated.

The federal push to tear down the roadblocks to women's progress in all areas of employment had begun almost a decade earlier. During the 1960s, Congress passed a number of landmark bills that would open the way for policewomen to be hired in large numbers. The 1963 Equal Pay Act prohibited sex-based wage discrimination in work environments where men and women performed the same jobs. The next year, Congress passed an updated Civil Rights Act, outlawing racial segregation in public places. Title VII of the 1964 act established the Equal Employment Opportunity Commission (EEOC) and prohibited employers from discriminating against people on the basis of race, color, religion, national origin, and—most important for policewomen—sex. Unfortunately Title VII didn't apply to state and local government agencies such as law enforcement organizations. The law would need to be expanded in a very specific way to force police departments not to discriminate against female candidates. Enter the Equal Employment Opportunity Act of 1972, which clarified Title VII. Now workplace discrimination requirements applied to "governments, governmental agencies [and] political subdivisions."

As he signed the bill into law, President Richard Nixon alluded to its powerful future impact: "By strengthening and expanding the government's powers against discrimination in employment, this legislation is an important step toward true equality on the job front," he said in March 1972. "Where promises have sometimes failed, we may now expect results. The most significant aspect of this legislation," continued the president, "is a new authority consistently advocated by this administration since 1969—a provision arming the Equal Employment Opportunity Commission with power to bring lawsuits in the Federal district courts to enforce the rights guaranteed by Title VII of the Civil Rights Act of 1964. Such actions are to be expedited by the courts whenever possible."[298]

Now women had a new weapon in the fight for equality in uniform. Armed with the 1972 law, the federal government cast a watchful eye over police departments across the nation. Meanwhile, policewomen who decided to go to court had a powerful partner backing them up.

A typical day for Martha Kinter, a 26-year-old officer in the Washington, D.C., police department. At the time these photos were snapped in June 1972, Kinter had been a cop for about two years. *(National Archives)*

It would take years for the new equal opportunity laws to filter down through the police ranks. Nevertheless, the changes, however small and slow, were significant. In 1972, for example, the Pennsylvania State Police became the first agency of its kind to have female troopers work the same jobs as the men. To the west, the Ohio State Highway Patrol had spent many years—1933 through 1976—relegating its female employees to clerical and support roles. With the advent of the equal opportunity laws, the highway patrol lowered its height requirement one inch, to five foot eight, and opened its academy to women. The badge worn by its officers changed as well. Instead of displaying the title *patrolman*, badges now sported the word *trooper*. Of a hundred interested female candidates, only one made it all the way through the academy in 1977. But Dianne Harris made it very clear that she wasn't trying to prove anything: "Somebody had to be first," she said at the time. "It just happened to be me. I focused on being a trooper."[299]

The old "boys' club" atmosphere was still quite evident in police departments across the nation. Case in point: a male officer in Seattle, Washington, made it crystal clear to rookie Mary Kulgren that he wasn't pleased that she had been assigned to him for her four months of field training. "[He] absolutely hated women," she recalled. "This officer repeatedly told me he thought women were to be fucked, and that was it. That's what he said as we were driving around the city and he was training me."[300]

When Philadelphia police commissioner Joseph O'Neill was asked why he thought women shouldn't be cops, he had a simple answer: "Because God, in his wisdom, made them different."[301]

O'Neill squared off against policewoman Penelope Brace in February 1974 when she filed a sexual discrimination suit against the city. Brace had been a cop for ten years. When she originally applied to be a police officer in the mid-1960s, she recalled being given an oral examination that included questions about her social life and whether she lived with her mother. Now, a decade later, she asked to test for detective and corporal but was told that she wasn't allowed to do so. In her lawsuit, Brace charged the Philadelphia Police Department with discriminatory practices and accused her superiors of harassment and retaliation after she complained about her situation. Brace's lawsuit was folded into a larger federal suit filed by the Department of Justice against the city of Philadelphia. The city admitted that discrimination did exist, but added that there was a good reason for it: women were physically unable to match the requirements of male police officers. The 75 women on the Philadelphia force were assigned to work juvenile cases only, and that was that.

After some finagling, the City of Brotherly Love cut a deal with the Justice Department: hire 100 women for street patrol during the next nine months, then study their progress for two years. Brace was incensed. Her attorneys labeled the settlement as "a transparent attempt to let the city save face" and concluded, "No study is necessary. It is an insult to women."[302] Brace noted that the agreement temporarily set aside the problem rather than attempting to solve it. "I would suggest the U.S. Justice Department conduct its own two-year study to determine why it cannot comply with its own civil rights obligations before it suggests that women are so inferior as a class that they must be studied," she said.[303]

Problems with paycheck discrepancies continued well into the 1970s and beyond. In Sheboygan, Wisconsin, policewoman Linda Achsel went to the state government regarding the pay differences between policewoman positions (with salaries ranging from $9,872 to

$12,225) and patrolman positions (with salaries ranging from $11,485 to $13,747). Because the job responsibilities were similar, argued Achsel, the pay rate should be the same. The city disagreed, and the state backed up the city. Although Achsel did have the power of arrest, "for the most part [she] works days as a secretary to the chief of police in the station house," argued the state. "While her duties do consist of responsible and difficult tasks, her function is more of an administrative assistant with a significant amount of clerical-related duties."[304] Patrolmen, on the other hand, operated outside of the station house and rode in a patrol car. Achsel received little help from the local media, which labeled her as the police chief's "girl Friday" who "serves as a receptionist and processes bills, besides her secretarial duties and those of a part-time policewoman."[305]

Many police departments were unprepared for the arrival of their first female officers, forcing the use of makeshift accommodations until a permanent solution was found. Brand-new officer Becky Downing walked into the York, Pennsylvania, station house in March 1974 and found nothing welcoming. "I knew no luxury as a shower, no separate locker room, no female uniforms," she recalled. "I wore all hand-me-downs, and I used hand-me-down equipment." She spent her first five years changing into her uniform inside a public restroom. When the department finally hired another female officer, Downing lobbied for a separate locker room and shower, pointing to the provisions of the 1972 Equal Employment Opportunity Act. Her superiors eventually relented, but it was an uphill battle. "Their thought process was that as long as they had a cot for women to lie down when they had menstrual cramps, they were in compliance," she explained. As the first female officer in York County, Downing took the brunt of the boys'-club mentality in the department. "I was thrown to the wolves," she said. "I went on patrol as an untrained rookie." Some of the male officers wouldn't work with her and even refused to help her when she called them on the radio. Wives phoned the department to complain about her presence on the force. But Downing persevered. "When I mastered all the skills easily, and was ready and willing to jump out of the car and run after a suspect, and physically take him down, I became one of the boys," she said.[306]

Locker-room language and off-color gestures, though often a part of male interaction, could be horribly out of place when a woman was in the room. In June 1974, Judy McCarr—one of Pennsylvania's first female troopers—filed suit against the department, citing "utter embarrassment and humiliation by the continuous use of crude, profane and obscene language by members of the Pennsylvania state police, including commissioned officers."[307] McCarr accused a retired lieutenant of improperly asking the chain of command to investigate her social life. The reason? She had dated the estranged husband of the lieutenant's daughter. Her commanding officer ordered her to stop seeing the man. An internal report accused McCarr of a "continuing, immoral relationship . . . with a married man." McCarr brushed it off. "It was my boyfriend," she said. "I am going out with him. I don't think that's immoral."[308] In an ironic twist, the man who had suspended her, police commissioner James Barger, pleaded guilty several years later to giving false testimony to a grand jury and conspiracy in tampering with public records.

Despite a wealth of stories to the contrary, many male officers did their best to integrate new female officers into their ranks. As a rookie with the Ohio State Highway Patrol, Virginia Fogt realized that she had more friends than she originally thought. In 1978, she was on her first day of duty, working the 8:00 A.M. to 4:00 P.M. shift by herself. She was called to an accident site of a single-vehicle crash. Though she worked the scene alone, help was right nearby. "What I didn't realize," said Fogt, "was that other troopers and my sergeant were intentionally positioned within a couple miles of my location, due to the uncertainty of how the public would react to a female trooper telling them what to do. This included issuing a citation or physically arresting someone. They were concerned for my safety."[309]

During their training at the Seattle academy, the female trainees were warned that male officers wouldn't support them in the field; however, the warning turned out to be a false alarm. "I never found it to be true," said Marsha Camp. "Once I got out of the academy, the men I worked around had the attitude of, 'Well, let's see. If she can do the job, then that's fine.'" It wasn't "wholehearted support," acknowledged Camp, "but they were willing to give me a chance."[310]

Sometimes well-intended efforts by male officers to accommodate new female recruits proved humorously awkward. When Kim Zangar became a Washington state trooper in June 1979, she was assigned to a male training officer who stood six foot seven to Zangar's five foot eight. "For six weeks I would drive and he rode with me," said Zangar. "I had a '79 Chevy and he rode on the passenger side. Since the car had a bench seat, his legs did not fit and it was really uncomfortable for him." Nor was the training officer used to working with a female subordinate. "When we met people, he would introduce me by saying, 'I'd like you to meet Kim. She's our female trooper.'" Zangar asked him not to do that. "I'm obviously female, so I thought it was funny, being introduced as a female trooper," she explained. "My training officer wasn't being critical; he actually liked having a female trooper around."[311]

After decades of tradition, the foundations of the department boys' clubs were beginning to crumble. Beginning in 1973, Los Angeles witnessed a groundbreaking court case that forever changed the police department's hiring practices. Fifty-two-year-old Fanchon Blake, a World War II veteran and 25-year veteran of the police force, filed a sex discrimination suit against the department, its chief, and the city itself. Blake noted that a lack of promotional opportunities, the five-foot-six height minimum, and a physical abilities test hindered women from joining the department. In addition, during a three-year-period—1970 to 1973—the department brought aboard more than 2,000 men while freezing its female hiring. When female officers heard a rumor that the department was thinking about phasing them out entirely, 100 women met with Ed Davis, the chief of police, to complain. "From the first day at the police academy," wrote Blake, "male officers made sure women in the Los Angeles police department were subservient to the men. . . . I developed a silent rebellion when denied choice assignments. It burned in me when I was told I couldn't take the lieutenant's exam, thus being denied promotion beyond sergeant."[312]

It took seven years for the Blake case to traverse the wickets of the legal system. Blake's complaint traveled all the way to the Supreme Court, which told the federal district court in Los Angeles either to go to trial or to put together a consent decree of some sort. So in 1980 a consent decree between the federal government and the Los Angeles Police Department reset a number of the entrance requirements and set hiring and promotion goals for the near future. The height requirement dropped to five feet, and the physical abilities test had to be programmed so that it didn't eliminate more than half of the female candidates who attempted it. The long-range goal: to place women in 20 percent of the sworn positions in the department. The Blake case remained open as the department struggled to meet the requirements of the consent decree. Unfortunately, Blake was unable to remain on duty. After suffering a stroke, she had to retire from the department. But her efforts to establish an equitable system of requirements for female officers would affect law enforcement organizations across the country for years to come.[313]

POLICEWOMEN IN TROUBLE

During a decade in which female law enforcement officers reached some important milestones, several high-profile incidents knocked policewomen's progress back several steps.

In one particularly horrifying case, a male-female pair of cops got into a fight and shot each other. Immediately questions began to fly. Was it racism? Sexism? Or just a case of bad temper? It was a Saturday in 1975, two days after Christmas. Two Flint, Michigan, cops walked to their patrol car to begin their shift. Madeline Fletcher was a 24-year-old African American officer. Walter Kalberer, 14 years her senior, was white and a former Marine. According to a policeman who was standing nearby, the events ensued as follows:

Fletcher got in the driver's side of the patrol car.

"Move your ass over," said Kalberer, incensed.

"Get your big fat ass on the other side," responded Fletcher.

Kalberer grabbed Fletcher and tried to pull her out of the squad car. Fletcher jabbed at Kalberer with her nightstick. Kalberer retaliated with his own nightstick. Fletcher unholstered her gun and fired at Kalberer, who pulled his own weapon and fired back four times. A nearby patrolman shot at Fletcher five times, missing every time. In the end, 14 bullets were fired from different guns. Fletcher suffered a gunshot wound in her left side. Kalberer held a bleeding thigh. Fletcher dashed behind some shrubs for protection. Then it was over.

The case was confusing, partly because the witnesses' statements didn't mesh. According to Fletcher's recollection, the incident occurred as follows:

Kalberer was standing near their assigned cruiser, holding his briefcase, not talking to anyone. Fletcher got in the driver's side, prompting Kalberer to approach her.

"Move over. I'm doing the driving," Kalberer said.

Fletcher shook her head. She had just completed her probationary period. "I've got my year in now, and whoever gets to the cruiser first does the driving."

Kalberer blew his top and slammed his briefcase on the top of the car. "[Then he] reached in and grabbed me around the collar," recalled Fletcher. "I leaned back in the seat and started kicking at him." Fletcher swung her nightstick at Kalberer but missed. Meanwhile, other police officers yelled at the two of them: "That bitch giving you any trouble? Snatch her black ass out of the car and whip her ass, man."

Kalberer whacked Fletcher over the head with his nightstick. She ran away, but he followed, continuing to beat her with the stick. Terrified, Fletcher pulled her service revolver and shot at Kalberer. When Fletcher looked around, her fellow officers were aiming their guns at her.

"Don't nobody move," Fletcher warned. Looking for cover, she moved toward some bushes perched at the corner of the building. At that point Kalberer shot her.[314]

Regardless of how the incident actually unfolded, both officers were rushed to the hospital. Fletcher was placed under guard after she received threatening phone calls and letters. One letter read, "It's too bad the white officer didn't kill that subnormal genetically inferior nigger animal. The policeman should have shot that nigger pig a dozen times." During her recovery and the media circus surrounding the incident, people raised funds for Fletcher's defense and slapped bumper stickers on their cars to show their support.

The police department suspended Fletcher and charged her with assault. The subsequent trial turned out to be almost as frightening as the incident itself. On the fourth day a gun went off in the packed hallway outside the courtroom, sending people screaming and scattering. The embarrassed policeman who was carrying the gun—and mistakenly thought the safety catch was on—was holding it for Kalberer, who was testifying inside the courtroom at the time.

Inside the courtroom, defense lawyers said that Fletcher was acting in self-defense. They read police radio transcripts out loud. Supposedly a dispatch officer had said, "Well maybe they'll get rid of the bitch now." During her testimony Fletcher said she had feared for her life. Six male officers testified against her. The jury acquitted Fletcher. In the end, the police department suspended Kalberer for five days and docked Fletcher two months' salary. Fletcher was "by far more guilty of infraction after infraction," explained the police chief.[315]

Meanwhile a police inquiry board recommended that Fletcher be fired. The police chief said no. Instead he added 90 days to Fletcher's suspension and allowed her to return to work in the fall of 1976. First, however, she had to attend refresher training since she had been off the job for ten months. But when Fletcher reported to the academy at Kalamazoo, she had "adjustment problems" and was eventually fired for failing to follow the rules there. Fletcher's list of infractions included driving 50 miles an hour in a 15-mile-per-hour zone, inappropriately loading additional bullets into her gun on the firing range and then refusing to give up the weapon, and driving to class in her patrol car with siren on and lights flashing. This time the police chief fired Fletcher outright. An arbitrator gave her another chance, ordering the police department to send her to the academy again. Fletcher had an appointment with the chief in October 1977 to make the proper arrangements, but she never showed up. "[She] is not interested in being recertified as an officer," said the chief.[316]

Just two years later came another highly publicized case involving policewomen. On August 26, 1979, a man stood in the middle of a street in Detroit, Michigan, a Doberman pinscher by his side. The man was naked and was busy setting dollar bills aflame. Policewomen Katherine Perkins and Glenda Rudolph came up to the man and tried to calm him down. Sergeant Paul Janness, their supervisor, arrived on the scene. Suddenly the nude man began beating up on Janness, knocking him down. Then came the worst part: After it was over, Janness accused the two female officers of doing nothing to help him.

What happened on that summer night in Detroit? Did the female cops stand by as a crazy man throttled their sergeant, as some witnesses said? Or did the women attempt to help, as another witness insisted? For their part, the policewomen had a simple explanation of what happened: "The sergeant put up his hand and said he was going to beat [the attacker's] ass," said Rudolph. So the two policewomen stepped aside.

After a January 1980 hearing the Detroit Police Department dismissed Perkins and Rudolph. The charge: cowardice in the line of duty. The women were devastated. Press photographs showed Perkins coming out of the dismissal hearing, holding her hat in front of her face. "I am not a coward," said Rudolph at the time. "I'm a fighter."

Two months later, in March, another police board convened to review the case. Five new witnesses provided testimony. Unfortunately the result was the same: the new review board upheld the original January decision, leaving the two policewomen out in the cold.

An incensed Rudolph railed against the review board: "A majority of the witnesses they used testified on stuff they read in the newspapers," she fumed.

Perkins's attorney noted that the decision wasn't surprising: police officers had lost 20 of the previous 21 cases brought before the board. "Our feeling has been that there may have been an element of racism or sexism," said Rudolph's attorney. (Both policewomen were African American.) "But we think the main brunt of the decision is a case of superiors against patrolmen."[317]

In May 1980, the seven-member board of police commissioners met to consider Perkins's dismissal. Neither the mayor of Detroit nor the police department thought that she should have been fired. But, said the city attorney, "there was shirking of duty during a time of danger." Perkins's attorney disagreed: "If these ladies were fearful they wouldn't have stopped. They could have locked the doors and waited for a backup unit. That wasn't the case." The severity of the punishment was unwarranted, he said.[318]

Eventually the board agreed to reinstate Perkins. Meanwhile, Rudolph decided to appeal through an independent arbitrator rather than the board of commissioners. Her case began on June 18, 1980. The department eventually reinstated her as well.

Looking back on the case, Perkins was very clear about what had happened. "It never entered my mind that I was guilty, and it never entered theirs that I wasn't," she said. "I may not be able to wrestle a two-hundred-pound nut, but a police officer has to have brains and common sense. I'm a professional, not just a dumb cop."[319]

"NEVER EXPECTED A WOMAN TO BE DOING THIS SORT OF THING"

Elsewhere in the 1970s, female cops were continuing to take on diverse roles as greater numbers of them joined police departments across the nation.

In August 1971, cameras clicked and whirred around the table where New York police commissioner Patrick Murphy perched in front of a bank of microphones. Next to him sat a 28-year-old woman wearing a black cloth over her face. Murphy praised the mystery woman for her work with the police department. The shrouded lady was an undercover police officer named Kathleen Burke. She was being promoted after nearly losing her life during a staged narcotics buy gone wrong. Three men had pulled her into an alley, stuck a knife at her throat, and grabbed $130 in cash along with her weapon. One of the men had jammed a gun against her head and pulled the trigger. Nothing happened. The other three undercover cops on Burke's team had come running into the alley and were able to grab one of the drug dealers, but the other two got away.

Writer Micki Siegel introduced Burke, undercover since 1969, to readers of *Parade* magazine: "She's dressed in cutoff jeans and a ratty t-shirt. Her hair is pulled into pigtails and there's real city dirt on her face. The thing about Kathy is this: She's scared, so scared that her hands are shaking. And that's good, because she's posing as a junkie and the shaking hands make her look even more convincing." Burke confided her fears to the journalist: being killed, being forced to take drugs, being raped. "I fear rape more than I fear death," she said. "More than I fear being shot or stabbed."[320] Eight weeks of additional undercover training had prepped Burke for her role as a drug addict. A senior undercover cop had showed her the ropes. "He taught me how to walk and talk like a junkie," explained Burke. "There's a certain downtrodden slump that they do. You know, they're beaten people and that's how they walk."[321]

Other undercover policewomen narrowly escaped death or dismemberment while working the streets. "After giving the signal once, I wasn't moving around the car fast enough to arrest the guy and he had a gun on me," recalled Baltimore officer Jean Mewbourne in 1978. A male plainclothes officer dashed out and jumped on the gunman in order to protect Mewbourne from getting shot.[322]

"The people on the drug scene never expected a woman to be doing this sort of thing," noted a 22-year-old female officer from St. Paul, Minnesota. In her guise as a junkie, the officer visited drug pushers and users all over the city. At a bar one night someone recognized her as a cop. She quickly got up and left the building. Five angry people followed her outside. She had to do something. "I turned around, pulled out a gun and told them I certainly couldn't outrun or fight all six of them," she recalled afterward. The officer got in her car, floored the accelerator, and hit all the green lights as her pursuers dashed after her. But her pursuers didn't have the same luck and eventually gave up the chase. "They weren't about to run red lights when they knew they were following a police officer," she explained.[323]

In the summer of 1979, in Trevose, Pennsylvania, a female state trooper went undercover in order to catch—believe it or not—a 25-year-old park policeman who had been attacking women on a local lovers' lane. The park policeman would separate couples, saying that the area was closed and that he had to talk to each lover separately. He would then escort the female half of the couple to his police vehicle and assault her. The undercover female trooper spent more than a month posing as a lover with a fellow trooper. Eventually, the park policeman who was the subject of the investigation separated the ostensible couple and took the female trooper aside. "He fondled the female trooper's breast and bottom and put her hand on his groin," a spokesperson related later. The park policeman was subsequently arrested.[324]

Female officers also continued to act as decoys for prostitution stings. A rookie policewoman, wearing a microphone inside her brassiere, spent an hour and a half on a Cincinnati, Ohio, street corner in April 1976. Twenty-five arrests later, she was done for the evening. "As soon as we put her out there, cars started lining up bumper-to-bumper," recalled a sergeant in the vice squad. "It was an instant traffic jam." The young officer found her experience as a decoy to be interesting. The men who propositioned her ran the gamut: they ranged in age from 17 to 55, held both white- and blue-collar jobs, and were as likely to be married as single. Although the typical prices on that particular corner were estimated to be between $5 and $20, the undercover cop received offers from $25 to $50—generous amounts that annoyed the real prostitutes working there.[325]

Kansas City cop Susan Johnston worked with eight male officers in the city's sex crime unit. When she ventured out to pose as a decoy, she left a sign in her office: "Out to Sex," it read. With other cops hovering nearby, Johnston would walk the city parks and streets until a suspect approached her. "At first my parents were very upset about my job," she said. "They were afraid I would be depressed by my work. But now that they have seen nothing bad has happened to me, they've changed their minds. My mother calls me the hired gun."[326]

In May 1970, *Time* magazine noted that not everyone was impressed with the decoy program in Washington, D.C.: "The new technique has upset civil libertarians," the magazine reported, "to say nothing of pimps, prostitutes and customers. Legal critics scent illegal entrapment. However, the policewomen have refined their techniques to avoid any overt welcome save their dress and location, and seventeen patrons have been convicted under a statute that makes solicitors liable for a $250 fine or ninety days in jail or both."[327]

The city of Chicago had the distinction of hiring a former nun, training her as a police officer, and using her as decoy prostitute. Cynthia Kane, formerly Sister Mary Anthony, had worked with young delinquents in a shelter prior to joining the force. "If prostitution is going to be illegal," she said, "then the patron is just as guilty as the women. And use of decoys to arrest these men is the most effective way to clear it out of residential areas." Among the undercover roles Kane played were a high-class hooker and a housewife with lesbian tendencies—all to lure drug dealers and pimps out into the open. Kane suffered a number of bumps and bruises while doing her job. A call-girl ringleader aimed a weapon at her, saying, "This is what I give to policewomen." A female prisoner beat her up, sending Kane to the hospital for a month.[328]

Not all policewomen liked being an undercover decoy. "It was boring," grumbled a Dallas policewoman in 1974. Posing as a prostitute, the policewoman sat at a local bar until a man sidled up to her and chatted for 45 minutes. "He just talked and talked and talked," she recalled. When he finally offered her $5 for sex, she was offended. On a different night, a potential customer wanted to give her $13.60—the amount left over after he paid for a hotel room with the $17 in his pocket. Despite the parade of cheap johns, the policewoman took pains to look classy. "I don't wear anything that's the least bit enticing," she said. "I dress just like the other customers in the bar I'm going to. If it's a higher-class bar, I dress accordingly. If it's a hippie bar, I dress like a hippie. The overdone-looking women are never the prostitutes."[329]

Perhaps the disgruntled policewoman could have refused her undercover assignment, as Gale Aldridge did in 1970. The Detroit

Police Department's ongoing decoy operation placed policewomen, dressed as prostitutes, on street corners. After several female officers complained, the department decided to take only volunteers. But Aldridge said she wasn't given a choice.

When she received her orders, Aldridge decided they were unlawful. "I went to Michigan State University for three years and I studied hard to be a policewoman," she said. "I just don't like the idea of being told to go out on the corner and make out as if I were selling my body. I just don't believe in such use of policewomen to combat prostitution." On May 16, 1970, the department promptly suspended Aldridge without pay. The police officers' association supported her, but her female boss didn't, saying that Aldridge should have complied with her instructions. In the end, Aldridge's gamble failed. A three-person police trial board fired her for refusing to follow lawful orders.[330]

Other female officers didn't feel quite as burdened when asked to pose as hookers. "It doesn't bother me when I'm mistaken for a prostitute," said a Dallas cop. "I feel like I'm succeeding in what I'm trying to do. It's not me they're talking to—it's what they *think* I am." But a former city councilman disagreed. "While burglars are literally carrying my neighborhood away," he complained, "the police are tying their officers up with a scheme like this. It just amazes me that the Dallas police department has so little to do that it can assign a woman and two officers to spend their time in bars."[331]

Apart from participating in undercover work, some policewomen in the 1970s played dual roles in real life. In an unusual twist, several women of the cloth joined the ranks of law enforcement officers. Like many police departments across the country, the Madison County, Illinois, force had a female police officer assigned to work juvenile cases. Unlike most such officers, however, this policewoman was also a nun known as Sister Fuzz. "That's what the kids call me," said Sister

Mary Cornelia, who lived at St. Elizabeth's Convent near St. Louis. "They yell to me when they see me on the street." A newspaper photo showed Sister Mary Cornelia in front of a police cruiser, wearing vestments and a habit, a gun belt around her waist.

The nation's capital also had its own police nun. Sister Eleanor Niedwick lived at the Daughters of Wisdom convent at Catholic University but spent most of her time visiting children, civic groups, and senior citizens in the rough-and-tumble Tenth Precinct in Washington, D.C. "This was the whole idea of the gospel," Niedwick said. "Jesus did not hide. He went to the people."[332] The former elementary school teacher, originally from New York, joined the D.C. police department in October 1969. Niedwick noted that she wore civilian clothes except when visiting retirement homes, when she would put on her habit. "They expect it," she explained.

Sometimes police officers heard a higher calling and left law enforcement for the church. In August 1964, Alice Cullen resigned from the police department in Providence, Rhode Island, to become a Roman Catholic nun. Cullen had joined the force back in 1934 as a clerk. Promoted to the city's first policewoman position, she spent three decades in uniform. But through all that time, the thought of becoming a nun stuck in the back of her mind. "Most criminals come from a background where there was a lack of affection and understanding," Cullen explained. "They felt left out of life. It sounds simple, almost corny, but most of them never had a home." Cullen seemed well suited for the religious life: one day she was speaking with a female prisoner who suddenly began to cry. "I asked her what I had said that was offensive," recalled Cullen. "She told me it was the first time anyone had said anything nice to her."[333] Like Susan Barney, the Women's Christian Temperance Union's prison missionary who had helped a female prisoner nearly 80 years before, Cullen was the latest in a long and proud line of women in law enforcement who provided care and direction for women and children who needed it.

HORSES AND OTHER HAZARDS

While the squad car was the most publicly recognized method of transportation for police officers, some female cops in the 1970s made use of horses as they patrolled their beats in the community. Putting a policewoman on a horse was not a new concept—recall Pearl Kray, who joined the mounted park police in Cleveland, Ohio, in 1914.

In 1969, 26-year-old Joanne Rossi applied to be the first female officer to ride a horse in the unit that patrolled Fairmount Park, the 9,000-acre system of public parks that winds its way through the city of Philadelphia. "After graduating from college I thought of what to do," said Rossi, "and I thought I'd like to be a Fairmount Park guard because I enjoy being in the open near nature and riding horses. And the pay's not bad either."[334]

The Fairmount Park Guard rejected her application. "We don't have any such classification as mounted policewoman," said the befuddled park police superintendent. "I don't think a woman could do the work. . . . It's just too dangerous."[335] Undaunted, Rossi appealed to the state human relations commission, which sponsored a hearing into the matter. "They have to patrol lonely areas at night," insisted the superintendent when he appeared before the commission. "I don't believe women are physically capable of pr

Felicia Shpritzer, who had successfully the New York Police Department in the r as well. "In New York we have to do all told the commission, "but chivalry prev most hazardous tasks, but if necessary w

In 1975, Chicago cop Gillian McLaughlin had better luck at getting approval to ride a horse on the job. After nine months in a patrol car, she was looking for a change of pace. McLaughlin applied to join the city's mounted police unit, which had 22 horses at the time. During training McLaughlin fell under her horse, Safeguard, who gave her a swift kick that damaged her shoulder and put her out of commission for three weeks. The lone woman in the mounted unit, McLaughlin noted that her police uniform sometimes created confusion among the public: "With my hair done up under my hat I've been mistaken for a man when I'm out riding, and that's brought some ribbing," she said. "The main thing is to keep the horse calm and under control because there are pressure situations—breaking up crowds, handling traffic and such," she explained. "And a horse may get bumped. Some motorists think the horses are raised in front of buses."[338]

Parking control officers—better known as meter maids—also faced certain dangers on the job. Forty-one-year-old Betty Ambrose, a former parking control officer, had switched jobs and spent two years working in the juvenile division of the Alexandria, Louisiana, police department. In 1977, she attended a three-month certification course at Louisiana State University and became a credentialed juvenile officer. But upon her return to the station, the police chief told her that she was going back to being a meter maid. Then things became even more confusing. While Ambrose was in school, the city had removed all of its downtown parking meters in order to encourage more shopping. So what was Ambrose supposed to do? The exasperated policewoman, the lone female in a force of 109 officers, was getting the runaround. "There are no meters—that's what I'm trying to get across to them," she explained. "They tell me the fire lanes need enforcing. But the men on the beat can do that—they can drive right up at them."[339] To add insult to injury, a male officer was already walking a beat in the downtown district and could check the fire lanes himself.

The novelty of women in uniform patrolling the streets on a regular basis caused a lot of head-turning among the general public. Kim Zangar described the phenomenon when talking about her time as a rookie with the Washington State Patrol: "I couldn't go anywhere without people staring at me like a Martian or two-headed calf. We couldn't even go to coffee without everyone staring at us."

Margaret Kline, a 21-year-old Hagerstown, Maryland, cop, had been a patrol officer for three months—the first female officer in her city. Her first days on the beat in January 1977 caused some confusion on the street. "We got lots of stares, especially from kids and teenagers," said her partner, Ronald Graves. "Guys you think would give her a problem don't. Others, well, it doesn't make one bit of difference. They treated her just like they treat any other policeman."[340] One day Kline brought in an unruly man who had resisted arrest. When she took off her hat, the man did a double take. "You're a woman!" he stammered. "I'm sorry. If I had known you were a woman, I wouldn't have given you so much trouble."[341]

From her first duty day in September 1973, Ethel Moore Diké, an African American officer in Columbia, South Carolina, said she experienced no discrimination, either racial or sexual. "When I came to South Carolina, there were no females," she said. "They had just opened the field to women in early 1973." Diké did notice, however, that the public was having a difficult time getting used the concept of a female officer. Diké, the first female cop in the city, had been issued the same uniform required of male officers, with one exception: a hat designed specially for women. But it was her hair that caught the attention of passersby: "Her stylish cut prompted [a] reaction recently from a local woman who thought it was disgraceful that a Columbia 'policeman' would have such an outlandish head of hair," noted a local reporter. "You should have seen her eyes widen when I turned around," said Diké. "You know, I think they really see only the uniform of a police officer. But I do get plenty of double takes."[342]

In California, Juanita Howard had a slightly different issue to deal with when she joined the Oakland force. The part-time model, wearing her regulation blue uniform, attracted a lot of attention out on the street. "I was on assignment at the St. Patrick's Day parade, and a group of little kids started shouting 'Charlie's Angels' and a group of guys said, 'Arrest me,'" noted a slightly flustered Howard. After graduating from the academy, Howard—the 17th woman on the Oakland force—headed out on the street with a field training officer. "When I was in the car I always had to wear black leather gloves," she said. "It didn't matter if it was a hundred degrees outside. I was told to wear the gloves because they made me look tough." Howard also had to drive with a bar of soap in her right hand to keep her from crossing her arms over the steering wheel. "The radio had a cord, and you could get caught in it," she explained.[343]

Meanwhile, the Detroit Police Department, which had wrestled with uniform designs since the 1920s—never quite getting it right— examined the use of pantsuits as an option for female officers. During the early 1970s, the police commissioner authorized their wear after a policewoman petitioned for it. But the head of the women's section, Dorothy Gay, had a few conditions. "Mrs. Gay made it clear that the pantsuit standards would discourage any crazy-looking styles," reported the *Detroit News*, "and would be geared to helping maintain the section's half-century reputation for conservative clothing."[344]

By 1974, with some of Detroit's female cops patrolling with male officers in radio cars, a real female uniform became a necessity. The department tried out a test pattern, fashioned out of polyester. It wrinkled badly. Another design, offered by a uniform supplier, fit poorly. Better received was an A-line skirt or flared pants topped with a short-waisted "Ike" jacket similar to the type popularized during World War II.

When she graduated from the academy in 1978, Ohio state trooper Virginia Fogt was faced with a fashion dilemma: "The tailor for the patrol had to take a male uniform and try to fit me to it," she remembered. "There were no darts in the uniforms."

Alice Scott, a Los Angeles county sheriff's deputy, recalled wearing skirts to graduation in 1980. For daily work the department issued its female deputies "girl pants" that lacked pockets. "That way they could have a nice tight fit," she said. Needless to say, Scott and her fellow deputies weren't happy with snug duty uniforms. "Whenever females went to patrol, we immediately bought 'boy pants' that had lots of pockets and were roomier," she said.[345]

Now that they had uniforms, what about their hairstyles? Indiana state trooper Shannon Spreckelmeyer had a short stature and a short haircut—both of which sometimes caused confusion on the street. One day she got a radio call from district headquarters.

"Did you just go to the grocery store?" asked the dispatcher.

"Yes," answered Spreckelmeyer. "For a loaf of bread."

"Okay. We thought it might be you!"

It was a case of mistaken identity. Someone had called the district complaining that a "little boy" had been seen driving a marked state police car.

The Ohio Highway Patrol required women to wear their hair short—off the collar and not extending below the earlobe. That restriction had an unintended effect. "It discouraged women to become troopers," explained Virginia Fogt. The superintendent finally changed the rules and allowed women to have longer hair—as long as it was worn off the collar, of course.

Though they expected that some male officers wouldn't be able to stomach having a woman working with them, newly minted female officers also ran into an unexpected foe: other women. For Donna Bacus, her first days in the Iowa state patrol were marked by distrust from the wives of male officers. "When I started in 1978, many of the trooper's wives did not want me riding in the car with their husbands," Bacus recalled. "I was called a 'woman's libber' and many other names of interest." Indiana state trooper Jill Rice remembered a further requirement when she joined that organization in 1979: "While I was being trained, I had to get written permission from the wives to let me ride with their husbands," she said.

When her training officer invited her for a party at his house, it was Kim Zangar's first time meeting the wives of the other officers on the Washington State Patrol. "I'm 24 and single and in top physical shape after getting out of the academy," said Zangar. "I get to the house and I'm dressed so conservatively—I had a blouse buttoned up to the top." While the men stood outside admiring her training officer's recently renovated back yard, Zangar was left inside with their wives. "I wanted to go out and talk with the men, but I couldn't," she explained. " I didn't want to give the wives any reason to worry about the fact that I worked with their husbands all night."

Dallas cop Norma Ferguson thought that the male officers' wives worried needlessly about mixed-sex partnerships on the force. "Nothing has happened," Ferguson said in 1974. We socialize in families now. The wives know us. They are more worried about those hookers who come on like they might take the men off against their will."[346] Things cooled down a bit as more women joined law enforcement and the spouses got used to the idea of their husbands having a female partner on the job.

POLICEWOMEN ON PATROL

Assigning female officers to a patrol beat seemed like a logical progression of responsibility, but not everyone agreed. Police departments in cities like Miami, Florida, and Peoria, Illinois, were ahead of the curve and had already allowed female cops on patrol duty. Many other law enforcement agencies were more tentative about it. The Dallas, Texas, police department, for example, tried out an experimental patrol program for female officers. Barbara Vandeventer and Norma Ferguson, recent graduates of the 18-week academy training program, took to the streets in 1972. "Both are involved in routine police work," said a supervisor, "including making arrests, traffic accidents and burglars in buildings, just like any other rookie policeman undergoing training."[347] The women officers each rode in a squad car with a training officer, .38-caliber revolvers strapped to their waists and a 12-gauge shotgun nearby.

In St. Paul, Minnesota, Deborah Gilbreath Montgomery made history on September 8, 1975, becoming the first female police officer in the city to complete the same training as the male officers. Montgomery, a 29-year-old mother of four, was a budget analyst and city planner when she applied for the police department in 1975. She was the only one of 450 females to pass the entire qualifying test. Montgomery recalled that her fellow classmates supported her throughout the five months of training. But once she was on the street it was a different matter: "None of the guys really wanted to work with a woman," she said, "and so I had a lot of shifts where I was a one-person unit when everybody else was a two-person unit."[348]

Policewomen in Los Angeles were just beginning to work in radio cars when Lynda Castro joined the sheriff's department in 1975. "It was demanding but so rewarding—and hard to admit you needed help or someone to talk to for fear of the perception of being weak," she said. Male and female candidates had always trained together at the sheriff's academy, but the women graduated after ten weeks of training and then "remained in custody [jail] assignments or working juvenile and sex crime assignments as detectives rather than being allowed to work the streets," explained Castro.[349] The men, on the other hand, stayed at the academy for the full 18-week course, which included patrol training. That changed in the mid-1970s when the women were finally allowed to complete the entire academy training program alongside the men.

In addition to hiring full-time officers, many police departments maintained an auxiliary or reserve force as well. New York, home to the Women's Police Reserve of World War I, boasted an auxiliary force of more than 4,000 members in the early 1970s. Five percent of the auxiliary cops were female. Edith Katz was one of them. Working half-shifts two nights a week in Prospect Park in Brooklyn, Katz and other auxiliary officers came in handy when the 74th Precinct's full-time force was cut nearly in half. "Sometimes there have been gang wars in the park," she noted. "Auxiliary police have made numerous narcotics arrests and have captured purse snatchers. But mostly our patrols are dull and routine. We feel what we do best is keep people from committing crimes, just because we're there."[350] Although the auxiliary police only carried nightsticks while on duty—they had no arrest authority, nor could they strap on a weapon—they were in radio contact with the full-time officers from their precincts.

By 1971 the New York Police Department had about 350 police-women—just 1 percent of the total number of cops on the force. Most of them worked in administrative jobs. With its women's bureau looking increasingly dated in an era of progressive female employment, the department launched an experimental program in 1972 called Policewomen on Patrol. Officers Lucille Burrascano and Kathaline Salzano were the first women in the city's history to work as partners in a radio car. Burrascano was looking for something new to do when she heard about the program. "At the time I wasn't in anyplace promising as far as my career went," she recalled. "I was searching prisoners and dead bodies." Under New York law, female police officers were required to examine the bodies of women who died under mysterious circumstances. Burrascano's other duties were less unpleasant but hardly pointed to career advancement. "We had a variety of work but there was no future," she recalled.[351]

Lucille Burrascano, one of New York's first policewomen on patrol, in 1972. She and partner Kathaline Salzano were assigned to the 77th Precinct in Brooklyn Heights. (*Courtesy Lucille Burrascano*)

Enter Gertrude Schimmel, who had broken down the promotion barriers with Felicia Shpritzer in the early 1960s. Schimmel was promoted to captain in August 1971. By that time the 53-year-old policewoman had served three decades on the force. "If there had been no sex discrimination in the department," the police commissioner said at the time, "Mrs. Schimmel might be receiving a star on her shoulder today."[352] Schimmel took command of the women's bureau that September.

Three months later she recommended to the police commissioner that women be allowed to go on patrol duty. Such a test program had worked well in England. Why not in New York, then? "Women might be better suited for some jobs than men," explained Schimmel. "They might not provoke things that men do. For instance, they might be able to avert some things, like assaults [on police] because they're women. Who'd slug a woman?"[353]

With the department's blessing, Schimmel sent questionnaires to all of the city's policewomen. She received just 17 responses and picked 15 candidates from the stack. "On the questionnaire I had said 'yes' all the way up and down, no questions," said Burrascano. This intrigued Schimmel, who brought in Burrascano for an interview. The two women clicked, and Burrascano was accepted into the program.

After interviewing with Schimmel, the 15 female candidates went through psychological testing—something not required of male applicants to the police department—and then participated in an intensive five-week training course to familiarize them with radio motor patrol car procedures. Then, for real-world orientation, the women rode as observers in squad cars with male officers.

Three city precincts—Brooklyn, Queens, and the West Village—hosted the Policewomen on Patrol program. Five female officers were farmed out to each precinct. Schimmel stopped short of putting male and female partners together in patrol cars. "The public might not like the idea of women answering their calls for help," she explained. "The policemen might not like the idea, either." Schimmel felt that two women in each car would be a better plan. Burrascano and Kathaline Salzano approached their precinct commander and asked to be paired. "He loved the idea," said Burrascano, "and so we became the first two women partners on patrol in New York City."

Thinking back to her experiences in a patrol car, Burrascano recalled that she and Salzano dealt with "family fights, dog bites, car accidents, deterring by driving around slowly, taking noise complaints—a lot of domestic issues." Working out of a radio car was an eye-opener. "I used to think the men went out and slayed dragons," said Burrascano. "It turned out not to be so spectacular, but it was wonderful anyway. You had to know the basics, and you had to love to be out there. And," she added, "you had to be a people person."

Partnering women officers also made the situation easier on the officers' wives. "The wives couldn't complain about us," said Burrascano, "and we didn't need the men to protect us." Nevertheless, the male officers still practiced a certain amount of chivalry. "When Kathy and I made arrests," explained Burrascano, "sometimes the men would get a little upset. They'd ask us, 'Why didn't you call for help?'"

During a late shift Burrascano and Salzano came upon two suspicious men sitting in a car. The vehicle turned out to be stolen, and then two men were holding drugs inside. The policewomen arrested the men and called for backup—not because they needed assistance with the two suspects, but so that someone could drive the stolen car back to the station house. When the call came in, half of the precinct responded. It was two o'clock in the morning. Later, as Burrascano and Salzano reached the station with their suspects in hand, the desk sergeant was visibly upset.

"Why didn't you ask us to help you?" he grumbled.

"We did," answered the policewomen. "We needed someone to drive the suspect's car to the station house."

Why did the arrest go so smoothly? The suspects didn't even attempt to put up a fight. When the female officers approached, the men got out of the car. One of them was six foot six and towered over the women. Later someone asked the man why he didn't just escape by running away from the female officers.

"Because," he said, "I knew that being women, they'd just take their guns out and shoot me dead."

When she heard about it, Burrascano shook her head. "The suspects perceived us as physically weak, so our last resort was to blow their brains out?" she said incredulously. But then she added, "If that's what he thought, why should I argue? There's no crime for them thinking that we're going to do that." And because of it, the arrest went without incident.

Burrascano credited age and experience with helping her and Salzano weather the ups and downs of the Policewomen on Patrol program. "Kathy and I came from the prison cell blocks," explained Burrascano. "For six years we'd searched some pretty terrible people—hookers, drifters, thieves." In addition, the women officers also escorted material witnesses and people in protective custody. "We did a lot of little stuff that many people didn't know about," said Burrascano. The two policewomen also had the benefit of life experience. "We were both 30 years old," said Burrascano. "We weren't babies on the job, and we weren't babies in life. Kathy was a wife and mother, and I'd traveled the world."

Public reaction to the women officers ran the gamut from mild amusement to death threats. As the women drove their squad car down the street, people would stop, point, and smile. "For some people it was puzzling, of course," said Burrascano. "We were two white women in a black neighborhood." The officers were sometimes on the receiving end of racial slurs. But quite often people from the neighborhood would come to their defense.

The 15 female officers in the Policewomen on Patrol program gathered together each month to receive evaluations and feedback about their performance. The women were closely watched and constantly evaluated. Two psychologists monitored them throughout the program.

"Two years after we started, we came out of it still standing when the smoke cleared," said Burrascano, who appreciated the camaraderie she shared with many of the male officers. "The men were wonderful—honest and hardworking and sincere," she explained. Even if the men didn't agree with what the women were doing, they backed them up anyway. During one shift, Burrascano recalled, one of the nicest male officers she knew opened up to her. "I still believe you belong in the kitchen," he said. "But that doesn't mean I don't respect you."

"THAT'S WHAT HELL IS LIKE"

As if working a stressful job and dealing with time-worn prejudices weren't enough, many policewomen also had to deal with life at home. Juggling children and a career was a constant challenge for female officers with families. It was one of the reasons that the number of women in law enforcement remained low, said Washington state trooper Kim Zangar. "If you want to have children you have to balance things out. Because you never know when you're coming home. With snow out there you could be three hours late. If you have a child in day care and they close at six o'clock, you're in a heck of a predicament."

Veneza Aguinaga was single when she started her career in the Austin, Texas, police department. She worked by herself in a patrol car on the evening shift. After she got married, she and her husband—also a patrol officer—had a daughter. "We decided that we only wanted one parent working on patrol," explained Aguinaga. Before she got pregnant, she requested to transfer from patrol duty to the recruiting office. Then she and her husband did their best to adjust. "Our schedules were crazy," she said, laughing, "but we made it work."[354]

In June 1988, Kim Zangar reluctantly moved a hundred miles away from her family to take a promotion. "That's what hell is like," she said. "I was a line sergeant, on call 24 hours a day, so I couldn't have my child with me." When Zangar came home for visits, her four-year-old daughter would grab her leg, hang on to it, and scream for her to stay.

Two months after Zangar began her long-distance job, she was called to the scene of an automobile accident where a mother and daughter had been killed. Zangar looked at the bodies. That was enough for her. The next day she walked into her supervisor's office and quit. "You know, I'm 32 years old," Zangar told her supervisor. "My mom is dead, and I can't change that. But my daughter isn't, and I'm not going to spend a year away from her." Though she moved back home, Zangar later returned to the state patrol, retiring after 25 years in uniform.

What happened when a female officer had a baby? In 1974, Lori Fry was a civilian working as a complaint desk coordinator for the police department in San Bernardino, California. She watched in awe as a coworker, Sue Dawson, battled to join the force. "Six weeks after delivering her sixth child via a C-section, she completed the same physical agility test required for all applicants," recalled Fry. "I was very impressed by her example." Dawson proceeded to pass the psychological and written tests with flying colors and was added to the rolls as a reserve officer—an unpaid position at which she excelled. "She literally showed many regular patrol officers how to write a good report, frisk a prisoner, many aspects of their job," said Fry. "She served on patrol competently, had excellent scores at the range and had shown herself over and over to be competent at the job of police officer, even though she was an unpaid volunteer."

Despite those strengths, Dawson was continuously passed over for appointment to a full-time position. When she turned 35, she hit the department's age limit and was unable to try again. "It was blatantly unfair," said Fry.

Meanwhile, in Washington state, Kim Zangar was the first state trooper to get pregnant. "I really got mistreated," she remembered. "They couldn't decide if they should take me out of the car, take me out of uniform, or whether I should wear a maternity uniform." Wanting to work regular hours, Zangar interviewed for a temporary desk job at headquarters. She was told she couldn't have the job because she was pregnant—"a decision that was illegal," she pointed out. But part of the problem was that no one knew what to do. "It was an educational process," she explained. "It wasn't meant to be malicious. After I had my baby they had me go back on the road to prove a point. They said, 'You have to because you're a girl.'"

Indiana state trooper Jill Rice kept her pregnancy a secret for as long as she could. "I had no idea what they would do with me, so I put off telling anyone about my pregnancy until I was six months along," she said. "I just kept getting bigger gun belts and my coat covered me. It was not a smart move, but I didn't want to lose my job or have to quit." Finally she told her lieutenant, who reassigned her to desk duty until she went into labor in March 1984. Over the next several years the department caught up with the times. "Today they have written standard operating procedures for troopers becoming pregnant," Rice said.

Could having a child improve an officer's marksmanship? Betty "Bull's-Eye" Hawk—who got her nickname during a May 1970 marksmanship contest—was one of two women on the Glendale, California, police force. She worked juvenile investigations for five years and then transferred to the operations desk when her first child was born. After completing her 10:00 P.M. to 7:00 A.M. shift, wrote reporter Avery Keener in a profile, "she wraps her pistols in a diaper, wraps her slender body in a mini, and schedules her naps with those of her curly-haired, laughing one-and-a-half-year-old son named Eric Dorian Hawk." Hawk attributed her precision on the firing range to extra practice and credited her son with making the difference: "The guns are heavy for a woman, but carrying a baby helps keep arm muscles strong."[355]

Although she was able to adjust her schedule to accommodate her growing family, Hawk ended up joining the growing number of female cops who filed discrimination cases during the 1970s. After six years on duty, she resigned, accusing the department of blocking her promotion to detective because she was a woman. She had scored higher on the detective's promotion exam than the five men who were eventually promoted. She was also expecting her second child. Was the timing a matter of simple coincidence—or did Hawk have to decide between her job and family?

BETTER FOR A WOMAN

As women cops gained ground in male-dominated police departments, they were often called upon to "talk down" irate or emotionally disturbed suspects. "I am pretty small compared to most male officers," said Veneza Aguinaga of the Austin, Texas, police force. "I learned to talk down a situation instead of having to fight someone."

Sheriff's deputy Roberta Abner, assigned to patrol the city of West Hollywood, California, saw this firsthand as well. "I responded to a rape call involving a mentally unstable woman who was found screaming in a bush," recalled Abner. "From the moment I started speaking to her, she wanted to sit on my lap and be held." Abner comforted the shuddering victim all the way to the hospital. Later, the woman calmed down. "Her brother thanked me for being so understanding, considering her mental limitations," said Abner.[356]

A case of attempted hijacking on a January night in 1973 aptly demonstrated not only the female officer's strengths in dealing with suspects but also her ability to be physical when the situation required it. It was a little after 9:00 P.M. and Louisville International Airport was bustling with Friday-night traffic. Passengers meandered through the terminal on their way to their flights. Suddenly a teenage gunman poked his head over a balcony and fired a shotgun at the ground floor below. Glass windows blew apart as the crowd screamed and scattered across the building. The gunman fired several more times, then dashed out of the terminal toward an empty Ozark Airlines DC-9 parked on the tarmac. He grabbed an aircraft mechanic as a hostage and climbed aboard the plane.

The local police and FBI started negotiations with the young gunman. They found out that he was a disgruntled soldier who was AWOL from Fort Knox, the nearby Army post. He wanted a getaway plan to take him to a country that would provide asylum. During the next six hours policewoman Marty Green, who usually walked a patrol beat in downtown Louisville, became his link to the outside world. Green strolled across the parking ramp and walked up the air stairs five different times to speak with the gunman. By trip number four she was fairly sure that the gunman wanted to turn himself in.

On Green's next visit to the airplane, the soldier made an offer to turn over his gun to her. Green walked carefully up the stairs to the entrance doorway. The gunman reached for her. As he grabbed her hand, Green yanked him to the ground. She held him there until other law enforcement officers rushed the aircraft and arrested him.

Then there were the unusual, lighter incidents—crying girlfriends, wacky drunks, kissing bandits—that balanced out the policewoman's more dangerous cases. During the 1980s, Kim Zangar was working the graveyard shift, 10:00 P.M. to 6:00 A.M. Driving on the highway, the Washington state trooper noticed a car swerving in and out of its lane. Thinking the driver was probably drunk, Zangar switched on her lights and pulled the car over.

The driver, a woman, jumped out and ran back toward Zangar's cruiser. "Don't you know this is a stolen car?" the woman yelled, pointing at her vehicle.

Zangar coaxed the woman over to the side of the road and into the back seat of the squad car. Once inside, the woman burst into tears. "We had a shield with holes on the sides between the front and back seat, and I'm stuffing kleenex through it," recalled Zangar. "I didn't want to put the window down."

Zangar checked with the dispatcher while continuing to comfort the crying woman as best she could. "I was a little bit frustrated," said Zangar. "Dispatch didn't get back to me quickly—it seemed like 15 minutes before they got the information on the 'stolen' car. It turned out that the car hadn't been reported stolen after all. Meanwhile the woman was crying in the back seat."

As it turned out, the car belonged to the woman. Her ex-boy-friend had swiped it from her house and given it to his *new* girlfriend. When the woman realized what her ex-boyfriend had done, she found her car, got in, and drove away as fast as she could. By the time Zangar stopped her, the woman was hysterical.

After the incident was over, Zangar reflected on how being a female cop probably helped the situation. "Guys don't deal with crying very well," she mused.

What about dealing with male suspects? Though she usually handled them just fine on her own, Zangar recalled an occasion when she had to ask for help. During a traffic stop Zangar was challenged by a drunk man who refused to get in her patrol car.

"You have to call for backup," he insisted, then stood still and refused to move.

After arguing with him for a while, Zangar finally threw up her hands and grabbed the radio. Since she knew another trooper was just a few minutes away, she called him. "I said, 'Do you mind driving over this way? No rush.'" The male trooper on the other end of the line was within five miles of the traffic stop. He agreed to drop by. When he arrived on scene, the drunk looked at him, nodded, and got into Zangar's cruiser with a satisfied look on his face. "He wanted a story to tell his buddies," explained Zangar. "'Look, I got arrested and it took two of them to get me into the patrol car!'"

Lonely male suspects, not used to seeing a woman in uniform, made for some entertaining traffic stops. In December 1977, Tulsa, Oklahoma, policewoman Perry Burnett pulled over a 24 year-old man for running a red light. When she walked up to the car, she realized the driver had been drinking. After she began writing a ticket, the man suddenly began fondling her hair. He pulled on her wrist, then started kissing her elbow. He went to court on an assault charge, pleaded no contest, and paid a $20 fine.

"One of the misconceptions that the general public has about female officers is that they mistake our sensitivity or concern for being weak," said Bernadette Jaramillo of the New Mexico state patrol. "The truth is that once a suspect crosses the line we know how to turn on our aggressive side. But more importantly, we know how to turn it off."[357]

POLICEWOMAN WITH A PEN

Like Mary Hamilton and Mary Sullivan before them, women officers with a talent for writing continued to put their thoughts down on paper. One of them was New York transit cop Dorothy Uhnak. "I had to hit this guy on my first arrest," she recalled. "He was a huge guy, an iron and steel worker, a thief. I saw him lifting wallets and pulled out my badge. He just laughed. I hit him on his big bald head and instead of falling in a heap on the floor, just like they do on TV, he stood there, turned to me and asked me what I had hit him with. It took six cops to get him. You see, I was supposed to shoot him instead of strike him."[358]

Uhnak joined the transit police in 1953 and stayed through 1967. With 15 years of story material in her head, she decided to start writing. She published her first novel, *The Bait*, in 1968, and followed it with nearly a dozen other novels, all drawing on her experiences as a cop. "With hardly a neighborhood left where people really feel at ease, it figured that there would be interest in just who policemen are and what they look like," explained Uhnak.[359]

Though one of her characters would inspire a television series called *Get Christie Love!*—which aired for a single season beginning in 1974—Uhnak wasn't terribly impressed by fictional portrayals of female cops in popular culture. "The profession has been all too romanticized, fantasized beyond recognition," she said.[360]

NBC's *Police Story* anthology series tackled the male-female partnership in a squad car in the episode "Collision Course," broadcast in 1973. Sue Ane Langdon played a rookie policewoman, with Hugh O'Brian as her training officer. The episode, Langdon said, deliberately avoided making a statement one way or the other. "Our show doesn't come up with an answer, and I really can't either. The purpose of the story is more to present the problem and let viewers decide."[361]

With the premiere of the TV series *Police Woman* in 1974, female law enforcement officers had a major hit series that, for better or worse, shone a spotlight on them and their daily lives. The series starred Angie Dickinson as Suzanne "Pepper" Anderson, a vice cop who did what needed to be done in order to bring in the bad guys.

Dickinson had turned down multiple offers to star in a series until *Police Woman* came along. She signed on because the role offered "a great deal of latitude," she said at the time. "An undercover policewoman works in many areas and all require a different approach." Although Dickinson wasn't interested in being a cop in real life, she respected those who were: "I can understand why women are attracted to the work," she said. "It certainly isn't dull." Dickinson noted that female roles on television were few and far between: "Despite women's lib, television is still a man's world."[362] Of her character's status as a divorcée, Dickinson said, "She's an adult and a liberal thinker. That's much more interesting. I told the producer I think it's time she gets involved again. I can't always be shooting a gun or catching a heroin pusher. She needs personal involvement."[363]

But it was the more salacious elements of the series that bothered some critics—and Dickinson as well—as the series moved through its four seasons on the air. "I don't mind wearing a short robe in a scene that will show off my legs and let everyone know that I'm still doing all right," said Dickinson in March 1978. "But I hate to tell you what I say when they ask me to take another bath in front of the cameras. And you should read some of the dialogue we wind up changing."[364]

Whether filing a harassment lawsuit, dealing with the reactions of the public and fellow officers to her new patrol beat, or working a dangerous undercover assignment, the policewoman of the 1970s made greater strides toward equality among her male peers than at any other time in history. But for female police officers across the country, things were about to get even more challenging. They had broken through the wall that had kept them from becoming full-fledged cops. Unfortunately, that wall was only the first of many. In the coming decade, policewomen would be promoted all the way to the top of the chain of command—chief of police—but with the new job would come new trials more difficult than anything they had faced in the past.

Every policewoman in the country has been asked, "What are you going to do if you meet a 350-pound drunk in an alley and you are by yourself? How are you going to take him into custody?"
— Penny Harrington, chief of the Portland, Oregon, police department[365]

A trooper asked me what the difference was between a male and a female trooper. My response was, "I have to take my gun belt off to use the restroom." To this day he said he knew I would fit in.
—Shannon Spreckelmeyer, Indiana State Police[366]

CHAPTER 6

Steady Movement (1980–2009)

AS LATE AS the 1980s—more than seven decades after Aurora Matilda "Lola" Baldwin became the nation's first sworn female officer, and in an era that would see the appointment of the first female police chiefs in the country—women in law enforcement were still an unusual sight in many areas of the United States.

When Judy Gerhardt joined her three older siblings in the Los Angeles County Sheriff's Department in 1983, she faced many of the same reactions from the public that her predecessors had. "Even then, women in law enforcement were somewhat of a spectacle," she said. "I remember people stopping me on the street just to take a picture." During her first four years in uniform, Gerhardt worked in a women's jail. When she switched to patrol duty, everything changed.

"I was the only female on my shift, in a male-dominated world," she said. Gerhardt's talent at writing reports gave her a slight advantage over some of the male officers, and she did her best to assist other officers whenever possible and asked for help when she needed it. Her efforts helped to establish trust and credibility with her partners. "That approval went a long way in keeping me sane," she said. "I saw other females who weren't as lucky. They struggled with writing and weren't helpful to the male officers, so they had a rougher road." Some of the women serving with Gerhardt quit in frustration.[367]

As always, traditional attitudes about women in the workplace were slow to change. When Rhonda Fleming applied to join the Texas Highway Patrol in June 1984, the recruiter was less than friendly. "He tried to steer my application into a position as a communications officer rather than as a police officer," she recalled. Early in her career, Fleming experienced sexism in a variety of forms—several times, for example, men she pulled over for speeding initially refused to sign the tickets she issued, saying they wouldn't do so for a woman.

In Indiana, state police officer Shannon Spreckelmeyer faced similar problems when male drivers couldn't fathom that a female officer was patrolling the highways. "I think the public can misinterpret a female taking charge of a traffic stop or arrest as being too aggressive," Spreckelmeyer noted. "And then you are labeled a 'bitch.' I'm sure there are some people who feel we shouldn't be out there, just like women shouldn't be allowed in combat, but I think most people accept us." On the way to booking after being arrested, Speckelmeyer recalled, some male suspects were so enchanted by the idea of a female cop that they could think about nothing else. "By the time we got finished talking about me arresting them, we were at the jail," she said, chuckling. Drunks proved even more entertaining: "They thought it was neat to get pulled over by a good-looking lady."[368]

In Washington state, Julie Myer patrolled a logging community during the late 1980s. "I stopped trucks for traffic violations and was known as 'Honey Bear,'" she recalled. "I didn't write any more tickets than my male counterparts, but the perception was that I wrote a lot more than anyone else."[369]

Elizabeth Whitfield, a state trooper who patrolled Gallup, New Mexico, with a male partner, saw the gender gap in action when she responded to radio calls. "When my male partner and I arrived, the reporting person tended to address his or her questions and issues to the male officer rather than at me," she recalled. The misconception, said Whitfield, was that female officers were not as knowledgeable and couldn't handle the job as well as male officers. "From my observations," said Whitfield, "those in the public that challenge authority will challenge a female officer more than a male officer. This might be because females tend to be smaller and may appear to have less confidence." Whitfield felt that, in general, female officers struggled more with emotional matters as they tried to balance personal and professional responsibilities—especially if they had children at home.[370]

For a number of women cops, proving to other officers that they could do the job was overshadowed by only one other thing: proving it to themselves. "You train and believe you can do the job," said Marilyn Baker, a Los Angeles deputy sheriff, "but until you are confronted with such a situation, it's hard to know for sure." One day during the early 1980s, Baker, partnered with a male officer, confronted a suspect who was wanted on kidnapping and rape charges. Baker's partner had to pull his weapon. As he was firing it, the suspect struggled with him over the gun. Baker managed to contact-shoot the suspect—firing her gun with the muzzle touching his body—and the officers were finally able to wrestle the man to the ground. That dangerous incident proved important to Baker's development as a law enforcement officer. "I knew I could handle any situation I was confronted with," she explained. But more important, the male officers in her department began to treat her differently. They now had proof that she could tough it out when needed.[372]

"THERE WAS NO SYMPATHY"

At the police academies, the rigorous physical demands of the training programs took their toll on some of the candidates, both male and female. Many women who entered the academies failed to graduate. "Out of one hundred recruits or more," wrote Mona Ruiz of the Santa Ana, California, police department, "there were just a dozen of us there at the end. I was the only female."[372] After Ruiz graduated seventh in her class in December 1989, the Los Angeles Police Department assigned her to a job as a parking control officer.

Adding to the stress of becoming a cop were the nagging questions about the policewomen's mental fortitude and overall presence on the job. "I don't think the physical requirements affected us as much as height, weight, and preconceptions about our emotional stability," noted Lori Fry, who joined the police force in Madison, Wisconsin, in January 1979. Fry recalled a height minimum of five foot eight and a weight minimum of 150 pounds. By those standards, she was too short and too light to join the force. So, when filling out paperwork, she found a way around it: "I would round up my five foot three to five foot four, then 'squiggle' the 4 to where it look like a 9. For weight, I made the 2 in *125 pounds* look like a 7." During the four years prior to her appointment to Madison's police force, Fry tried to get into other departments around the country. Many of them waved her off, refusing to let her take the physical agility or written exams because of her size. When they did allow her to test, the male officers were quite amused that a petite woman wanted to join them. "They expected that I would never push a car the length of half a football field, lug a 150-pound dummy from a car and pull it 20 or more feet, scale a six-foot or higher fence, jump a series of hurdles, or run distance in the required time," said Fry. "They thought I'd simply look silly." But Fry would tackle the physical tests and pass them— only to be told that, once again, she was too small to do the job.[373]

In Nevada, Lori McGrath battled similar preconceived notions about her physical capabilities. When she was in the second grade, McGrath knew she wanted to be a state trooper. Her father, a Nevada highway patrol officer, encouraged her to apply. In 1984, when she was just 18 years old, she became a dispatcher. Three years later she applied to go to the academy. Some of her family and friends were worried about her. "I was only five foot three and 105 pounds. They were afraid that I would be hurt or killed," said McGrath. Her physical fitness test involved carrying metal weights that weighed as much as she did. "I had to pick up these weights and carry them up a simulated embankment, over a guardrail, then down the embankment," she said. Her solution? "I tied them to my wrists and carried them across my hips, walking with my back arched." It worked.[374]

Training went well for Rhonda Fleming, a natural athlete, but it did have its challenges: During classes in defensive tactics at the Texas Highway Patrol academy, Fleming was paired in a boxing match with a male candidate who towered over her. Fleming gamely went into the ring. During the subsequent sparring match she suffered a concussion, bruised ribs and a swollen jaw. "I never went down, though," she said.[375]

Shannon Spreckelmeyer also suffered injuries during her academy days in Indiana: "During riot training my partner hit me with a large baton and broke my knuckle. Troopers do not cry, and I was off to the hospital." Coincidentally, the accident occurred on the first night in 12 weeks that the trainees were allowed some time off. While her classmates visited friends and relatives, Spreckelmeyer sat in the hospital nursing her broken finger. She was back at the academy the next day—just in time for boxing classes. "There was no sympathy," she recalled. "You just tried to block out the pain."[376]

Then came weapons training. In Los Angeles, Lynda Castro had never fired a gun in her life. After several attempts at the firing range, she was barely hitting the target. "One of the crusty range masters saw my frustration and lack of technique," she said. "He asked me if I wanted to be the top shot in the class." She said yes, and with his help she continued practicing for the next several weeks. On graduation day her aim was much better: she was able to split a three-by-five-inch index card sideways. Castro was so thrilled that she later framed the card and hung it on the wall in her office.[377]

Second generation: Lynda Castro (right) of the Los Angeles County Sheriff's Department with her daughters Carey (left) and Sara (center). Sara joined the Los Angeles Police Department in October 1997.
(Courtesy Lynda Castro)

Firearms training proved difficult for Julia Grimes, who joined the Alaska State Troopers in January 1983. "I had never fired a gun before the academy," she recalled. "I had very small hands for the size of the weapons—an L frame .357 revolver and a Remington model 870 shotgun. It was a new problem that was eventually resolved with better weapons—Glock 10-millimeter semiautomatic pistols—and better training for our firearms instructors."[378]

By contrast, Peggy Fox was lucky; she didn't need much practice at all. Fox grew up in rural Kansas and was familiar with firearms by the time she joined the police department in Topeka in 1987. "There are a larger percentage of women who have trouble with firearms mostly because they have a lack of exposure to weapons prior to hiring on," said Fox.[379]

For academy graduates new and old, on-the-job harassment was still very much in evidence. As a rookie in Madison, Wisconsin, Lori Fry wanted to ask for feedback from her fellow officers but couldn't always get it. "There was a group of men on one side of town who would not meet with any of the women," she recalled. "If they saw a woman in a car that came alongside their squad to 'coffee up,' the men would drive off and never talk to her. It wasn't personal—it was how they treated all women rookie officers." However, male officers were more than happy to coffee up with the male rookies.

Fry got fed up and decided to make a point. During the next coffee break she drove her patrol car in front of the male officers' bumpers, blocking them from moving anywhere. Then she got out of her car and asked them the questions she'd been storing up. When she was done, Fry got in her car and left—no chitchat or further conversation. The male officers were so astounded that they finally responded to her, providing answers and guidance, however reluctantly.

But after Fry had performed her blocking maneuver several times, one of the male officers lost his patience. As she pulled her squad car in front of his, the male officer leaned out the window, fuming. "Stop!" he yelled. "What the fuck are you doing?"

"I'm trying to learn the job better," responded Fry, "which is pretty hard to do when people keep driving off. And if I complain to the sergeant I'll be labeled a crybaby."

"Well," he said with an admiring smile, "you are a brazen little bitch, aren't you?"

Fry shrugged. "Would you prefer to be backed up by a crybaby or a brazen bitch?"

The male officer burst out laughing. "Tell you what," he said. "I'll talk to the guys. If you have any more drive-offs, let me know, okay?"

"Okay."

"And by the way," he added, "I take my coffee black."

On her next visit to the male officer, Fry brought the coffee. After that they took turns buying, and no one ever drove away from Fry again.[380]

The repercussions of the federal amendments to the Civil Rights Act of 1964 took time to filter down through police departments across the country. For the time being, tradition held sway in many law enforcement organizations. In 1976, Beth Bradbury moved from a reserve officer position to full-time dispatcher in the tiny town of Priest River, Idaho. "There was actually a mark on the door frame to the department," she recalled. "It was set at six feet. If you were shorter than that they wouldn't hire you as a police officer."[381]

That issue was mild compared to what some other policewomen went through as they entered the male-dominated offices and squad cars in their cities. As one of the first vice presidents of the Wisconsin Association of Women Police, Lori Fry heard stories of female officers who received threatening phone calls, found used condoms in their department mailboxes, and saw dead cats tied to their cars. Their complaints to the brass often went unheeded. One male officer in Madison came on very strong to several women in the department. "I usually was able to tell any interested males to forget it," said Fry, "and they were fine with a 'no' and respected it. Not this guy." Eventually, the male officer crossed the line: he forced himself on a young woman driver in lieu of issuing a ticket, and the driver filed suit against him. Three other women filed harassment complaints as well. The officer was convicted of rape and fired from the department.

However, Fry was quick to point out that not all of the male officers treated women badly. "Although it may sound like a lot of harassment," she explained, "actually it was only a handful of older male officers that were really outwardly rude toward the idea of women officers. For every one that was not supportive there were others who were really helpful. But as reluctant as they may have been, in my department, I do not think if there had been a call for an officer in trouble that there would not have been backup. I always knew that if need be, those men would put their lives on the line for me just as I would for them. Most of them did not do anything but wait and see how women would work out on the department. Only a few were outwardly hostile or nasty, but even those would not let a fellow cop go down—male or female."[382]

In Idaho, Beth Bradbury filed several harassment complaints against supervisors during her tenure in the state police. "It cost me a lot initially," she explained. "I left the road because of it and went into investigations." But Bradbury soon realized that there was a silver lining to the pain: her new duty hours meshed better with her responsibilities as a mother to two children, the pay was better, she enjoyed the work as a detective—and, in the end, the supervisor who harassed her was eventually dismissed from his job. "Helping to get rid of those 'good old boys' definitely opened doors for more of us to become police officers," Bradbury noted.[383]

The battle against discrimination continued in the courts. Six years after Fanchon Blake's discrimination lawsuit shook the Los Angeles Police Department to the rafters, the *Bouman v. Block* case had a similar impact on the county sheriff. Susan Bouman became a Los Angeles sheriff's deputy in 1971 and tested for promotion to sergeant in 1975. She made it on the promotion list, from which deputies would receive their stripes as positions opened up. But when she asked about when she might get her shot, Bouman found that no one was in a hurry to move a woman up the ladder. She heard rumors that she wouldn't be promoted—and she wasn't. A frustrated Bouman skipped the 1977 exam but decided to try again in 1980. In the interim she filed complaints with the California Division of Fair Employment Practices and the Equal Employment Opportunity Commission, then launched a federal class action lawsuit on April 7, 1980. Among other things her case charged that "Bouman was not permitted to serve in a solo radio car at night in certain areas because her supervisors felt it would be inappropriate. Meanwhile, male deputies were allowed to serve in such areas. The station commander also had a policy of having women deputies rotate on the station complaint desk. At one point, she was told to leave a radio car and work the station front desk"—something the male officers didn't have to do.[384]

After appealing the case all the way to the state supreme court, the sheriff's department found itself operating under a consent decree to reform its employment practices, "along with a set of judgments and orders so complicated that they fill a binder four inches thick," wrote Beth Shuster in the *Los Angeles Times*.[385] Bouman got her promotion and $200,000 in back pay, but she soon retired for health reasons. Lee Baca, elected sheriff in 1998, inherited much of the fallout from the *Bouman* case from his predecessor, Sherman Block. "My belief is that we need more women in the department than we have now," said Baca in 2000. "Women are excellent leaders, as are men. But this organization has been dominated by men historically. The men and women in the department must share in [solving] the problems of the past."[386]

During the years that followed, reactions were mixed regarding how much progress the sheriff's department was making. "We were under court scrutiny for issues related to hiring, assignment to coveted positions, promotions and harassment investigations," said Roberta Abner. "As a result, more women have been promoted, hired and placed into coveted positions."[387]

Another deputy, Sheila Sanchez, noted some progress as well. "By the time the case had gone through the court system, the department had made great strides in rectifying what had led to the *Bouman* lawsuit. However, those strides were not taken into consideration and the department was painted with one stroke of the gavel." Sanchez noted an unfortunate side effect of the *Bouman* case was that some women as well as men received promotions before they were ready. "The gender of the employee should not be the main criterion," said Sanchez. "It should be the best-qualified deputy sheriff. I guarantee the crook doesn't care what the numbers are. And when a citizen calls with an emergency, he or she won't care who responds as long as they are qualified and able to handle the emergency."[388]

A graduating class of the Washington, D.C., metropolitan police academy in 1980. The officer in the front row wearing civilian clothes is not in uniform because she is pregnant. *(Metropolitan Police Department, Washington, D.C.)*

Issues of sex and gender were also paramount in the debate over civil unions and gay marriages, as a number of lesbian police officers sought equal recognition and legal protection not only as women in uniform but also as partners in marriage. In March 2004, after a circuit court judge in Multnomah County, Oregon, struck down a state law prohibiting same-sex marriages, over 3,000 gay couples rushed to secure marriage licenses. Not everyone agreed with the Multnomah County ruling, and a legal battle ensued. In April a circuit court judge ordered a temporary halt to the issuing of marriage licenses while the case moved through the legal system. In the meantime, however, the judge ordered the state to recognize the marriage licenses that had already been granted in Multnomah County.

While the window was still open, Katie Potter and Pam Moen, two Portland, Oregon, cops who had been together for nearly 15 years and had two daughters, got married. Potter had a close supporter in her father, Tom Potter, a former police officer himself. He began his career on a street beat in 1967, making his way up to chief in 1990;

he also was elected Portland's mayor in 2004. While he was chief of police, Potter participated in the city's annual gay pride parade, wearing his police uniform. Some people criticized him for doing so, but Potter wasn't concerned. "I'm the police chief for all the people," he explained. "I've marched in St. Patrick's Day parades, Fourth of July parades and parades against racism, all in uniform. It's only the gay pride march that set people off."[389] As opponents of same-sex marriage worked to amend the state constitution, Katie Potter felt that the people of Oregon would show their support for gay rights, as they had in the past. "People are going to see that gay marriage has no effect on their own marriages," she said.[390]

However, the state supreme court disagreed. In April 2005, the court ruled that same-sex marriages were invalid. "Today," the ruling read, "marriage in Oregon — an institution once limited to opposite-sex couples only by statute — now is so limited by the state constitution, as well."[391] As the debate continued, members of the state legislature worked on a bill to authorize civil unions instead. "I'm not supporting this legislation to give special rights to gays and lesbians," said state senator Ben Westlund. "I'm supporting it because gays and lesbians are human beings."[392] The bill sparked a lot of debate over what rights to grant same-sex couples and, in the end, died in committee. The legislators tried again, and May 2007 the governor signed a law that allowed gay couples limited rights under the banner of domestic partnerships.

The situation was markedly different in Los Angeles, where police officers Sara and Helen Jaramillo married in June 2008. "The Los Angeles Police Department and the city provide the same benefits to domestic partners as they do to married couples," said Sara. "There's no distinction whatsoever." The couple, who had twin daughters, were entitled to the same insurance and pension benefits as other married couples. After the couple decided to marry, Helen left the police force to become a full-time mother. Sara continued in her job as a tactical flight officer in the air support division. "I'm actually a street cop," Sara explained, "except instead of driving around in a car I ride in a helicopter." Her duties involved providing assistance to officers on the ground during incidents like shootings as well as vehicle and foot pursuits.

Have lesbian policewomen faced any greater discrimination than policewomen in general? "I've never experienced any negativity or discrimination," said Sara. "I've never been made to feel that being a lesbian has kept me from being promoted or anything else. It's been a non-issue throughout my career." If anything, said Sara, being a gay officer has proved to be an asset because it allowed her and her fellow officers to focus more effectively on the job. "I've almost always worked with men, and my being gay takes away the sexual dynamic you might have with a male partner," she explained. "We're just like two buddies working together."[393]

Whether by force of law or by recognition that they were making significant contributions to police work, female officers were gaining stronger footholds among their coworkers and in their communities as well.

"I THOUGHT I WAS GOING TO DIE"

As policewomen moved from welfare service to light investigative work, to assignments as undercover decoys and street patrol in squad cars, the dangers they faced continued to increase. Whether dealing with looters, murderers, or terrorists, policewomen in the late 20th century risked injury every day. Some made the ultimate sacrifice in the line of duty.

In April 1992, South Central Los Angeles resembled a war zone—burned-out buildings, people running through the streets, fiery wreckage everywhere. A Los Angeles policewoman sighed heavily as she surveyed the destruction. "It's like shooing flies away," she told a reporter. "As soon as we leave, they come right back."[394] She was talking about looters who were scrambling through local stores, grabbing everything from televisions and microwaves to diapers and groceries. "People are just tired," one man told a reporter. "There are no jobs, no work. . . . They played the game. It didn't work."[394] The rioters were incensed that the four Los Angeles police officers accused of assaulting motorist Rodney King had just been acquitted by a jury.

In March 1991, King, driving under the influence of alcohol, was chased down the highway and onto surface streets by a husband-and-wife team of California Highway Patrol officers, Tim and Melanie Singer. Once King stopped, the Singers approached his car. Soon a group of Los Angeles police officers arrived and waved off Melanie Singer, who had drawn her gun when she thought King was reaching for a weapon. Singer then watched in surprise as the police officers beat King repeatedly—all documented on video by the resident of a nearby apartment. "There was blood dripping literally from his mouth, and there was a pool of blood beneath his chin," a tearful Singer later recalled. She wanted to provide medical help to King, but she saw other officers watching and joking. Singer stayed put. "I didn't want them to start heckling me," she explained.[396] It was a painful decision on her part. Going against fellow cops—even a group of officers who were beating a suspect—was a dangerous proposition.

Debate over the use of physical force was nothing new to female officers. After years of being told that they wouldn't be able to handle angry suspects, policewomen were proving that they could. But now they had to deal with a follow-up issue: How much force was necessary—and how much was *too* much? "Bad guys have to go to jail. And the truth is that no matter how fit or strong an officer is, there is always someone bigger who can defeat you physically," noted Julia Grimes, director of the Alaska State Troopers. "We don't want our troopers being hurt on the street, so we've prioritized risk management in our use of force. That is why we provide so many non-lethal tools—pepper spray, steel batons, the Taser—in addition to firearms." Most important, added Grimes, was that law enforcement officers were trained to verbally "de-escalate" high-tension situations when they made arrests.[397]

Jennifer Crews-Carey, a police officer in Annapolis, Maryland, understood this all too well. During a domestic disturbance call in 2002 she nearly had to shoot a 16-year-old boy. An argument between the teenager and his father escalated into a fight. When Crews-Carey knocked on the door of their home, the son answered. "He was grasping gas stove burner grates in both hands," said Crews-Carey. Standing on the tiny porch, she was forced to pull her weapon. The son ran inside the house, with Crews-Carey right behind him. Inside, the teenager "started hitting his father in the face and head with the iron grates, backing the dad into a very small kitchen." Crews-Carey knew she couldn't fire her weapon without risking injury to the father. "All I could think of was this father called the police for help, and I am going to have to shoot his kid," she said. Suddenly the son whirled around and advanced on Crews-Carey. She ordered him to stop, but he kept coming. Just as she was going to pull the trigger, the teenager threw the grates at her. She ducked and the grates flew by, barely missing her head. Instead of firing at the boy, Crews-Carey decided to use one of the other tools on her belt. "I holstered my weapon and sprayed him with mace," she explained. "Then the fight was on until help arrived." Crews-Carey struggled to hold the teenager down. Her backup arrived quickly and helped her take the son into custody—without having to hurt him physically.[398]

In undercover work, to maintain the appropriate illusion, some policewomen cannot use physical force or even carry a weapon. State trooper Jill Rice undertook such a vulnerable position in 1993 when the Indiana State Police launched an undercover drug investigation in Indianapolis. A drug smuggler from Mexico was bringing large amounts of marijuana into Indiana. His girlfriend, whom Rice identified only as Roxy, was a cocaine addict who lived with her young son in a duplex home. Rice posed as a health care provider for the elderly and moved into the other half of Roxy's duplex. Whenever she visited her neighbor, Rice wore a hidden microphone to record their conversations for evidence. "One day when I was gone, her son went crazy and was shooting his gun inside their half of the double," remembered Rice. "It was a little scary there."

The state police coordinated the case with the U.S. Drug Enforcement Agency, the Internal Revenue Service, and the Marion County Sheriff's Department. They eventually arrested Roxy. Faced with prison time, she agreed to become an informant instead.

Soon Roxy's drug-smuggling boyfriend asked her to pick up a load of marijuana in Brownsville, Texas, and drive it back to Indianapolis. Rice and Roxy flew to Brownsville on a commercial airliner. At a local motel the two women met with the boyfriend, who tossed them a set of car keys. "There are only ten pounds in the trunk," he told them. "I need you to drive the car back to Indiana." The boyfriend, of course, planned to fly back on a commercial flight.

Rice and the girlfriend looked at the car he had provided. "It was a junker and it was falling apart," recalled Rice. "We couldn't start the car with keys—we had to use a screwdriver. Fortunately, the Texas Rangers were assisting us in the investigation, so if the car broke down we would have them there to pick us up." Rice and Roxy drove off, pretending to be heading back to Indianapolis as the boyfriend had requested. Instead the two women drove to Amarillo, where the Air National Guard loaded the automobile onto a C-130 cargo plane. But after the aircraft had left Amarillo, one of its engines died in flight. "The Guard said not to worry," said Rice. "The plane could fly on three engines, but we needed to make an emergency landing." They touched down in Corpus Christi. "The runway was lined with police cars and fire engines," Rice recalled. "I thought I was going to die in this plane with this female cocaine addict!"

After the Air National Guard swapped the crippled C-130 for a fully operational one, the trip resumed. Once the airplane reached Indianapolis, the crew unloaded the drug-laden car. Then Rice drove it to the state police garage, where investigators conducted a thorough search of the vehicle. Roxy's boyfriend-smuggler had lied to her. The car held a little more than the ten pounds of marijuana that he had mentioned—in fact, the drug was packed into every crevice available. "Marijuana was hidden in the bumpers, side panels, quarter panels, tires, and engine—all throughout the car," said Rice. "It was a huge load. The boyfriend didn't want us to know about all of it because he thought we would steal it from him."

After unloading most of the drugs, Rice and Roxy drove the car to the rendezvous point, a small apartment in the city, where they were supposed to turn the car over to the boyfriend. "When he arrived with his friends to take the car and unload the marijuana, we surprised him," said Rice. As soon as the boyfriend got in the vehicle and started to drive away, law enforcement officers swarmed over the car and arrested him.

But the case wasn't over just yet. The police wanted to know who was buying the drugs from the boyfriend. "We got the other drug dealers to come to the duplex," explained Rice. "I was there with Roxy, and we sold marijuana to the dealers." One of the dealers had driven all the way down from Michigan to get his share of the marijuana. As each of the three dealers left the duplex, they were met by representatives of the Indiana State Police, its drug enforcement section, and the IRS. On three different meetings they were able to arrest three different drug dealers. All of the suspects later served time in federal prison. Rice's quiet determination in the undercover assignment helped make it a success.[399]

Sometimes a rough climate has had a great effect on the recruiting of new female officers. Alaska's state troopers, for example, work in a challenging terrain that requires abilities not necessary in most other law enforcement units: flying through the bush in a small plane, riding snowmobiles over icy ground, working alone with backup many hours away, and rescuing lost hunters. "We'd always had a low percentage of female troopers," said Julia Grimes, "but it was due to the difficult nature of trooper work in Alaska and not because the agency didn't welcome them. We asked them to live in places—remote 'bush areas'— that municipal officers never dreamed of." Grimes, a former pilot for United Airlines, joined the state troopers in January 1983, rising to the rank of colonel and director of the organization.

On a spring day Grimes was airborne in her Cessna 185, on her way back to her home base in Dillingham, near Alaska's southwestern coast, when she got a call. She and her sergeant diverted to coordinates near Manakotak, a village with a population of 400. A local pilot and his friend had been practicing tight turns in their Piper Super Cub near the village. During their maneuvering the aircraft stalled and spun straight downward into the tundra. The plane slammed propeller-first into the ice-crusted ground and burst into flame.

Alaska state trooper Julia Grimes, who piloted this Cessna 185 aircraft as part of her duties. Her K-9 partner, Yambo, was a drug detection dog and her co-pilot. "He loved to fly," said Grimes. *(Courtesy Julia Grimes)*

Grimes landed her plane on a small frozen pond nearby, the wheel skis gliding over the shiny surface, and came to a stop. "Eskimo villagers from Manakotak had already arrived on snow machines and communicated with us via handheld radio," she recalled. When Grimes came upon the accident site, the wreck was still burning. The pilot and passenger had not survived the crash. "We couldn't have gotten to the scene any more quickly than we did," she said, "but we could not save the victims."

After grabbing a fire extinguisher out of her Cessna, Grimes sprayed the smoldering crash site. Time was running out—the sun was descending over the horizon. "We struggled to get the bodies out of the wreckage, and were forced to cool the remains on the tundra before placing them in the 185 for transport," recalled Grimes. "It was important to the family that we bring them home that night. We couldn't leave them there or risk a takeoff from a pond in the dark."

Although she was unable to save the crash victims, Grimes never forgot what happened in Manakotak. "The overall intensity of the scene and circumstances of that recovery will never leave me," she said. "This was the brutal reality of life and death in remote Alaska."[400]

For female officers who experienced life-and-death issues first-hand, their perspective on the job was forever changed. In Columbia, South Carolina, Ethel Diké and her fellow officers lost one of their own on a dark night in 1973. During their shift Diké and her partner received a call that a male suspect had abducted a prostitute and dragged her into the driveway behind a local business. Diké and her partner pulled up in their squad car, got out, and crouched with guns drawn as the terrified prostitute, now nude, ran out of the backyard. The man they were hunting was still in there, hiding in the darkness.

"Come out with your hands up!" yelled Diké's partner.

But the suspect had dashed through a hole in a fence and was gone. Diké and her partner spent the rest of their shift looking for him, to no avail. The next day's shift picked up the trail but also had no luck. Then the midnight shift came on. Several officers caught a glimpse of the suspect and put out a description. Everyone was on the lookout.

One of the lieutenants was on the street and saw the man head down some stairs next to a building. Curious, the lieutenant shined his flashlight down the stairs. He saw the suspect looking back at him. The man was holding a shotgun. He shot the lieutenant in the chest, killing him.

Diké had lost a fellow cop. The memory stayed with her long after she left the department. After all, any of the officers might have come across the suspect that night. And they might have died the same way as their lieutenant did. "It could have been us," said Diké. "It could have been us."[401]

Death in the line of duty highlighted the dangers inherent in wearing a badge. The 1998 shooting death of Idaho state trooper

Linda Huff was significant not only because a female officer made the ultimate sacrifice but also because it happened under frighteningly bizarre circumstances. Huff, who had begun her career as a dispatcher for the Payette County Sheriff's Department, later went on patrol and earned promotion to sergeant. In February 1997 she and her husband both graduated from the Idaho State Police Academy— the first married couple ever to have done so. They were stationed at state police regional headquarters in the resort town of Coeur d'Alene, Idaho, about 30 miles east of Spokane, Washington.

On a summer night in June, a man named Scott Yager hopped on his bicycle and pedaled to the building that housed the state police headquarters. It was a little after 11:00 P.M. In the parking lot behind the building, Huff was on her way to her squad car. Suddenly Yager opened fire. Huff's bulletproof vest caught two of the bullets, but Yager fired again and again, severing Huff's spinal cord. She collapsed on the ground but got off two shots from her .45-caliber pistol, hitting Yager in the throat and shoulder.

Yager continued firing, reloading once to pump a total of 17 rounds into Huff's body. Satisfied, he walked away, leaving Huff dying on the ground of the asphalt parking lot. The 33-year-old mother of three had been an Idaho state trooper for just 14 months. Troopers chased down Yager and arrested him. Eight months later, Yager was sentenced for Huff's murder: life without parole. He didn't receive the death sentence due to a technicality. The judge said that the state hadn't proved that Yager killed Huff under aggravating circumstances.[402]

Several years after Huff's murder, another female cop perished in the worst terrorist attack in American history. At about 4:00 A.M. on March 20, 2002, recovery workers at the burned-out crater where the World Trade Center once stood found the remains of Officer Moira Smith. The only city policewoman to perish in the September

11, 2001, attack—and the second female New York police officer ever to die in the line of duty—Smith had volunteered to help rescue people after the airliners hit the World Trade Center. "Her voice was heard over a police radio," reported the *St. Petersburg Times*, "directing people out of the burning buildings as she helped an asthma victim." The recovery workers first saw her collar insignia—a gold *13* representing the precinct she served—and then uncovered Smith's badge and name tag, which were buried in the rubble.

A 13-year veteran of the police force, Smith left behind her husband—also a police officer—and a two-year-old daughter. Smith saved a number of people on 9/11, including insurance broker Edward Nicholls. She escorted the injured Nicholls to nearby medics, then dashed back into the building to help others. "Don't look, keep moving," Nicholls recalled Smith saying over and over, moving people toward an exit.[403] One of the police dispatchers, Modesto Muniz, remembered receiving Smith's call on the day she died. "Help me, please," she told him. Muniz said he may have been the last person to talk to her.[404]

The various tools designed to protect a police officer—weapons, communication strategies, and so on—are sometimes at the mercy of uncontrollable factors. Body armor, an indispensable part of the police officer's gear, is a picky beast. It protects portions of the body, but it can't cover everything. But when it works, it works well. In November 2008, the International Association of Chiefs of Police and the DuPont Corporation celebrated the 20th anniversary of the Kevlar Survivors' Club by naming Officer Jennifer Moore as its latest inductee.

Moore, a Phoenix, Arizona, officer who had been with the department for less than a year, was riding shotgun with a partner late on a Saturday night. The officers stopped a car for a license plate violation. One of the two men in the car pulled a handgun and fired at Moore. The bullet sliced through her right ring finger and hit her in the chest, where the body armor swallowed it and prevented additional damage. As the gunman ran away, Moore's partner fired his weapon but was unable to bring the man down. The gunman took a hostage and barricaded himself in a nearby apartment. When he called his family to tell them what he'd done, they encouraged him to surrender. After almost five hours, the gunman gave up. Moore eventually recovered from her injury.[405]

Lauretha Vaird, a Philadelphia cop and proponent of the bulletproof vest, died on duty—shot in the chest—on the one day she failed to wear the Kevlar plates that might have saved her life. "She was wearing the shell minus the panels," her supervisor recalled after Vaird was killed while trying to prevent a bank robbery on January 2, 1996. Two local music artists were arrested, along with a third man. They had stolen a minivan and, brandishing guns, got inside the bank before its scheduled opening time. When Vaird responded to a silent alarm, one of the men fired his weapon at her.

Vaird, who worked as a teacher's aide prior to joining the police force, left behind two orphaned sons. "Laurie was the one who would remind people, don't forget your vest," said her supervisor. So why was she only wearing the cloth vest but not the plates? Some people theorized that Vaird had omitted the Kevlar because the vest was uncomfortable. Lighter models were on the way—in fact, Vaird was in line to receive an upgraded vest in the near future.[406]

"I'm sure you've noticed that women are built a little differently," noted Jonelle Greear, an Idaho state policewoman. "Several years after I started in the 1990s I was finally issued a ballistic vest that was actually designed for a female. It had darts and everything." Greear noted that many women officers she knew didn't want to complain about ill-fitting vests. "We just wanted to fit in," she said," so we dealt with it."[407]

Christy Lynn Hamilton was 45 when she graduated from the Los Angeles Police Academy in February 1994. She had waited 23 years, raising a family before pursuing her dream of being a cop. Hamilton was in her second month of patrol duty when she and her partner responded to a disturbance call. A high school senior and his father hadn't been getting along. The 17-year-old repeatedly threatened to kill his father. One day, he made good on that promise. Hearing gunfire, neighbors called the police. Squad cars arrived at 1:20 A.M. Through the darkness officers saw the teenager's stepmother in the street, screaming that the young man had fired on his father.

Then things got worse. "As the officers got out of their cars they were immediately met with a fusillade of shots—at least five, six or seven shots," said the police chief after the incident was over. After the shooting started, a bullet plowed through the window of the squad car door and hit Hamilton through the armhole of her bullet-proof vest. She died after arriving at the hospital. Her father, a retired detective, was by her side. Meanwhile a special weapons and tactics (SWAT) team that entered the house recovered an AR-15 rifle—and the bodies of the teenager and his father. The incident was over, but another female cop had died needlessly in the line of duty.[408]

"ENTERTAINING BUT NOT REALISTIC"

The real-life struggles of policewomen were highly dramatized by their fictional counterparts in movies and television. Flipping away from the TV news during the 1980s, viewers could find escapist entertainment featuring stories that stretched credibility to the limit and female characters who barely resembled the real cops on the street. "There were very few TV shows, if any, at the time that accurately depicted women in law enforcement," said Cheryl Sanders, a Tennessee Highway Patrol officer who came on board in the early 1980s. "Shows like *Charlie's Angels* and *T. J. Hooker* were entertaining but not realistic."[409]

Fortunately, not all of the entertainment was so unrealistic: perhaps the best example of female TV cops in the 1980s was *Cagney and Lacey*, a weekly CBS drama about two New York policewomen who worked as partners. Initially the network tested the concept with a two-hour TV movie and a short-run series. Ratings were poor. Supposedly the viewing public had difficulty dealing with female cops who came on too strong. *TV Guide* quoted a network executive: "They were too harshly women's lib, too tough, too hard, and not feminine."[410] After one of the roles was recast with actress Sharon Gless, the show found a faithful viewing audience; when the series was cancelled again, a storm of viewer protest led to its revival, and it finally ran for six years.

Other television shows—for example, *Hill Street Blues*, *Law & Order*, and the reality program *Cops*—got the viewing public used to a harder-edged, more realistic type of female cop. "The ascendance of women in police dramas is unequivocal and pretty much television-wide," notes historian Peter Horne. "It has occurred in movies as well. The media attention has helped promote favorable attitudes toward female officers among the general public, prospective police candidates, and even police officers themselves."[411]

Homicide: Life on the Street, based on Baltimore journalist David Simon's book *Homicide: A Year on the Killing Streets*, premiered on the NBC network in 1993. The series featured actress Melissa Leo as Kay Howard, an independent, resourceful female detective. The writers of *Homicide* based the character on a real-life police officer, Bertina "Bert" Silver, who was featured in Simon's book. Silver boasted a strong reputation—and the dubious distinction of being the only female among 36 employees in the traditionally all-male homicide unit. Wrote Simon: "Her arrival in homicide did little to change the prevailing political view among many detectives, who regarded the decision to give badges to women as unequivocal evidence that the barbarians were rattling the gates of Rome." The "accepted equation" in the homicide unit, explained Simon, was that "the women officers are secretaries, but Bert is Bert. Partner. Cop."[412] In order to work with a woman, noted Simon, the male officers divorced her sex from her job performance, rendering her, in a sense, neither man nor woman, but a police officer all the same.

The new dynamic in male-female partnerships could be found in the bookstore as well. Lisa Desimini's children's book *Policeman Lou and Policewoman Sue*, published in 2003, traces a typical day for a male-female duo. Desimini was inspired by children she knew who wanted to be police officers when they grew up. "It was actually my editor's idea to do a book about police officers because there weren't many books on the subject," explained Desimini, who has written and illustrated a variety of children's books. "I decided to make it about a man and a woman because I liked the balance." To construct a story about a typical day of policing a local neighborhood, Desimini consulted with a cousin who was a former chief of police. "He taught me how to depict an arrest procedure, among other things," she said.[413]

Various media portrayals began to show female cops as equivalent to the men with whom they worked. "The mass media has put a positive spin on the portrayal of policewomen," said Peter Horne. "Today the print media does not run the sensational front-page stories about the first policewoman hired or promoted. Articles about women in policing are more matter-of-fact or routine these days."[414]

While women were gaining more visibility within the police ranks, some female officers were more visible than others. Perhaps the female cop with the worst luck ever was Anita McKeown, a 25-year-old rookie in Santa Monica, California. "Determined to be a policewoman even if it kills her," said the *New York Times*, McKeown spent ten months of her probationary year "hospital-ized, in casts, nursing bruises or just plain out of action." During her academy training McKeown suffered a dislocated shoulder and a bite from a rattlesnake. Out on the street, she struggled to control a drunk driver and was rewarded with a back injury and a broken finger. People took to calling her "Calamity Jane."[415]

One late night in 1985, McKeown responded to a noise com-plaint. When she approached the suspects, a pair of boys, one of them came toward her, stabbing her in the hand and shoulder with a knife. The other boy attempted to execute her by shooting her in the head, but the gun malfunctioned. So instead the boy hit her with the gun, rendering her unconscious. McKeown's run of bizarre luck didn't stop there. After recovering from the stabbing, she responded to a three-car collision. As she was trying to get one of the cars off the highway, a drunk driver hit her. This time she suffered a torn kidney and broken ankle. When she returned to duty, she made a traffic stop and had to dodge bullets fired by the irate driver. "It was the one time I came close to quitting," she commented.[416]

After that, McKeown pursued a stolen vehicle in a high-speed chase and banged her vehicle into a wall. In 1986, she tried her pro-bationary period again, and all seemed to be going well—until the end of the year. She was searching a suspect and dug around inside a bag he was carrying. Inside was a razor blade. Thirty-two stitches later, McKeown was back on duty.[417]

Several other policewomen garnered media exposure that not only caused headaches for their supervisors but also brought dubious publicity to police departments in general. In Springfield, Ohio, Barbara Schantz wasn't interested in being a secretary, so she applied to join the police department and was accepted. The year was 1979; there were two women and 148 men on the force. After a few years, the media came calling. In November 1981, Schantz asked police chief Winston Stultz if she could participate in an interview for *Playboy* about female police officers. Stutz was noncommittal. "I didn't tell her she could do it or she couldn't," he recalled later. *Playboy* then offered Schantz $20,000 to pose nude in the magazine, and Schantz accepted. Her pictorial, "Beauty and the Badge," appeared in the May 1982 issue. The accompanying text portrayed Stultz as being incensed about Schantz's contact with *Playboy*. It was this attitude, said the magazine, that compelled Schantz to agree to the pictorial. With all of the media attention bearing down on her, Schantz stayed off the job for two days, calling in sick. "One minute they're saying it's sickening and terrible, and the next someone's running up and saying, 'Can I have your autograph? You're a star,'" lamented Schantz. Meanwhile the police department suspended her without pay while the city manager pondered what to do next. Officer Douglas Radel, who also posed in the magazine—albeit clothed—was also suspended.[418]

In New York, police officer Cibella Borges had a skeleton in her closet: before she joined the department, she had participated in a photo shoot for a hardcore pornographic magazine. A year and a half after she had put on the uniform, a fresh issue of the magazine hit the newsstands—with Borges's photo layout inside. Borges lost her job but didn't give up. Eventually the state's appellate division voted three-to-one in favor of reinstating her with back pay. The police department had no jurisdiction, they said, to punish Borges for things that happened before she joined the police force. She returned to duty in April 1985. That November—more than three years after she was suspended—a judge for the state supreme court awarded Borges back pay to the tune of $80,000.[419]

Carol Shaya appeared in *Playboy* magazine's August 1994 issue. "NYPD Nude," blared the cover—an allusion to the popular television series *NYPD Blue*, which was airing at the time. The New York policewoman, who had been on the force for four years and was assigned to the 45th Precinct in the Bronx, received $100,000 for a nude pictorial. Publicity savvy, Shaya made media appearances prior to her appearance in the magazine. Asked about the situation, the deputy commissioner for public information was almost dismissive: "If this woman, who is a police officer, is willing of her own volition to take on the potential anxiety and abuse that will arise from this, either from the other officers she works with or the public she serves," he said, "then what she thinks of our reaction is going to be academic. . . . Still, it's a matter we're going to weigh when it hits the stands, but I don't expect we'll be doing official somersaults over it."[420]

Higher-level officials made their position clear: "The reputation of the New York police department is not for sale," said police commissioner William Bratton, "and there's no room in our organization for anyone who would attempt to do so."[421] During a three-day disciplinary hearing in January 1995 that reviewed 20 counts of misconduct, the police department slammed Shaya for participating in unauthorized off-duty employment and for using the official uniform and logo in her magazine pictorial. The photo layout was, in the words of the judge, "about sex with a New York City cop."[422] Then on March 7, 1995, Bratton fired Shaya. She struck back with a $10 million lawsuit. Having been through a similar process, Cibella Borges was blunt: "If [Shaya] wants this job, let her fight like I did.

I did what I did before I came on the job. She used her uniform and shield for personal gain," said Borges.[423]

Not to be outdone, a male officer decided to pose as well: *Playgirl* forked over $5,000 to Eddie Mallia for a nude layout. Mallia said he would donate the money to the police widows' and orphans' fund, but in the end his generosity mattered little. In March 1995, the *New York Daily News* reported that it had presented Bratton with an advance copy of the 11-page layout, but that Bratton wouldn't look at it. "If, in fact, the article or pictorial is in violation of our department and procedures, it will be similar to Carol Shaya," he told the *Daily News*. "We will initiate that type of activity against the officer."[424] Mallia was unrepentant. "I'm proud of my job and my body," he said. "Why shouldn't I model? It was all done for art."[425] Knowing that disciplinary action was around the corner, Mallia soon quit the force.

Los Angeles police officer Ginger Harrison would also pose for *Playboy*. "The Arresting Officer Ginger" layout appeared in the July 2001 issue. What was her reason for doffing her clothes? "To show a positive side to being a female police officer that you can be feminine and you can have your own thing going on," she said. Unlike Carol Shaya, Harrison avoided using any official uniforms or gear in her pictorial. "We learned from her experience. We didn't use anything of mine. Everything was rentals or props," she said.[426] "I hope the [police] department looks at this in a positive way. Maybe it can bring us into the twenty-first century where women don't fit a stereotypical role. Lighten up. It's just nudity."[427]

One police pinup appeared in a magazine layout fully clothed— and received just as much publicity as the nude officers had. Jacqueline Phillips Guibord, a 30-year-old undercover narcotics cop in Provo, Utah, became an overnight sensation in 1990. The Martin Agency, a Virginia-based advertising firm, was looking for models for a Wrangler jeans campaign. Someone recommended Guibord, who accepted the offer. She posed in front of a patrol car, fully clothed, proudly displaying her Wrangler jeans. The advertisement featuring Guibord was published in magazines like *People* and *Rolling Stone*. It would have been just another advertisement for clothing, except for one thing: American soldiers serving in the Gulf War, restricted from displaying nude women while in a Muslim society, really wanted a pinup of some type. Someone came across the Wrangler advertisement, and a new celebrity was born. "A sex object?" asked the *New York Times*. "A woman fully clad in thick denim and leaning against her patrol car with a shotgun?"[428]

Giubord, daughter of a retired Air Force navigator who had served in Vietnam and wife to a former Marine, wasn't sure what to make of her sudden stardom. "I was shocked, I was flattered. It was hard to envision that was something they would hang up," she said at the time. "I've gotten a lot of positive feedback from females," she added, "who were delighted that a fully clothed woman could be considered beautiful."[429]

PIONEER IN PORTLAND

After policewomen had jumped so many hurdles to gain the respect of the officers they served alongside, it was only a matter of time before a policewoman made it all the way to the top and became chief of police. It happened in January 1985, and her name was Penny Harrington. America's first female chief of police was 44 years old and had spent two decades in the Portland, Oregon, police department. She fought her way up not only by advancing as fast as she could but also by filing a series of sexual discrimination complaints, which created animosity within the department long before she took over as chief. "I loved my career," she later wrote, "despite all the inherent traumas of being a woman in a man's world. I felt I was doing something important, that I was helping people."[430]

Although she had always dreamed of becoming a chief, Harrington never thought she would see it happen. "For all my dreaming, I was still a woman," she wrote. "And I knew that regardless of talent, regardless of ability, regardless of how hard I worked, I would never be given that opportunity, even though I fought for women's rights in the department."[431] Time would prove her wrong. Portland held the distinction of hiring Lola Baldwin, the first policewoman with arrest authority, back in 1908. Now it had hired the nation's first female police chief of a major city. The media scrutiny that whirled around Harrington was unyielding. She was interviewed almost 200 times, not always politely: one television correspondent asked Harrington if it was all a "stunt."[432] Undaunted, Harrington moved into the chief's office and got to work.

Harrington inherited a department buckling under budget constraints and overflowing prisons. During her first month she was forced to lay off 16 officers to save money. Another 60 positions were left unfilled as the budget crisis unfolded. Along the way Harrington angered her personnel—90 percent of whom were men—by cracking down on smoking while on duty and banning the carotid ("sleeper") hold after two officers accidentally killed someone while using it. To help fulfill the mayor's promise to reduce burglaries, she established a new division to battle juvenile truancy, but in doing so she had to double some officers' workloads by deleting the vice and drug division.

Then her husband, also a police officer in the Portland department, was accused of tipping off a friend about a law enforcement operation to bust cocaine suppliers. The friend ran a restaurant that allegedly counted members of the local mob among its loyal clientele. Government hearings followed, initially at Harrington's request. She wanted to avoid the appearance of unfair bias. But as the investigation gained momentum, Harrington came under increasing scrutiny about how she was running the police department.

In 1986, the city fired Harrington. She had been chief of police for just 18 months. "I went from being a celebrity to a pariah," said Harrington. "I opened many doors to policing for women, only to have them slammed shut in my face. In only one year, I went from being *Ms. Magazine*'s Woman of the Year and one of Harvard Law School's Top Ten Most Influential Women in Law, to *Time* magazine's label of Portland's Tarnished Penny."[433] Despite her fall from grace, Harrington put her law enforcement experience to good use after she left the department. She served as the director of the National Center for Women and Policing from 1995 to 2001 and opened a consulting business, Harrington & Associates, in Morro Bay, California.

Though her career was pockmarked with some rough spots, Harrington had as many supporters as detractors. Charles Moose, who served as Portland's chief of police from 1993 to 1999, defended Harrington as a pioneer in a field where the deck was stacked against her. "[She] has never understood her place," he wrote. "She has always sought another place, and the scars have become part of her. When we consider how difficult it is to change a law enforcement agency, Penny's efforts really begin to take shape. Her ability to break through so many barriers in less than twenty-five years is the stuff of legends."[434] Harrington's dream of becoming a police chief would be carried on by others. By 2006—twenty years after she left Portland —two other women had served as the city's chief of police.

CONFLICT IN HOUSTON

In the 1990s, women continued to face obstacles on the path to becoming police chiefs. In January 1990, Kathryn Whitmire, the first female mayor of Houston, Texas, assigned Elizabeth Watson to be the city's chief of police. When she promoted Watson to run Houston's west side, Whitmire had expressed "trepidation" about placing a woman in a supervisory role. "I was concerned about the support she would get there," Whitmire said. However, a relieved Whitmire later reported that Watson received very strong support from that predominantly male staff. "I expect her to receive the same support as chief," said the mayor. Unfortunately, things did not go well for the new hire During an annual evaluation in December 1991, Whitmire gave Watson a "needs improvement" rating and refused to add a merit pay raise to her $95,000 annual salary. Two months later, the city's newly elected mayor, Bob Lanier, fired Watson. "The new administration would be better off with a new police chief," Lanier explained, "and break clean [from] whatever may have been the problems in the past, whether they were Chief Watson's making or not."[135]

For her part, Watson had entered the job confident about supervising a primarily male police department. As a rookie in 1972, she was forced to sew her own uniform from a pattern provided to her. Her subsequent track record was peppered with firsts: first female captain, first female deputy chief, and finally female chief of police. "Look where I am now," she said. "Heck, obviously I haven't been too put upon."[436] But she did acknowledge that the road ahead might be difficult: "The feeling was, whoever took the job was doomed to failure," she told *Time* magazine in 1990. "Police morale was as low as any of us had ever seen it, and community tensions were higher than any of us could remember."[437]

The *New York Times* noted that Watson had "occasional con-flicts" with the city council and "other public relations problems, but no major crises."[438] A Philadelphia native, Watson came from a large family that counted among its ranks a female sheriff's captain, a ser-geant, and various others in law enforcement. When she surpassed her husband's rank of sergeant, she praised him for supporting her: "I have been above his rank for many years, and I would not be above his rank if he had not insisted. I did not get here by myself."[439]

Watson had strong support from the Houston Police Officers Association. "I can't think of anything bad to say about her," said its president, Mark Clark. One of Watson's initiatives was the neighbor-hood-oriented policing strategy, a holdover from the previous police chief. The approach was being implemented in police departments across the nation. "Under that concept," explained the *Times*, "police officers are assigned to community beats with the intent of develop-ing local contacts that can help prevent crime."[440]

But Watson also took on the mayor in public: "At a recent city council meeting," noted *Time* magazine, "the police chief stood by her rank and file and politely dissented from portions of the may-or's proposals to the state legislature." A councilman noted that he didn't think the mayor was "real pleased." Watson acknowledged that police chiefs had a short life span. "I remember saying before I took the job that I needed three years to retirement, and the average chief lasts two and a half," she told *Time*. "I guess I'll need six months somewhere," she added with a smile.[441]

So what happened to Watson's skyrocketing career? Her dis-missal from such a public post was attributed to various issues: conflict with the mayor, a shortage of police personnel, a less-than-competitive salary, and an increasing crime rate. "There are always problems," she admitted. "In a city of this size and complexity there are no periods of time where everyone is happy. I am not intimidated."[442] Despite some very public setbacks, in the end Watson set the stage for a greater number of female police chiefs to follow.

"THE WEIGHT OF ALL THE WOMEN
OF THE WORLD"

"We will be the model police agency in this country," promised Ella Bully-Cummings. It was November 23, 2003, and the 46-year-old African American woman had just taken over as the chief of police in Detroit, Michigan. It was a bittersweet promotion for Bully-Cummings. The previous chief, Jerry Oliver, had reluctantly submitted his resignation after being charged with a misdemeanor for carrying an unlicensed .25-caliber pistol in his luggage at Detroit Metropolitan Airport. After only a year as chief, Oliver faced charges from the county prosecutor and a fine from the Transportation Safety Administration. He said he could no longer run the department effectively and soon put in his papers for retirement. He had carried the sidearm for many years and hadn't thought to license it when he arrived in Detroit.

Bully-Cummings inherited a department of 4,200 personnel in one of the most dangerous cities in the United States. Multiple consent decrees issued by the U.S. Justice Department required an independent monitor to keep an eye on the embattled police force. "Because I am a female, I have the weight of all the women of the world on my shoulders right now," she said. "My biggest challenge is getting to understand that, as a woman, there is no difference between me running the police department than a man."[443]

As a teenager Bully-Cummings worked in a local movie theater, where she saw her first uniformed policewoman. The sight inspired her: "I was sitting there selling tickets one day and I saw a police car pull up and a female in full uniform stepped out of the police car . . . and it struck me as really strange because all your life you grew up thinking that this was a man's job."[444]

She had joined the department in 1977 when she was just 19 years old. After helping five of her siblings go to college, Bully-Cummings went herself, receiving a degree in public administration and later a law degree from Michigan State University. She served in the Detroit police department until 1999, when she retired at the rank of commander and put her law degree to good use as a private attorney representing managers in discrimination cases.

When 31-year-old Kwame Kilpatrick was elected mayor of Detroit in 2002—the youngest mayor in Detroit's history—he rounded up a number of his friends to help him run the government. One of them was Bully-Cummings, whom he appointed as assistant chief of police. During the Jerry Oliver scandal Bully-Cummings was bumped up to interim chief, then permanent chief.

Unfortunately, Bully-Cummings's accomplishments as police chief would be severely affected by the public shenanigans of the mayor's office, as the Kilpatrick administration turned out to be rife with corruption. Prior to becoming chief of police, Bully-Cummings had spent a year and half working on the more than 900 disciplinary cases within the department, so she was familiar with malfeasance on the part of police officers. Unfortunately, that knowledge proved fairly useless as the problems in the Kilpatrick administration spun out of control.

On the night of June 21, 2004, officers Zack Weishuhn and Patrick Tomsic pulled over a prominent city official for speeding. When they approached the woman's car, she yelled at them, "Do you know who the fuck I am?" The driver was Christine Beatty, the mayor's chief of staff. Beatty pulled out her cell phone and called Bully-Cummings, who instructed the officers to back off. Later, when asked about the incident during a radio appearance, Mayor Kilpatrick made a misstep: "It sounds like a setup to me," he said.[445] Bully-Cummings claimed that the officers were harassing Beatty. Weishuhn and Tomsic felt they were being slandered. They sued the city, Kilpatrick, and Bully-Cummings.

Meanwhile the *Detroit Free Press* ran a story that caught the mayor's office off guard: During their testimony in another case during the summer of 2007, Kilpatrick and Beatty were asked if they were romantically involved with each other. They denied it under oath. The *Free Press* begged to differ, pointing to its review of text messages that Kilpatrick and Beatty had sent to each other on their city-issued pagers during 2002 and 2003. The messages made it clear that Kilpatrick and Beatty were having an affair.

"At this point the whole landscape has changed," the police officers' attorney told the *Free Press*. "It is my opinion that the mayor has committed perjury and anyone who thinks otherwise is delusional."[446] The house of cards came crashing down quickly. Beatty saw the writing on the wall and resigned in February 2008. Seven months later, Kilpatrick resigned his office, pleading guilty to two counts of perjury. Bully-Cummings followed suit and announced her retirement several minutes later. After fighting her way to the top, another high-profile female chief found herself unable to stay there.

"WOULD YOU BE THE NEXT POLICE CHIEF?"

Other women were more fortunate in taking leadership positions. On a November day in Washington, D.C., in 2006—just three days after Adrian Fenty was elected the city's new mayor—policewoman Cathy Lanier entered his office and closed the door. She wasn't sure why Fenty wanted to see her. But after 16 years with the police department, Lanier was used to surprises. For the past 11 months, she had been ensconced in the office of Charles Ramsey, chief of police, serving as commander of the Office of Homeland Security and Counterterrorism. She had coordinated investigations with the FBI joint terrorist task force and had created field training exercises for major law enforcement agencies. She was no rookie.

Fenty looked at her. "Would you be the next police chief?" he said.

At first Lanier thought the mayor was pulling her leg. Ramsey had served the city for eight years. To put Lanier in charge would mean that Fenty had to dismiss Ramsey. And even more important were the issues of sex and race: There were more than 4,000 personnel assigned to the department in a city that was 75 percent African American. Lanier was not only a woman; she was also white. How would she fare in that kind of environment? Surely Fenty was asking about someone else.

"Are you kidding me?" asked Lanier.

He wasn't. Once she realized that Fenty was serious, Lanier accepted his offer. The unexpected announcement was released to the press on November 20, and over 250 interview requests poured into Lanier's office during the next two months. It was an unprecedented promotion for a female cop. No one was more surprised than Lanier. Ten years before, she had told a local TV station, "I don't think I'm chief of police material. You need a lot of political savvy for that, and I've got a little too much street cop in me." (She later admitted that it was a "goofy" thing to say.) Lanier took charge of the D.C. police force on January 2, 2007.

Fenty had taken office at the age of 36, becoming the youngest D.C. mayor in history, and had immediately started shaking the foundations of the city government. A biracial candidate in a tight mayoral race, Fenty had promised more hands-on governing of the city. In addition to handpicking Cathy Lanier to run the police department, Fenty tapped Michelle Rhee, a Korean American woman in her thirties, to run the gigantic D.C. public school system.

Lanier's story echoed those of her fellow female police chiefs. Their appointments were sometimes surprising, often unexpected, and always pioneering. The National Center for Women and Policing noted that fewer than 10 percent of officers ranked at least a captain were female. It was somehow fitting that the nation's capital was installing its first woman chief. "Washington, D.C., was one of the first places to utilize females on the street," noted Ethel Diké, who served in the police department in the early 1970s. Jerry V. Wilson, the chief of police, increased the roster of assignments that women could have. During the first three years of his tenure, Wilson opened up new venues to women, including investigative work and the tactical squad. He capped that progress by hiring a hundred women for patrol duty in 1971.

Now, 36 years later, the city government had taken another bold step in hiring Cathy Lanier. In the media frenzy that erupted after her appointment, the press spotlighted Lanier's rise to chief as an example of what self-determination could bring. A tomboy who grew up with two brothers—one of whom became a police officer and the other a firefighter—Lanier became pregnant when she was just 15 years old. She dropped out of high school and had her baby, marrying and soon divorcing the father. She held down jobs as a waitress and a secretary, collected her GED, and attended community college classes when she had the money to do so. In 1990, when she learned that the D.C. police department reimbursed college tuition for its officers, Lanier let go of her dream job as an attorney and signed up with the police force. She found herself loving the new job.

As a beat cop in D.C., Lanier and her fellow female officers faced the same kind of prejudices that policewomen had battled since their first days on duty. In 1995, after finding no solution through the Equal Employment Opportunity Commission, Lanier and an officer named Lena Johnson filed a sexual harassment suit in district court. The case alleged that Lanier and Johnson's supervisor, a male lieutenant, had made crude remarks and behaved in a manner that denigrated them because they were women. It wasn't the first time that Lanier found herself harassed, but it was the first time she decided to take legal action. "I just thought at some point somebody has to stand up and say something," she explained.[447]

Life as a female rookie was difficult for Lanier. Sexual comments were an ongoing part of the daily routine. In her court deposition Lanier recalled the day she arrived for duty in the fourth district in May 1991: When she walked into the roll call room, she was greeted with "hooting and hollering, 'fresh meat' comments by the officers in front of the officials—nice ass, damn she's built like a black girl, that kind of shit that went on."[448] A sergeant in the department continually asked Lanier out, even after she told him that she didn't date police officers.[449]

Lanier would remain in the fourth district until November 1994, when she received her promotion to sergeant and transferred to the sixth district. There she was subjected to even worse treatment at the hands of her supervisor. Lanier accused her lieutenant of sexually harassing behavior including an incident where he pulled her ponytail "in a room full of peers, making the comment about pulling a woman's hair while having sex."[450] The married lieutenant would call her into his office for brief meetings during which he would ask her out on dates. In 1997, the case was settled out of court; the city promised to improve its sexual awareness training and Lanier and Johnson received $75,000 for their troubles.

Ten years later and in her new position of authority, Lanier paid close attention to harassment cases in her department. Soon after her appointment she demoted and removed Robin Hoey, who had been commander of the sixth district since 2004, due to a series of sexual harassment complaints dating back a decade. Hoey called the accusations "garbage" and attributed the problems to his aggressive leadership style.

After Lanier told Hoey of her decision to demote him to captain, he protested and she ordered him to undergo a medical evaluation. Hoey claimed that Lanier sent him to the doctor after he threatened her and another top-level supervisor in the department. In April 2007, Hoey ended up as a captain in charge of the city's main lockup facility. It was a hard fall for an officer who was credited by residents with cleaning up a residential area of violence and drug dealing. During his stint as inspector in charge of the Georgia Avenue substation in the northwest section of the city, Hoey oversaw the neighborhoods of Park Morton, Pleasant Plains, and Columbia Heights. The president of the Park Morton Citizens Association praised Hoey as a "people person." The press reported that residents of the sixth district were shocked at his demotion, noting that he participated in community meetings and was viewed favorably by community leaders.

Lanier faced public outcry over her decision. During a safety meeting at a local church in early May, she rose to speak and was greeted with boos from the audience. Rumors abounded, especially since Lanier had offered no official explanation of why she halted Hoey's career. One theory held that Hoey had called Lanier a name at the end of a conference call after he thought she had hung up. But Lanier denied the story. "I've made a decision, and it won't be changed," she said.[451] As the new police chief, it was her option to move people around.

After decades of having male supervisors make decisions regarding their careers, policewomen were now in positions of power, directing male and female officers alike. Things had certainly changed.

SHOW OF FORCE

Meanwhile, more women stepped into the role of police chief in cities across America. Orlando, Florida—home to Disney World, flocks of family tourists, and sun-seeking retirees—welcomed its first female police chief in December 2007. Val Demings was also African American, the first to be appointed as chief of the thousand-member force. It was a family legacy of sorts: Demings's husband Jerry had held the post for four years beginning in 1998, then supervised the public safety division before running for Orange County sheriff.

Like Cathy Lanier, Demings came from an impoverished background. She grew up in Jacksonville, crammed into a two-bedroom house with her six brothers and sisters. After a brief tenure as a social worker, Demings joined the Orlando police department in 1983 and worked her way up through the ranks. She supervised Operation Delta, a program to reduce street-level drug trafficking in the city.

What about the traditional reluctance of male police officers to follow a female supervisor? "When I worked for her and I was a watch commander on the street on the midnight shift, she would come out to those calls late at night, shootings, serious calls," said Brian Gilliam, who worked for Demings. "The officers here really believe she cares and they know she's no-nonsense. She's going to get out there and make some decisions, so I think there's a lot of support within the ranks and, I think, in the community."[452]

Following the 9/11 attacks, Demings, then a captain in charge of the patrol division, sent police officers armed with machine guns to patrol the local airport. Despite concerns from local officials about such a public show of force, Demings was undeterred. According to a November 2007 article in the *Orlando Sentinel*, "It was that take-charge attitude from the twenty-three-year veteran and deputy police chief—who has overseen much of the city's violent-crime initiative during the past two years—which led Orlando mayor Buddy Dyer to tap Demings as the city's first female police chief." She had a huge challenge ahead of her: "Demings inherits a department in the midst of a battle to control street violence, especially robberies, shootings and murders."[453] During the previous year, 49 people were murdered in Orlando—a city record. A confident Demings said she was ready to tackle the issue: "Let me make one thing perfectly clear," she said after the mayor announced her appointment as chief. "I am up to the challenge, and I am prepared for a time such as this."[454]

Whether they were serving as rookie patrol officers or chiefs of police, women were making their mark on law enforcement organizations across the United States. Over the years, the opportunity to improve their communities, to make things right, drew many women into the law enforcement field. They had come a long way from their initial efforts at battling sexual harassment, fighting for promotion opportunities, and demanding the right to patrol the streets. Along the way they earned the respect of their male peers and the people they served. The glass ceiling wasn't completely broken, but it was cracked enough to let plenty of opportunity shine through.

They think you can't do the job like a man can.
You absolutely can.

> —Capt. Teresa Galloway,
> Kokomo, Indiana, police department[455]

We were not hired to be pretty and smell nice.

> —Michelle Cotten, Virginia State Police[456]

CHAPTER 7

Summing Up and Looking Ahead

DESPITE THE FACT that women have been in law enforcement for over a century and a half, and even with laws specifically dictating fair hiring procedures, policewomen are still continuing their quest to break through the walls that have hindered their progress in a male-dominated profession.

The earliest reformers in the women's movement lobbied to install matrons in prisons and police departments while at the same time pushing for temperance, equal treatment under the law, and the right to vote. As police matrons became a firmly established part of the law enforcement system, their duties expanded to include the supervision of women and children in their communities. The first sworn policewomen soon followed—female officers with the power to arrest criminals. Over the years—through discrimination, harassment, inequality in pay, wars, changing sexual mores, and rising crime rates—the policewoman's authority and responsibilities grew steadily. Female officers were placed in their own single-sex bureaus, which were later disbanded as male and female cops were consolidated under the same umbrella. The traditional notion that women were too emotional, too slight, too scared to do the job, became an outmoded way of thinking. For the most part, female cops showed that they could perform on par with their male counterparts.

But while police departments—and many male officers— had become better acclimated to the women in their ranks, old attitudes still haunted the station houses. There were more policewomen in the United States than ever before, but they still faced the discrimination and harassment that had been a part of the job ever since the first police matron signed up for duty back in the 19th century. As they had many times before, policewomen continued to go to court to ensure fair treatment on the job. As recently as 2006, the American Civil Liberties Union and six female officers filed a lawsuit against the Suffolk County, New York, police department for refusing to reassign pregnant employees to desk duty—effectively forcing them to resign from the force. Over the years female officers had succeeded in improving their status in society, but in some ways there was still a long way to go.

The population of female cops in the United States has experienced a slow but steady growth. According to a 2006 article by historian Peter Horne, women comprised about 7 percent of the police officers in state agencies, while they comprised around 13 percent of municipal police departments. The FBI noted that for the country's 18,000 law enforcement agencies, women had gained about half a percentage point each year. By those numbers, Horne estimated that the country had about 100,000 female police officers on the job.[457] Overall, women over the age of 16 made up only 7 percent of the

American workforce in 1900; in 2007, that figure was 46.5 percent—meaning nearly half of America's workers were now women.[458]

Over time, relationships among male and female police officers have markedly improved. Some of this progress has been due to the retirement of older male officers who felt that women didn't belong in the police force. Newer generations of male officers have more readily accepted women in their ranks, partly because the policewoman was less of a novelty. "Women just became mainstream after a while," said Elizabeth Robinson, one of the first female police officers assigned to regular patrol in a squad car. "The younger men who came on [the force] were used to it."[459]

And though it still exists, on-the-job sexual discrimination has become less prevalent. "I don't believe it is intentional as much as it is a matter of circumstance," said one female officer in confidence. "Women don't always have the same opportunities to network as their male colleagues, which can be limiting in transfers or promotions." But their smaller numbers could actually be a detriment. "Some people feel that, in an effort to comply with the court, certain women are being promoted or transferred to specialized units before they are qualified, essentially setting them up for failure," continued the officer. "And some women's credibility is questioned because others feel they were promoted or transferred to 'get the numbers,' not because they were qualified." Thus, in leveling the playing field, some police departments have inadvertently created the situation they were trying to avoid. In doing so, the departments have unintentionally forced policewomen to face the same doubts and debates over their capability of performing the job all over again.

Nevertheless, the signs of progress are everywhere. Out on the street, the public has become more accepting of female cops. Whereas people previously refused to take them seriously, policewomen have gradually become a recognized part of everyday life in most cities in the United States. "We aren't treated as the weaker sex or pigeon-holed into certain jobs like juvenile or sex crimes or as school resource officers," observed Peggy Fox of the Topeka, Kansas, police department. And, said Fox, the women's locker room has finally become larger than the tiny bathroom-sized area that many early female officers were provided when they arrived for work.[460]

In addition, male officers—rather than doing everything they can to keep women off the force—are now helping pave the way for equality. "As we have evolved," said Lynda Castro of the Los Angeles Sheriff's Department, "I now see males calling in to take time off with child care responsibilities. It's not just the woman being held accountable for the needs of the children." It's a good sign, Castro added, that the playing field had become equal in many respects, not just with regard to pay and assignments.[461]

On the other hand, some old habits are hard to break, particularly for older generations who witnessed the policewoman's coming of age but still had a difficult time adjusting to the new ways of doing business. Sometimes hanging on to the past has led to rather humorous incidents in public. "I still have elderly ladies give me a dirty look when I go into the women's restroom," said Donna Bacus of the Iowa State Patrol. "They just see the uniform and think that a male trooper went into the wrong restroom."[462]

The belief prevalent in the 19th century that women possess empathy to a greater degree than men do, and are therefore better suited to tasks like taking care of wayward women and children, still holds sway among some law enforcement officers today. David Couper, former chief of the Madison, Wisconsin, police department, believes that the inclusion of women in the male-dominated law enforcement profession led to an improvement in the style of policing as well as an expansion in demographics. "Women brought a different contribution to policing than men," said Couper. "For example, they handled violence with a more sensitive and managing style, and they responded to sexual assault victims in a better way." Generally speaking, said Couper, women officers are more compassionate in the ways they do their job. However, he cautioned, this happens only if they do not get "co-opted into being *police* women rather than police *women*."

How many more challenges are there for female law enforcement officers to overcome? "The history of women in policing is nearing the time when there will be no more 'firsts,'" notes Horne. "Many police agencies have already experienced the first woman hired, the first woman to be promoted to whatever rank, the first woman on the SWAT team, the first woman commander, and so on."[462]

Indeed, major cities like Boston and Chicago have already brought aboard their first female SWAT team members, but Los Angeles—home of the nation's first SWAT team, formed in the late 1960s—remained a holdout. In 2008, the Los Angeles Police Department announced that it had cleared the first woman to train for its SWAT unit. Jennifer Grasso would vie for one of the 60 elite positions. The announcement generated as much discord as praise. According to the *Los Angeles Times*, "The new selection criteria angered many current SWAT officers, who accused Police Chief William J. Bratton and his command staff of watering down the process in order to make it easier for a woman to join the demanding unit, which specializes in resolving standoffs with barricaded suspects and other high-risk operations."[464] However, officers who had watched Grasso tackle the obstacle course and the other physical tests admitted they were impressed with her performance.

Grasso's admission into SWAT training was a vicarious victory for Nina Acosta, who had sued the department in 1994 when it refused to let her apply for the SWAT team. When the department finally demurred, after much back-and-forth discussion, a fed-up Acosta said no thanks and quit. Still, despite being accepted into the training program, Grasso faced a number of hurdles: even if she completed her training successfully, she wasn't guaranteed a spot in the SWAT unit. Like the male officers hoping to join SWAT, Grasso would have to go through yet another selection process. In the end she made it, opening the doors for future female candidates.

Changing times: Darla Sudderth of the Tennessee Highway Patrol in 2008. The Massachusetts State Police hired the first two female troopers in the United States in 1930. Back then female officers weren't issued uniforms. *(Tennessee Highway Patrol)*

"YOU SAVED MY LIFE"

Whether battling to move up the ranks or simply trying to do the best job possible each day, police officers often carry with them remembrances of incidents that resonate years after they originally occurred. "I have many memories," said Julie Myer of the Washington State Patrol. "Sad instances where I told a family their child had died in a crash, the feeling of not having options for response when one of my troopers and I were involved in a shooting, the good times and camaraderie with coworkers, the energy and satisfaction running from crash to crash on a stormy night."[465]

Michelle Cotten of the Virginia State Police found the most difficult part of her job to be death notifications: "It's difficult to tell a family member that their loved one was killed in a traffic accident, for example. I remember all of those like they happened yesterday. It's painful, the way people react to seeing you in the middle of the night."[466]

Some policewomen have found that even routine contact with the public leaves a strong impression. "Many times we interact with people and never know the impact that we have on their lives," said Donna Bacus. Bacus pulled over a female drunk driver on the south side of Des Moines one night. The woman shoved Bacus away from her, called the trooper names and refused to surrender. After a heated conversation, Bacus was able to calm the woman down and get her to the station. After her arraignment the next morning, the woman was instructed to attend a treatment program and pay a fine. She also lost her driver's license for 180 days.

A year later Bacus received a message to return a phone call. When she did, the female voice on the other end of the line didn't sound familiar—at first.

"This is Trooper Bacus. I was asked to call you."

"You probably don't remember me," said the voice on the other end of the line.

"I'm sorry, I'm afraid I don't."

"You saved my life a year ago," said the woman. "I wasn't very nice to you."

As the woman continued her story, Bacus realized who she was.

"I got drunk that night and was going to run my car into a bridge," explained the woman. "I wanted to kill myself. My husband had left me. My life was a mess. I just felt that life had nothing to offer, so I was going to end it"—she took a breath—"until you showed up and stopped me."

The woman invited Bacus to the one-year anniversary of her sobriety. "She was back with her husband, was continuing her education, and she was incredibly happy," recalled Bacus. "It meant a lot to me that she called and wanted to include me."[467]

Female officers have long recognized the courage of the women who made it possible for them to wear the uniform. "I can honestly tell you I love my job and enjoy coming to work every day," noted Shannon Spreckelmeyer of the Indiana State Police. "I truly appreciate the women who have come before me—the trailblazers. They certainly made it easier for me."[468]

Aside from the celebrated pioneers—the women whose names are featured prominently whenever the history of policewomen is discussed—there have been thousands of unsung heroines who, though they never had a spotlight shone on them, nevertheless helped advance the cause, whether they knew it or not. "Not to be forgotten are the women who were desk coordinators, clerks, matrons, juvenile officers, worked undercover in drug enforcement situations, acted as decoys to catch sexual predators, and yet were not allowed to carry a gun," said Lori Fry, who served on the police force in Madison, Wisconsin. Also toiling away quietly in the background have been the clerks and secretaries who listened as police officers dictated their reports. "They were the first to hear of a horrific accident, sexual assault, or death investigation," explained Fry. "They were the first to offer support to an officer who had just witnessed a nightmare, and the first to give comfort. They were our sisters, our friends, and people to whom we could confide the things we—as men or women officers—could not talk about with our spouses, family and friends who were not a part of the police family."[469]

Camaraderie, so much a part of life for those who serve the public every day, can keep police officers going even during their worst days on the job. Sometimes the family atmosphere in a police department has inspired women to consider a career in law enforcement. Married to a New Mexico State Patrol officer, Bernadette Jaramillo saw the rigors and joys of the job firsthand. When she lost her husband to cancer, Jaramillo was grateful for the support she received from his coworkers. "The law enforcement family was so good to my family and me," she recalled. "And I was able to see how tight-knit law enforcement officers stick together." In December 2004, Jaramillo followed in her late husband's footsteps and joined the state patrol herself.[470]

Despite the hardships, the discrimination, the very nature of the job itself—what kept the women pioneers in law enforcement going to work every day? "We loved it," said Elizabeth Robinson. "It was an adventure and we loved doing it."[471]

Jonelle Greear of the Idaho State Police summed it up this way: "I work in a beautiful area. I get to be outside in all kinds of weather, and a sunrise on the mountains or a sunset on the lake can make the whole day. I love to drive—sometimes really fast. I meet lots of people— some even like me. I feel like I can make an impact every day."[472]

Throughout their history, women in law enforcement have recognized their unique roles not only in serving their communities but also with regard to their impact on society as a whole. Back in 1946, as she prepared to retire after more than three decades of service, Mary Sullivan, chief of the New York Policewomen's Bureau, made a fervent wish for the future: "And may there be many more policewomen—not only in New York, but all over the world."[473]

ACKNOWLEDGMENTS

I'M VERY HAPPY to have had the privilege of sharing this history with you. I think it's critically important to thank everyone who contributed in ways large and small to turn a massive collection of research into a solid volume. There are many people who—directly or indirectly—encouraged my love of history and, whether they know it or not, helped me complete this book. Ron Goad, the high school English instructor who loved my writing? Your encouragement back then has kept me putting pen to paper all these years. Jody Wheeler, the best friend who gave me feedback on my earliest stories? You encouraged me to keep trying, so I did. And on and on—so many people who, just by being there for me, have led me to this: doing what I love.

I'm grateful to the law enforcement officers who spent time with me talking about the job, about their reasons for doing it, about their families and friends. The individual anecdotes and opinions supplied by these participants have brought history to life: Roberta Abner, Veneza Aguinaga, Christine Bailor, Donna Bacus, Marilyn Baker, Lucille Burrascano, Beth Bradbury, Lynda Castro, Michelle Cotten,

Jennifer Crews-Carey, David Couper, Juanita (Howard) Darbonne, Ethel Moore Diké (Greene), Rebecca Downing, Rhonda Fleming, Virginia Fogt, Peggy Fox, Lora Lee (Lori) Fry, Judy Gerhardt, Jonelle Greear, Julia Grimes, Joan Halloran, Bernadette Jaramillo, Sara Jaramillo, Lori McGrath, Julie Myer, Geraldine Perry, Jill Rice, Elizabeth Robinson (and her husband, Donald Goeden), Sheila Sanchez, Cheryl Sanders, Alice Scott, Shannon Spreckelmeyer, Elizabeth Whitfield, and Kim Zangar. Thanks also to those who are no longer with us but left behind their stories for us to hear about from their families and friends—or to read about in newspapers, in magazines, and on the Web.

Guardians of our past, museum and historical society personnel ensure that future generations will know how we lived. I'm grateful to them not only for helping me produce this book but also for the daily conservation work in which they engage. Without them, we wouldn't have a history to look back upon. Thanks to Liz Dormady, manager/curator of the Portland Police Museum; Alan March, president of the Greater Cincinnati Police Historical Society; Glynn Martin, executive director of the Los Angeles Police Historical Society; Brent Shepherd, curator and director of operations at the American Police Hall of Fame and Museum; and Beth Spinelli, registrar at the New York City Police Museum.

During my adventures in research, I connected with spokespersons and media relations officers at a number of law enforcement organizations, including David Bursten of the Indiana State Police; Christopher Childs of the California Highway Patrol; Pamela Cruz of the Michigan State Police; David Couper, former chief of the Madison, Wisconsin, Police Department; Hal Dalton of the Annapolis, Maryland, Police Department; Courtney Greene of the Iowa State Patrol; Don Kelly of the Baton Rouge, Louisiana, Police

Department; Laura McPherson of the Tennessee Highway Patrol; Ronald Miller, chief of the Topeka, Kansas, Police Department; Nancy Mulroy of the Hartford, Connecticut, Police Department; Jessica Pierson of the Ohio State Highway Patrol; Sonny Smith of the Columbia, South Carolina, Police Department; Roger Spurgeon of the Indianapolis Police Department; Jim Sughrue of the Raleigh, North Carolina, Police Department; and Paul Thompson of the Indianapolis Police Department.

Other authors were a huge help as well: Lisa Desimini, author of the children's book *Policeman Lou and Policewoman Sue*; Jack French, retired FBI agent and author of *Private Eyelashes: Radio's Lady Detectives*; David Griffith, editor of *Police Magazine*; Professor Peter Horne of Mercer County Community College in West Windsor, New Jersey; and Dr. Kathleen Kiernan, founder of the website SameShield.org.

My friend Eric Ford, a deputy sheriff for Los Angeles County, was enthusiastic about the book when I first pitched it, and was even more enthusiastic after it found a publisher. Eric connected me with female law enforcement officers who provided a wealth of technical knowledge and personal stories that enriched this history.

Thanks to my friends, coworkers, and supervisors during my 11-year stint as an officer in the U.S. Air Force. Whether you knew it or not, you encouraged my interest in history and provided a solid foundation for writing about it.

I'd like to single out a few more people who have greatly affected my career as a writer:

- Ben Ohmart, who published my first book, *The 12 O'Clock High Logbook: The Unofficial History of the Novel, Motion Picture, and Television Series*, through his company Bear-

Manor Media. In working with Ben, I learned how to make a book—and how to make it better. This new volume wouldn't exist had it not been for Ben's nurturing of me as a brand-new author.

- Professor David Ralston at the Massachusetts Institute of Technology. Though I was in college to study electrical engineering, I took a number of Professor Ralston's history courses as well. During lectures, when he asked a question and no one had an answer, his usual retort was classic: "Your silence is eloquent," he'd say with a chuckle. Then he'd continue from where he had left off. His office was difficult to visit, as the floor was always layered with stacks of books. I soon realized that his deep love of history meant that he read . . . a *lot*. And that I should follow his example, which I did.

- Professor William M. Fowler, Jr., a wonderful, engaging historian and my old boss at *The New England Quarterly*. Bill— who exudes a furious love for history—was a guiding force when I was attending graduate school at Northeastern University in Boston, and continues to be a mentor today.

- Equally important, Linda Smith Rhoads, the editor of the *Quarterly*, showed me how the industry worked and gave me my first shot at getting published when she offered me a book review to write.

- The rest of the teaching staff at Northeastern also contributed to my compulsion to write about history.

- The two other editorial assistants with whom I shared a tiny office, Anne Decker Cecere and Michele Foster Lineaweaver, were also wonderful and helped make my experience at the *Quarterly* two of the best years of my life so far.

- My father, Les, a former special agent with the Office of Special Investigations—the FBI-type unit of the U.S. Air Force— who instilled in me a sense of justice and a passion for getting the story right. I also inherited his love of history.

- My mom, Maria, who encouraged me to write books from the time I was, what, six years old? You were right, Mom. (I bet you never thought you'd see that in print.)

- The executive editor at Kaplan Publishing, Don Fehr, and editorial assistant Rachel Bergmann, who oversaw this book through the long and fruitful process of research, writing, revising, and revising again. Thank you for seeing the potential in this project and for believing in the story I wanted to tell.

- Kim Bowers, production editor at Kaplan Publishing, Janet Renard, copyeditor, and proofreader Nancy Gillan. Thanks for strengthening the manuscript and helping craft the finished product.

Warm thanks to my agent, Jane Dystel of Dystel & Goderich Literary Management in New York, who shepherded this project, guiding its author through the roller-coaster ride of crafting a book from scratch. Thanks also to Adina Kahn, who saw the potential in the initial pitch and helped me navigate the proposal and sale of the concept.

Finally, thank you to my wife, Michele, who has the same strength, courage, and innovative spirit embodied by the police-women portrayed in this book. More than that, she recognized that I was a writer long before I'd figured it out myself. Without her, my life would be . . . well, what's the point of wondering? I'm grateful to have the opportunity to love her, each and every day.

For anyone I haven't listed here, I apologize for missing you, and thank you as well for making this history come to life.

Allan Duffin
Los Angeles, California
September 2009

BIBLIOGRAPHY

BOOKS

Almodovar, Norma Jean. *Cop to Call Girl: Why I Left the LAPD to Make an Honest Living as a Beverly Hills Prostitute*. New York: Simon & Schuster, 1993.

American Social Hygiene Association, *Journal of Social Hygiene, Volume I*. New York: Waverly Press, 1916.

Appier, Janis. *Policing Women: The Sexual Politics of Law Enforcement and the LAPD*. Philadelphia: Temple University Press, 1998.

Belknap, Joanne. *The Invisible Woman: Gender, Crime, and Justice*. Belmont, CA: Wadsworth/Thomson Learning, 2001.

Bloch, Peter B., and Deborah Anderson of the Urban Institute. *Policewomen on Patrol: Final Report*. Los Angeles: Police Foundation, 1974.

Brooks, Tim, and Earl Marsh. *The Complete Directory to Prime Time Network TV Shows, 1946–Present*. New York: Ballantine Books, 2007.

Burke, Kathy. *Detective: The Inspirational Story of the Trailblazing Woman Cop Who Wouldn't Quit*. New York: Scribner, 2006.

Cavinder, Fred D. *The Indiana Book of Records, Firsts, and Fascinating Facts*. Bloomington: Indiana University Press, 1985.

Chapin, Clara C. *Thumb Nail Sketches of White Ribbon Women*. Chicago: Woman's Temperance Publishing Association, 1895.

Collins, Max Allan, and John Javna. *The Best of Crime & Detective TV*. New York: Harmony Books, 1988.

Dantzker, M.L. *Understanding Today's Police*. Monsey, NY: Criminal Justice Press, 2005.

Desimini, Lisa. *Policeman Lou and Policeman Sue*. New York: Blue Sky Press, 2003.

Farrington, Brenda, and Gordon Morris Bakken, Editors. *Encyclopedia of Women in the American West*. Thousand Oaks, CA: Sage, 2003.

Fletcher, Connie. *Breaking & Entering: Women Cops Talk About Life in the Ultimate Men's Club*. New York: HarperCollins, 1995.

Freedman, Estelle B. *Their Sisters' Keepers: Women's Prison Reform in America, 1830-1930*. Ann Arbor: University of Michigan Press, 1984.

French, Jack. *Private Eyelashes: Radio's Lady Detectives*. Albany, GA: Bear-Manor Media, 2004.

Gallo, Gina. *Armed & Dangerous: Memoirs of a Chicago Policewoman*. New York: Tom Doherty Associates, 2001.

Gold, Marion E. *Top Cops: Profiles of Women in Command*. Chicago: Brittany, 1999.

Harrington, P. E., and K. A. Lonsway. *Investigating Sexual Harassment in Law Enforcement and Nontraditional Fields for Women*. Upper Saddle River, NJ: Prentice-Hall, 2006.

Harrington, Penny. *Triumph of Spirit: An Autobiography*. Chicago: Brittany, 1999.

Hays, Gayleen, with Kathleen Moloney. *Policewoman One: My Twenty Years on the LAPD*. New York: Willard Books, 1992.

Hays, Thomas G., and Arthur W. Sjoquist. *The Los Angeles Police Department*. Mount Pleasant, SC: Arcadia, 2005.

Hosansky, Tamar, and Pat Sparling. *Working Vice: The Gritty True Story of Lt. Lucie J. Duvall*. New York: HarperCollins, 1992.

Jenks, Mary A. *Behind the Bars; or, Ten Years of the Life of a Police Matron*. Pawtucket, RI: Salisbury Manufacturing Company, 1902.

Lardner, James, and Thomas Reppetto. *NYPD: A City and Its Police*. New York: Holt, 2001.

Lichtenberger, William. *Indianapolis Police Department History Book*. Evansville, IN: M.T. Publishing Company, 2006.

Martin, Katherine. *Women of Courage: Inspiring Stories from the Women Who Lived Them*. Novato, CA: New World Library, 1999.

Martin, Susan Ehrlich. *Doing Justice, Doing Gender, Second Edition: Women in Legal and Criminal Justice Occupations*. Thousand Oaks, CA: Sage, 2006.

McNeil, Alex. *Total Television*. New York: Penguin, 1997.

Myers, Gloria. *A Municipal Mother: Portland's Lola Greene Baldwin, America's First Policewoman*. Corvallis: Oregon State University Press, 1995.

Miller, Susan. *Gender and Community Policing: Walking the Talk*. Boston: Northeastern University Press, 1999.

Painter, Nell Irvin. *Standing at Armageddon: The United States, 1877–1919*. New York: W. W. Norton, 1987.

Parsons, Deborah, and Paul Jesilow. *In the Same Voice: Women and Men in Law Enforcement*. Santa Ana, CA: Seven Locks Press, 2001.

Remmington, Patricia W. *Policing: The Occupation and the Introduction of Female Officers, an Anthropologist's Study*. Washington, D.C.: University Press of America, 1981.

Rhode Island State Police. *Rhode Island State Police: 75th Anniversary, 1925–2000—In the Service of the State*. Paducah, KY: Turner, 2002.

Ruiz, Mona, with Geoff Boucher. *Two Badges: The Lives of Mona Ruiz*. Houston, TX: Arte Público Press, 1997.

Schertzing, Phillip D. *Preserve, Protect and Defend: An Illustrated History of the Michigan State Police in the Twentieth Century*. Paducah, KY: Turner, 2002.

Schnabel, Martha. *Officer Mama*. San Antonio, TX: Naylor, 1973.

Schulz, Dorothy Moses. *Breaking the Brass Ceiling: Women Police Chiefs & Their Paths to the Top*. Westport, CT: Praeger Publishers, 2004.

___. *From Social Worker to Crimefighter: Women in United States Municipal Policing*. Westport, CT: Praeger, 1995.

Segrave, Kerry. *Policewomen: A History*. Jefferson, NC: McFarland, 1995.

Simon, David. *Homicide: A Year on the Killing Streets*. New York: Ivy Books, 1991.

U.S. Bureau of Labor Statistics. *Women in the Labor Force: A Databook*. Bureau of Labor Statistics, 2007. http://www.bls.gov/cps/wlf-table11-2007.pdf.

Ware, Susan, and Stacy Braukman, eds. *Notable American Women: A Biographical Dictionary, 5, Completing the Twentieth Century*. Cambridge, MA: Belknap Press, 2005.

Wells, Sandra, and Betty L. Alt, *Police Women: Life with the Badge.* Westport, CT: Praeger, 2005.

Wilbanks, William. *True Heroines: Police Women Killed in the Line of Duty Throughout the United States, 1916–1999.* Nashville, TN: Turner, 2000.

Willard, Steve. *The San Diego Police Department.* Mount Pleasant, SC: Arcadia, 2005.

PERIODICALS

Chapter 1

"Brevities." *Davenport (IA) Tribune,* July 3, 1889, p. 2.

"The Connecticut Prison: Two of the Attaches Suspended by the Acting Warden." *New York Times,* May 14, 1893, p. 20.

"The Cost of Flogging Women." *New York Times,* March 3, 1881, p. 2.

Editorial. *Fitchburg (MA) Sentinel,* August 11, 1887, p. 2.

"Equal Suffrage or Blood: Mrs. Goldzier of Bayonne Counsels Women to Arm and March on Trenton." *New York Times,* August 26, 1909, p. 1.

"The First Municipal Woman Detective in the World." *New York Times,* March 3, 1912, p. SM1.

"Flogged Young Girls: Cruel Charges Against a Prison Matron in Indianapolis." *Anaconda (MT) Standard,* January 29, 1901, p. 4.

"The House of Detention." *Davenport (IA) Tribune,* March 7, 1891, p. 2.

Howard, Joseph. "About Two Women: Prison Matron Foster and Prima Donna Patti." *Syracuse (NY) Herald,* February 7, 1892, p. 7.

"Inspecting Prison Work: A Visit to the Kings County Penitentiary." *New York Times,* January 5, 1883, p. 8.

Lugara, Joe. "Women in Blue." *NY Metro Parents,* May 21, 2004. http://www.nymetroparents.com/newarticle.cfm?colid=7239.

"Managed by Women: They Preserve Model Discipline in the Prison for Women at Auburn." *Waterloo (IA) Courier,* February 5, 1896, p. 2.

"Matron Campbell Dead." *New York Times*, June 3, 1907, p. 7.

"Miss Wilder's Appointment." *Newary (OH) Daily Advocate*, June 19, 1897, p. 6.

"A Month of Bourbon Rule: Making and Grabbing Offices Under Gov. Cleveland." *New York Times*, February 5, 1883, p. 1.

"Mrs. Webb Resigns: The Best-Known Police Matron in the Country About to Retire." *New York Times*, June 4, 1890, p. 8.

"New Jersey Prison Matrons Resign." *New York Times*, March 12, 1898, p. 2.

"A Police Matron." *Decatur (IL) Morning Review*, September 17, 1890, p. 3.

"A Police Matron: Influence of a Womanly Woman over a Despised and Hardened Outcast." *Lima (OH) Daily Times*, July 29, 1891, p. 2.

"Wants Women Police: Mrs. Julia Goldzier Lays Her Plan Before Secretary of State Koenig." *New York Times*, February 25, 1909, p. 2.

"Wed His Prison Matron." *New York Times*, February 9, 1898, p. 2.

Chapter 2

"Abraham Van Winkle Dies." *New York Times*, October 1, 1915, p. 11.

"Aid Ossining Policewoman: League Members Ask Her Retention, as She Chases Soldiers." *New York Times*, December 17, 1917, p. 20

"Arrest by Policeman: Exhibition in Madison Square Garden Enlivened by Bluecoat in Skirts." *New York Times*, October 8, 1902, p. 9.

Baldwin, Lola. "Our Policewomen." *Oregonian*, May 1953.

"Bandits Trailed by Policewoman." *Oakland Tribune*, August 31, 1917, p. 10.

"Bayonne's Policewoman: When Mayor Appointed R. McAdie He Didn't Know Applicant's Sex." *New York Times*, April 25, 1914, p. 6.

"Boudoir for Policewomen." *New York Times*, January 7, 1921, p. 2.

"Brokers in Theatre Tickets Arrested: Policewoman Mary Sullivan Tours Times Square District and Arrests 3 Speculators." *New York Times*, November 8, 1919, p. 18.

"Butte's Woman Officer Authorized to Carry Gun." *Anaconda (MT) Standard*, December 3, 1913, p. 7.

"Call for Policewomen to Protect the Boys: Why Not? Asks Mrs. Goldzier, 'Clubwoman' of Bayonne." *New York Times*, March 7, 1907, p. 9.

"Chicago's First Policewoman." *Lowell (MA) Sun*, June 28, 1909, p. 14.

"Chicago's Policewoman." *Frederick (MD) Daily News*, December 6, 1907, p. 3.

"'Copette' in Films, New Comedy Star: 'Zone Policewoman' at Fair Expert as Mother-in-Law." *Oakland Tribune*, April 22, 1916, p. 18.

Craydon, Barbara. "High Jinks in the English Surf." *Fort Wayne (IN) Sentinel*, August 16, 1919, p. 10.

"Duties of Women Police." *New York Times*, July 28, 1918, p. 31.

"Famous Policewoman Urges Prevention of Crime." *New York Times*, December 22, 1912, p. SM13.

Feiner, Richard. "Blanche Payson." http://www.laurelandhardyarchive.com/stills/1-laurel-hardy/379-46-l32-07/associated/people/all/item/26-blanche-payson.

"Female Copper Was Humiliated." *Logansport (IN) Daily Reporter*, May 12, 1909, p. 6.

"First Arrest by New Policewomen." *Fort Wayne (IN) Sentinel*, August 8, 1913, p. 6.

"First Policewoman in State Died in Jamestown Hospital." *Dunkirk (NY) Evening Observer,* July 13, 1944, p. 13.

Fong, Tillie. "Capitalist and Humanitarian: Coal Mine Owner Fought for Workers' Rights." *Rocky Mountain News*, July 13, 1999.

"Girl Cops Keep New York Women in Narrow Path." *Lincoln (NE) Daily News*, October 23, 1913, p. 3.

"Girl Given 8 Years for 1924 Robbery Try." *San Mateo Times*, February 21, 1930, p. 1.

"Girls Are Gaining." *Emporia (KS) Gazette*, May 13, 1909, p. 1.

"A Gun? Too Heavy to Lug, Says Police Woman." *Lima (OH) Sunday News*, December 12, 1926, p. 11.

Harnisch, Larry. "The Vexations of Research: Alice Stebbins Wells." *Los Angeles Times*, August 19, 2007. http://latimesblogs.latimes.com/thedailymirror/2007/08/the-vexations-0.html.

Haskin, Frederic J. "Police Women in Washington." *Fitchburg (MA) Daily Sentinel*, December 27, 1918, p. 4.

"Hats Off to the Lady Cop!" *Big Pines (WY) Examiner*, August 28, 1913, p. 6.

"Have Appointed 'Policewoman.'" *Cedar Rapids Evening Gazette*, August 5, 1910, p. 1.

"Healer Lays Curse on Police Woman: Anathema Against Miss Preiss Published in 'Ram's Horn,' Schlatter's Paper." *New York Times*, June 14, 1916, p. 6.

"How New York's Policewomen 'Spot' German Spies." *Washington Post*, September 15, 1918, p. 1.

"Husky Women Sought for the Police Force." *Atlanta Constitution*, July 10, 1913, p. 2.

"Jersey Policewoman Quits: Miss McAdie of Bayonne Tired of Spying on Spooners." *New York Times*, July 8, 1914, p. 20.

"Keep Back Men! Hoseless Bath Suits Upheld." *Oakland Tribune*, August 17, 1919, p. B-5.

"Lady Coppers in Quaker City." *Fond du Lac (WI) Daily Commonwealth*, February 5, 1913, p. 2.

"Lieut. Van Winkle Ready for Fight." *Washington Post*, March 25, 1922, p. 1.

"Loiterers to Workhouse." *New York Times*, November 12, 1913, p. 3.

"Los Angeles Policewoman Tells of Work." *Oakland Tribune*, June 18, 1911, p. 10.

"Masher Tried to Date Woman Cop—Arrested." *Des Moines News*, May 8, 1913, p. 8.

"Mayor Hylan Leads City Police Parade." *New York Times*, May 12, 1918, p. 16.

"More Skirted Cops: Colored Women to Be Appointed with Full Police Power." *Washington Post*, August 2, 1918, p. 1.

"The Mother Police." *Washington Post*, July 30, 1916, p. 8.

"The Only Policewoman." *Iowa State Press*, May 3, 1899, p. 7.

"Persecution Drove Policewoman from Racine, She Claims." *La Crosse (WI) Tribune and Leader-Press*, October 16, 1922, p. 6.

"Pinch for a Pinch." *Logansport (IN) Pharos-Reporter*, March 5, 1919, p. 9.

"Police Recovered Thirty-One Cars Stolen in 1923, Report Says." *Appleton (WI) Post-Crescent*, February 19, 1924, p. 7.

"The Policewoman." *Middletown (NY) Daily Times-Press*, August 12, 1913, p. 4.

"Police Woman and Her Duty." *Oshkosh Daily Northwestern*, May 18, 1915, p. 9.

"Policewoman at Movies." *New York Times*, June 19, 1914, p. 4.

"Policewoman Doing Satisfactory Work." *Salt Lake Tribune*, May 4, 1916, p. 12.

"Policewoman Follows Up Violations." *Olean Evening Herald*, February 18, 1919, p. 5.

"Policewoman for Sacramento." *Lincoln Evening News*, April 14, 1910, p. 12.

"Policewoman Is a Sphinx." *Stevens Point (WI) Daily Journal*, August 11, 1910, p. 3.

"Policewoman, Not Scared, Says 'Rest Easy, I Pack a Gun.'" *New York Times*, May 17, 1922, p. 18.

"Policewoman on the Trail." *New York Times*, May 23, 1917, p. 17.

"Policewoman Rides Horse: New Guardian of Cleveland Parks Will Make Young Men Behave." *New York Times*, June 7, 1914, p. 12.

"Policewoman's Service." *Indianapolis Star*, March 3, 1911, p. 8.

"Policewoman Subdues Man: Pulls Fighter from a Chicago Street Car and Arrests Him." *New York Times*, December 27, 1913, p. 4.

"Policewoman Takes Rap at Those Prohibitionists." *Des Moines (IA) National-Democrat*, June 1, 1916, p. 4.

"Policewoman to Sterilize Music." *La Crosse (WI) Tribune*, December 2, 1912, p. 1.

"Policewoman Tries to Enforce Laws." *Salt Lake Tribune*, May 22, 1916, p. 10.

"'Policewoman' Wanted." *Stevens Point (WI) Gazette*, March 3, 1909, p. 9.

"Policewomen." *New York Times*, March 31, 1880, p. 4.

"Police Women Not a Failure." *La Crosse (WI) Tribune*, April 7, 1914, p. 1.

"Police Woman on Motorcycle." *Ogden (UT) Evening Standard*, December 7, 1912, p. 14.

"Police Women on View." *New York Times*, April 6, 1909 p. 6.

"Policewomen Wash Rouged Girls' Faces." *New York Times*, November 30, 1918, p. 4.

"The Port of Missing Girls." *San Antonio Light*, July 25, 1920, p. 10-C.

"Postpone Policewoman Exams for Age 'Errors.'" *Oakland Tribune*, November 16, 1913, p. 2.

"Proper Policewoman." *Rochester Herald*, July 16, 1910, p. 4.

"Puts Ban on Tango." *Oelwein (IA) Daily Register*, January 13, 1914, p. 2.

"Racine's 'Copette' Attracts Interest." *Racine (WI) Journal-News*, May 14, 1914, p. 10.

"Refuse Job to Mrs. O'Shea." *New York Times*, March 31, 1918, p. 14.

"Regarding Policewomen." *Lowell (MA) Sun*, November 11, 1914, p. 6.

"Rochester Gets a Policewoman." *New York Times*, September 23, 1913, p. 1.

"R. Wanamaker Made a Police Deputy." *New York Times*, February 26, 1918.

"Should Policewoman Wear Uniform? Delegates at Sea." *Indianapolis Star*, May 11, 1916, p. 4.

"Slave Ring Is Investigated by Policewoman." *Des Moines News*, April 28, 1916, p. 10.

Smith, James Walter. "Enter the Lady Cops of Gotham." *Boston Evening Transcript*, May 18, 1918. http://www.sameshield.com/press/sspresso9aa.html.

Steele, Louise Egan. "Policewoman's Lot Not an Ordinary One." *Pasadena (CA) Star-News,* July 28, 1977, p. B-2.

"Suzanne Frances Napton Is Appointed W.C.T.U. Policewoman for Missouri." *Chillicothe (MO) Constitution*, September 24, 1915, p. 5.

"Take Suffragists at the Capital." *Stevens Point (WI) Journal*, June 23, 1917, p. 4.

"Tells Why Police Women Are Needed: Intelligent Handling of Social Evil Demands Them, Says Miss Milholland." *New York Times*, March 7, 1913, p. 20.

Thierry, E. M. "N.Y. Policewoman Sets Off Bomb." *Wisconsin State Journal*, December 19, 1920.

"This Female Sampson [*sic*] to Guard Visitors at the Panama Expo." *Bismarck (ND) Daily Tribune*, February 19, 1915, p. 1.

"This Grandmother Totes a Real Gun." *Oneonta (NY) Daily Star*, May 17, 1922, p. 1.

"This Is the Costume for Chicago Policewomen." *Racine (WI) Journal-News*, August 21, 1913, p. 10.

"Truck Injures Policewoman." *Washington Post*, November 12, 1918, p. 18.

"Trudged Back in Rainstorm." *Fort Wayne (IN) Sentinel*, June 5, 1914, p. 1.

"Two of Police Women Refuse to Surrender." *San Antonio Light*, February 1, 1919, p. 3.

"Want Policewomen on the City's Force." *New York Times*, October 28, 1916, p. 4.

"Warren's Police Woman Success." *New Castle (PA) News*, September 11, 1917, p. 6.

"Washington's Interesting Policewoman." *Mexia (TX) Evening News*, April 18, 1922, p. 5.

"Washington's Valiant Policewoman." *Brownsville (TX) Daily Herald*, November 15, 1923, p. 4.

"Wealthy Girl a Policewoman." *Washington Post*, January 21, 1909, p. 2.

"Welfarer." *Time*, November 26, 1934.

Wells, Alice Stebbins. "Personal History of Los Angeles' First Policewoman." *Los Angeles Police Association's Bulletin*, October 1940, pp. 5, 10.

"What One Woman Did to Become a Policewoman." *Hamilton (OH) Daily Republican-News*, July 15, 1914, p. 1.

"Why I Want to Be a Policewoman." *Oakland Tribune*, May 5, 1907.

Wilson, Ella. "A Woman Tells Some of Her Interesting Experiences as Mayor of a City." *New York Times*, September 24, 1911, p. SM8.

"Woman Cop Cures Man of Flirting." *Logansport (IN) Pharos-Reporter*, May 17, 1919, p. 9.

"Woman Medium Sues for Police Raid." *New York Times*, June 1, 1913, p. 10.

"Woman Policemen to Protect Women." *Bismarck (ND) Tribune*, December 5, 1923, p. 7.

"Woman Refuses to Stop Spooners." *New Castle (PA) News*, July 13, 1914, p. 8.

"Woman Wants Police Job: Mrs. O'Shea, Who Fought 'Spooning' in Ossining, Would Come Here." *New York Times*, November 12, 1921.

"Women Police Needed in Harlem, Declares Woman 'Cop.'" *Syracuse (NY) Herald*, January 23, 1910, p. 65.

"Women's Auxiliary for Police Reserve." *New York Times*, May 10, 1918, p. 11.

"Women to Be Cops," *Syracuse (NY) Herald*, September 19, 1911, p. 10.

"Women to March in Police Parade Today." *New York Times*, May 11, 1918, p. 11.

"Women Vote in Ossining: Mrs. O'Shea, ex-Policewoman, Fails to Beat Her Opponents." *New York Times*, March 13, 1918, p. 4.

"The Work of a Police Woman Discussed by One of Them." *Kokomo (IN) Daily Tribune*, May 6, 1916, p. 7.

"Work of Policewomen: Miss Bixby Tells of Duties." *Indianapolis Star*, December 4, 1910, p. 39.

"Young Policewoman, Fired for Efficiency, Is Now Back on the Job." *Fort Wayne (IN) Sentinel*, May 27, 1913, p. 8.

Chapter 3

Allen, Mary Cherry. "Retired Policewoman Worked Around the Clock." *Petersburg (VA) Progress-Index*, August 18, 1963, p. 14.

"Appleton's New Policewoman." *Appleton (WI) Post-Crescent*, April 6, 1922, p. 9.

"Army Resists Disease Spread." *Ogden Standard-Examiner*, August 4, 1942, p. 5.

Barber, Joseph. "Get Tough, Lady, If Molested, Says Policewoman in Salt Lake." *Ogden Standard-Examiner*, March 5, 1943, p. 1.

Bird, Carol. "Policewomen's School." *New York Times*, July 31, 1921, p. 74.

"Birth Control Raid." *Time*, April 29, 1929.

Boardman, Larry. "Automobile and Liquor Termed Foes to Morals." *Ogden Standard-Examiner*, July 17, 1925, p. 1.

Brice, Anna M. "Must Eliminate Politics in Chester to Cope with Crime, Policewoman Says." *Chester (PA) Times*, July 27, 1945, p. 1.

"Charge Mystic Bilked Film Stars." *Cumberland (MD) Evening Times*, May 17, 1930, p. 5.

"Chicago Cops to Quit April 1." *Lima (OH) Daily News*, March 23, 1920, p. 1.

"Chief Asks Council to Exonerate Police in Beating of Wife." *El Paso Herald-Post*, November 28, 1944, p. 1.

"Chief Considering Moving Policewoman from Military Work." *El Paso Herald-Post*, December 1, 1944, p. 1.

"Chief Opposed to Policewoman." *Hagerstown (MD) Daily Mail*, January 21, 1947, p. 1.

Civil service advertisement. *Benton Harbor (MI) News-Palladium*, October 9, 1947, p. 13.

Cook, Ben. "Says Greedy Gang Bosses Bit Off Too Much in Los Angeles." *Tucson Daily Citizen*, December 18, 1949, p. 31.

"Crank Tells Girls to Report to Policewoman." *El Paso Herald-Post*, August 26, 1947, p. 5.

"Crime Is a Medical Problem." *Elyria (OH) Chronicle-Telegram*, October 4, 1924, p. 10.

"Crime Show Makes Actors of Police." *New York Times*, August 2, 1939, p. 22.

"CWAC in New York Leads Cops' Chase." *Panama City News-Herald*, October 24, 1943, p. 7.

Deck, Arthur V. "Fan Dance Is Art; Jury Frees Girl." *Oakland Tribune*, June 8, 1935, p. C-2.

"Dope Traffic Today." *Olean (NY) Evening Times*, August 25, 1928, p. 12.

"Downey Offers Motorcycles for Use of Policewomen." *Lowell (MA) Sun*, February 21, 1929, p. 1.

"Fan Dancer Says Act Is Art." *Zanesville (OH) Times Recorder*, November 14, 1946, p. 2.

"Finds Loaded Pistol." *Billings Gazette*, March 23, 1943, p. 2.

"Four Little Boys Found Left Without Food, Fire or Sufficient Clothing." *Syracuse (NY) Herald*, January 14, 1936, p. 3.

"Fresno Teacher Is Named City Policewoman." *Fresno Bee*, July 4, 1944, p. 1.

Gaines, Judith. "Tough Love: The Massachusetts State Police." *Boston Globe Magazine*, 2001.

"The Girl Who Always Wanted to Be a Cop." *Syracuse (NY) Herald*, October 5, 1924, magazine section.

Graham, Sheila. "Hollywood Today: Ann Sothern." *Kingsport (TN) News*, November 1, 1946.

"Guilt Admitted in Lewd Picture Case." *Long Beach (CA) Press-Telegram*, July 27, 1948, p. B-2.

Hamilton, Mary E. "Identify Yourself." *Billings (MT) Gazette*, October 1, 1933, 3, p. 13.

Harrison, Paul. "Big Thrills of New York's Three Feminine Detective Chiefs." *Wisconsin Rapids Daily Tribune*, November 12, 1932, p. 5.

"'Hi Chubby,' No Way to Speak to Lady." *Troy (NY) Times Record*, July 12, 1947, p. 1.

"High Wages Blamed for Delinquency." *Chicago (IL) Southtown Economist*, July 21, 1943, p. 1.

"Hollywood Vice Queen Freed on Court Writ." *Lima (OH) News*, September 2, 1949, p. 27.

"I'm No Greenhorn, Says 'Moll Buzzer,' Picked Up by Cops." *Waterloo (IA) Daily Citizen*, October 3, 1941, p. 12.

"In New York." *Fitchburg (MA) Sentinel*, November 17, 1924, p. 14.

"Infant 'Bandit' Gang Disbanded." *Eau Claire (WI) Leader*, June 10, 1923, p. 5.

"Jobs Seeking Graduates as Result of War." *Tucson Daily Citizen*, July 14, 1943, p. 9.

"Judge Announces Qualifications for Policewoman." *Wisconsin State Journal*, February 27, 1943, p. 2.

"Jury Is Confused After Seeing Dance." *North Adams (MA) Transcript*, May 20, 1948, p. 10.

Kerr, Adelaide. "Women at Their Work, Lady Cop Likes Job." *Council Bluffs (IA) Nonpareil*, June 11, 1946, p. 6.

"Lack of Courtesy Disturbs Women Who Drive Cars." *Montana Standard*, April 14, 1929, p. 7.

"Lady Cops Shriek 'No!' as Toy Unveils Uniform." *Detroit Free Press*, May 3, 1949. Via Criminal Justice and Law Center, Lansing Community College.

"Learn Jiu-Jitsu, Advice of Veteran Policewoman." *Monesson (PA) Daily Independent*, March 13, 1936, p. 2.

"Madison Not Jeep Track, Judge Rules." *Wisconsin State Journal*, June 4, 1943, p. 18.

"Masher Tries to Flirt with Wrong Woman." *Estherville (IA) Daily News*, September 12, 1946, p. 1.

"Military Helps as 'Jivers' Go Berserk." *Lowell (MA) Sun*, August 6, 1942, p. 1.

Millett, Ruth. "We, the Women: Mary Shanley." *Wisconsin Rapids Daily Tribune*, February 1, 1939, p. 3.

"More Room at Bedford: New Dormitory Is Opened at State Reformatory for Women." *New York Times*, June 18, 1922, p. 16.

"Most of Woman Cop's Hard Work Comes Before the Appointment." *Galveston Daily News,* February 2, 1939, p. 9.

"Most Girls Picked Up by Vice Squad Are Juveniles." *Corpus Christi (TX) Tribune*, July 16, 1947, p. B-1.

"Mother, Policewoman Two Weeks to Feed 5, Killed." *Syracuse (NY) Herald*, March 13, 1930, p. 20.

"Mrs. Guynes, Chief Differ on Armament." *Wisconsin State Journal*, June 22, 1943, p. 2.

"Mrs. Kate O'Connor Stricken in Midwest." *Oakland Tribune*, November 11, 1938, p. 12.

"Mrs. Reese to Resign Police Job." *Wisconsin State Journal*, February 5, 1944, p. 1.

"My Most Thrilling Moment: Mary E. Hamilton." *Oakland Tribune*, February 28, 1926.

"Narcotics Are Seized." *Kingston (NY) Daily Freeman*, May 20, 1948, p. 17.

"Nice Work If You Can Get It! But Beauty Contest Ends in Court." *Nevada State Journal*, May 7, 1938, p. 1.

"No Bare, Dimpled Knees May Dazzle: 'Fags' Also Are Taboo." *Waterloo (IA) Evening Courier and Reporter*, July 8, 1921, p. 3.

"Novice 18 Months Ago, Champion Today to Defend Title at Meet." *Oakland Tribune*, September 22, 1938, p. 13.

"Nude Woman Seized Taking Capitol Building Sun Bath." *Indiana (PA) Evening Gazette*, 3 September 1948, p. 2.

"Officer Talks to Galion Club." *Mansfield (OH) News-Journal*, April 18, 1941, p. 3.

Othman, Frederick C. "Disgusted Judge Discharges Girl Contest Jurors." *Fresno Bee*, May 10, 1938, p. A-2.

"Parents to Blame for Runaway Girls, Says Policewoman." *Wichita Daily Times*, May 16, 1921, p. 8.

Parks, Amy. "Mrs. Fairley Is Challenge for Any Age." *El Paso Herald-Post*, March 9, 1962, p. 12.

Plummer, Mary Elizabeth. "Nurses, Pianists, Lawyers Hold Jobs on Force." *Nebraska State Journal*, April 25, 1941, p. 2.

__. "Women Cops Varied Lot." *San Antonio Express*, May 4, 1941, p. 11.

__. "Women Invade Police Ranks." *Mansfield (OH) News-Journal*, August 27, 1950, p. 7.

"Police Are Called, Not Undertaker." *Ogden (UT) Standard-Examiner*, December 30, 1928, p. 7.

"Police Arrest S.F. Man Over Lewd Pictures." *Oakland Tribune*, June 29, 1952, p. D-25.

"Police Force Rejects WCTU Leader, 87." *Oakland Tribune*, May 2, 1948, p. 4-A.

"Police Pair Has Tough Job, Must Read Comic Books." *Lima (OH) News*, May 13, 1949, p. 15.

"Police Prepare to Protect N.Y. Visitors from Crooks." *Maryland Times-Signal*, June 22, 1924, p. 6.

"Policewoman Blames Parents for Deliquency." *Syracuse (NY) Herald*, June 26, 1922, p. 10.

"Policewoman Captain Tiny Phi Beta Kappa." *Lima (OH) News*, September 6, 1940, p. 11.

"Policewoman Cracks Link in Dope Chain." *Lima (OH) News*, March 21, 1949, p. 1.

"Policewoman Defends Sally [Rand] in Nude Dance." *Oakland Tribune*, September 26, 1933, p. B-10.

"Policewoman Denies She Was Drunk While Firing Gun in Bar." *Galveston Daily News*, April 30, 1941, p. 12.

"Policewoman Exams to Be Held July 25." *Fayetteville (AR) Democrat*, July 11, 1923, p. 2.

"Policewoman Finds Duties Are Mystery." *Portsmouth (OH) Times*, March 16, 1936, p. 10.

"Policewoman Gets Status of Man." *Oakland Tribune*, May 26, 1938, p. D-15.

"Policewoman Holds Angry Mob at Bay to Avoid Lynching." *Indianapolis Star*, May 5, 1921, p. 1.

"Policewoman Is Animal Protector." *Massilon (OH) Evening Independent*, October 19, 1929, p. 3.

"Policewoman Is a Student Now." *Portsmouth (OH) Times*, January 17, 1937.

"Policewoman Just Puts Gun on Them And . . ." *Uniontown (PA) Morning Herald*, October 8, 1932, p. 5.

"Policewoman Killed in Saving Children." *New Castle (PA) News*, March 13, 1930, p. 1.

"Policewoman Kills a Negro Purse Snatcher." *Oshkosh Northwestern*, November 19, 1934, p. 1.

"Policewoman Leaves Force." *San Antonio Light*, November 8, 1945, p. 11-A.

"Policewoman Proves Need, Official Says." *Blytheville (AR) Courier News*, August 16, 1928, p. 3.

"Policewoman to Give Radio Talks." *Hagerstown (MD) Daily Mail*, November 23, 1932, p. 4.

"Policewoman to Recover Books." *Appleton (WI) Post-Crescent*, July 7, 1922, p. 9.

"Policewoman Rapid-Fire Expert." *Hayward (CA) Review*, December 21, 1934, p. 1.

"Policewoman Rewarded." *Newark Advocate and American Tribune*, February 6, 1930, p. 6.

"Policewoman Shows Gun to Twins; Shot in Hand." *Joplin (MO) Glove*, December 19, 1948, p. 22.

"Policewoman's Job Unchanged by War, Declares Mrs. Dukes." *New Castle (PA) News*, May 4, 1945, p. 11.

"Policewoman Takes 'Count,' But Floors Man." *Salt Lake Tribune*, December 20, 1933, p. 24.

"Policewoman Will Carry Blackjack." *Wisconsin State Journal*, June 23, 1943, p. 1.

"Policewomen Busy in 1932, Report Shows." *Wisconsin State Journal*, January 19, 1933, p. 20.

"Policewomen Don Navy Blue Dress." *Detroit News*, July 29, 1942. Via Criminal Justice and Law Center, Lansing Community College.

"Policewomen Will Meet in S.F. June 25." *Oakland Tribune*, May 12, 1929, p. A-7.

"Pretty Policewoman Quits on Eleven Charges of Drinking, Petting." *Decatur (IL) Evening Herald*, April 16, 1930, p. 1.

Quinby, Ione. "University Town Puts 'O.K.' on Fan Dance Chicago Barred." *Massillon (OH) Evening Independent*, October 13, 1933, p. 7.

Ragsdale, Eleanor. "Capital's Juvenile Deliquency No. 1 Policewoman Headache." *Kingsport (LA) Times*, July 17, 1942, p. 2.

"Riding Motorcycle, Policewoman Here on 12,000-Mile Trip." *Modesto (CA) News-Herald*, August 4, 1929, p. 3.

"Sally Rand Still Says She's Artistic." *Idaho Falls (ID) Post-Register*, July 16, 1950, p. 6.

Scharfenberg, Doris. "'The Division Has Become a Necessity.'" *Michigan History Magazine*, November–December 2002, p. 76.

"Score Taken in Raids on Slave Rings." *Helena (MT) Independent*, January 27, 1938, p. 1.

"Scratch 'Em First; Then Pinch." *Lincoln (NE) Star*, March 21, 1924, p. 16.

"She Quits Boston Police." *New York Times*, February 1, 1922, p. 17.

"Shirley a Policewoman." *Jefferson City (MO) Daily Capital News*, January 6, 1938, p. 10.

"Shooting Wins Job for Policewoman." *Ogden Standard-Examiner*, December 20, 1928, p. 10.

Simpson, Bessie. "Great-Grandmother of Eight Feted as 'Mother of the Year.'" *El Paso Herald-Post*, May 11, 1963, p. 8.

"Smashing a Masher." *San Antonio Light*, March 10, 1941, p. 8-A.

"Starving Baby." *Davenport (IA) Democrat and Leader*, February 20, 1949, p. 6.

"State Is Closing Against Pantages." *Galveston (TX) Daily News*, October 15, 1929, p. 1.

"Stenos in Police Department Start Gun Firing Study." *Abilene Daily Reporter*, May 8, 1936, p. 16.

Sugrue, Thomas. "The Perfect 36—The Rockettes." *Modern Mechanix*, December 1936, p. 66.

"35 High School Students Riot in Vacant House." *Fresno Bee*, October 24, 1929, p. 13.

"This Dressing in Public in Atlanta Just Has to Stop, That's All." *Modesto Bee*, October 9, 1948, p. 1.

"Uniformly, the Gals Get Last Word." *Detroit News*, November 19, 1948, via Criminal Justice and Law Center, Lansing Community College.

Unsigned review of *My Double Life,* by Mary Sullivan. *Time*, July 11, 1938.

"Vamps Who Oggle Auto Drivers to Be Caught in Chicago Grill; Drive." *Modesto Evening News,* July 27, 1922, p. 1.

"Very Few Women Are Bootleggers, Policewoman Says." *Bridgeport (CT) Telegram*, November 18, 1926, p. 16.

"Virginia Has First Negro Policewoman." *Wisconsin State Journal*, April 20, 1921, p. 7.

"Washington Police Jobs Are Offered to Charleston Women." *Charleston (WV) Gazette*, November 11, 1928, p. 8.

"Washington's $1,440 Girls Confront a War of Nerves." *Oakland Tribune*, December 27, 1942, Magazine Pictorial, p. 1.

"Webs to Catch the Broadway Butterflies." *Oakland Tribune*, April 13, 1930, p. 59.

"What They Found in New York's 700 Dance Halls." *Syracuse (NY) Herald*, November 9, 1924, magazine section.

"Woman Brings 'Lunch' to Her Prisoner Husband; Dope Found in It." *Valparaiso (IN) Didette-Messenger*, July 11, 1929, p. 1.

"Woman Dies to Save 3 Children." *San Antonio Express*, March 14, 1930, p. 4.

"Woman Dressed 'Coast Style' Is Arrested." *El Paso Herald*, July 7, 1945, p. 1.

"Woman Guards GI Equipment, with a Ready .45 at Her Hand." *Wisconsin State Journal*, July 10, 1944, p. 14.

"Woman Held on Charges of Abortion." *Nevada State Journal*, June 16, 1949, p. 1.

"Woman Rescued from Window Ledge." *Elyria (OH) Chronicle-Telegram*, November 8, 1932, p. 4.

"Woman to Be L.A. 'Mother.'" *Oakland Tribune*, February 8, 1930, p. B-6.

"Women Advised That Screams Rout 'Mashers.'" *Lima (OH) News*, December 8, 1936, p. 16.

"Women Hoot, Jeer; Put Out of Courtroom." *Sioux City (IA) Journal*, April 25, 1929, p. 1.

"Women Sherlocks Making Good in New York City." *San Antonio Express*, April 27, 1924, p. B-5.

Chapter 4

"Auto Marker Sticks; Policewoman Is Pulled from Cycle." *Modesto Bee*, October 1, 1953, p. 27.

"Belly Dancer Convincing Witness." *Long Beach (CA) Press-Telegram*, May 14, 1960, p. 1.

"Brunette Decides She'll Wrestle with the Boys." *Abilene (TX) Reporter-News*, August 9, 1968, p. 6-A.

Carder, Joe. "Policewoman Fulfills Girlhood Dream." *Albuquerque Tribune*, June 25, 1965, p. B-2.

"Charge Parents Sold Girl, 11, for $5, Gasoline." *Dixon (IL) Evening Telegraph*, January 30, 1951, p. 9.

"Couple Tries to Trade Baby for New Car." *Appleton (WI) Post-Crescent*, November 9, 1961, p. B-8.

"Court Spurns Policewoman Claim of Discrimination." *Kittanning (PA) Leader-Times*, May 9, 1967, p. 3.

Davila, Vianna. "Pioneer Female Officer Faced Down Fears." *San Antonio (TX) Express-News*, November 5, 2006.

"Dope-User Suspects Lured into Arrest." *Arizona Republic*, December 15, 1959, p. 14.

Dixon, Victoria. "Martha Schnabel: Wife, Mother, Police Sergeant, Judge." *Wilson County News,* November 29, 2006, p. B1.

"Eleven-Year-Old Girl Says Parents Sold Her for Five Dollars and Tankful of Gas." *Lowell (MA) Sun*, January 30, 1951, p. 18.

Farmley, Helen. "Policewoman Helping Teenagers." *Prospect Heights (IL) Herald*, July 5, 1967, p. 1.

"Former Policewoman Files Federal Suit." *Indiana Gazette*, June 6, 2002, p. 12.

Forrester, Betty. "The Suburban Policewoman: Chic and Sympathetic." *Chicago Daily Herald*, October 6, 1966.

"Frankie Lured by Lady Cop." *Brownsville (TX) Herald*, March 8, 1957, p. 1.

Fuller, Tony. "Yips Told to Bring Weapons to Riot Area." *Dunkirk-Fredonia (NY) Evening Observer*, October 4, 1969, p. 1.

"'Girl Gangs' Rivaling Boys in Philadelphia." *Monesse (PA) Daily Independent*, November 24, 1953, p. 1.

"Grand Rapids Policewoman Describes Her Activities." *Holland (MI) Evening Sentinel*, October 26, 1967, p. 7.

"Grilling Is Man's Job, Boy Insists." *Lubbock (TX) Avalanche*, April 13, 1954, p. 9.

Griswold, Earl. "Women Gains in Police Jobs Told." *Long Beach (CA) Press-Telegram*, October 29, 1968, p. A-15.

Gunby, Phil. "Champs Rarely Come Prettier." *Billings (MT) Gazette*, October 17, 1963, p. 14.

Harnisch, Larry. "Chasing Marilyn Monroe." *Los Angeles Times*, June 2, 2007. http://latimesblogs.latimes.com/thedailymirror/2007/06/marilyn_monroe.html.

"Heel Fells Policewoman." *San Antonio Express*, October 28, 1969, p. 3-A.

Heilman, Adam. "Focus: Women in Blue." *Daily Pennsylvanian*, February 24, 1992.

Heisler, Judy. "Policewoman Is First Again." *Phoenix Gazette*, March 9, 1965, p. 49.

Honan, William H. "Felicia Shpritzer Dies at 87; Broke Police Gender Barrier." *New York Times*, December 31, 2000.

Hospodar, Paul. "Speaking About L.A. Police Job Opportunities." *Van Nuys (CA) News*, November 14, 1968, p. 2-A.

"It's the Law: Policewomen Must Enroll in Judo Class." *Black Belt Magazine*, December 1966, p. 50.

Johnson, Erskine. "Female Friday Will Prowl." *Rhinelander (WI) Daily News*, September 26, 1957, p. 6.

Joseph, Frank. "Suburb Gets First Girl Cop." *Appleton (WI) Post-Crescent*, September 29, 1964.

Kidder, Karl. "Fresno Policewomen Find Job Rough on Complexion." *Fresno Bee*, July 21, 1953.

Leedom, Robert. "First Woman Detective Joins Pasadena Police." *Pasadena (CA) Independent*, March 28, 1968, p. B-7.

"LSD, Heroin Easy to Get in Portland." *Pasco, Kennewick, Richland (WA) Tri-City Herald*, January 19, 1968, p. 24.

Maddock, Don. "Policewoman Still Typical Women." *Long Beach (CA) Independent-Press-Telegram*, March 31, 1963, p. A-3.

"Masquerading Fugitive Seized By Policewoman." *Zanesville (OH) Times Recorder*, June 27, 1953, p. 1.

McLoughlin, John. "Mrs. Barnes Wins Suit but Resigns as Cohoes Policewoman." *Troy (NY) Times-Record*, February 14, 1966, p. 1.

Messerly, Grant V. "Daughter for Car? Pair Held." *Salt Lake Tribune*, November 9, 1961, p. B1.

"'Meter Maids,' Policewoman Suggested in Haughey Plan." *Berkshire Eagle*, August 6, 1960, p. 13.

Miller, Laura J. "Frances Glessner Lee: Brief Life of a Forensic Miniaturist: 1878–1962." *Harvard Magazine*, September–October 2005.

"Minneapolis Policewoman Killed." *Scottsbluff (NE) Star-Herald*, August 3, 2002, p. 4C.

"Miss Police Becomes Detroit Policewoman." *Logansport (IN) Press*, October 18, 1950, p. 3.

"Miss Police Joins Up." *Wisconsin State Journal*, November 19, 1950, p. 5.

"Most of New Drug Addicts Juveniles, Policewoman Says." *Corpus Christi (TX) Times*, March 21, 1957, p. 7.

"Mother's a Cop on Night Shift." *Long Beach (CA) Independent-Press-Telegram*, November 22, 1959, p. A-12.

"New Program: Women Placed in Patrol Cars." *Morgantown (WV) Dominion News*, September 25, 1968, p. 9-B.

"New Teen-Age Fad: Carve or Sear Initials on Arms." *Albuquerque Journal*, August 22, 1952, p. 22.

"Nudist Colony Flourishes Within L.A. City Limits for Eleven Years." *Modesto Bee*, September 11, 1946, p. 2.

"N.Y. Policewoman Collects $3,018 for Maternity in Line of Duty." *El Paso Herald-Post*, June 18, 1965, p. D-14.

"N.Y. Policewoman Spurned Quiz Spot." *Syracuse (NY) Herald-Journal*, November 4, 1959.

"Obituary: Clare W. Faulhaber." *New York Times*, February 3, 2008.

"Omnipotent Youth Seized After Chase." *Eau Claire (WI) Daily Telegram*, July 27, 1968, p. 8B.

"125-Lb. Policewoman Throws Husky Mugger Down Subway Stairs." *North Adams (MA) Transcript*, October 11, 1955, p. 1.

"One Man's Army." *Time*, March 1, 1954.

Padgitt, James. "Around Hollywood." *New Castle (PA) News*, July 17, 1950, p. 9.

Pauley, Gay. "Petite Policewoman Has Long Record in Crime Prevention." *Coshocton (OH) Tribune*, October 20, 1959, p. 7.

"Peephole-Drilling Milkman Meets Chicago Policewoman Eye to Eye." *Terre (IN) Haute Star*, January 12, 1950, p. 1.

Plummer, Mary Elizabeth. "Women Invade Police Ranks." *Mansfield (OH) News-Journal*, August 27, 1950, p. 7.

"Policewoman Assists in Arrest of Fugitive Dressed as a Female." *Logansport (IN) Pharos-Tribune*, June 27, 1953, p. 14.

"Policewoman Cracks Smuggled Baby Ring." *Statesville (NC) Daily Review*, February 20, 1954, p. 1.

"Policewoman Defends the Female Cruiser Partner." *Cedar Rapids (IA) Gazette*, September 25, 1968, p. 12B.

"Policewoman Dies on Job." *Nashua (NH) Telegraph*, December 27, 1967, p. 34.

"Policewoman Does Routine Patrol Duty." *Troy (NY) Record*, November 29, 1969, p. B-22.

"Policewoman Earns Badge, Makes Uniform." *Hammond (IN) Times*, July 3, 1966, p. 1.

"Policewoman Files Suit for Promotion." *Jefferson City (MO) Post-Tribune*, September 7, 1961, p. 10.

"Policewoman Fired as Red." *Troy (NY) Times Record*, January 27, 1954, p. 19.

"Policewoman Has Own Cruiser." *Massillon (OH) Evening Independent*, July 22, 1965, p. 5.

"Policewoman Helps Save Airman from Death Leap." *Corpus Christi (TX) Times*, June 1, 1956, p. 1.

"Policewoman in Nun's Habit Halts Shakedown Plot." *Cedar Rapids (IA) Gazette*, March 4, 1969, p. 11A.

"Policewoman Quits, Accuses Chief of Making Advances." *Wisconsin State Journal*, July 18, 1953.

"Policewoman Quits Before Demotion Hits." *Jefferson City (MO) Sunday News and Tribune*, April 27, 1958, p. 16.

"Policewoman Quits in Huff at St. Louis." *Chillicothe (MO) Constitution-Tribune*, August 3, 1954, p. 3.

"Policewoman Retires but Stays Active." *Troy (NY) Times-Record*, January 20, 1968, p. 16.

"Policewoman Says Calls for Aid Bring Help Fast." *San Antonio Express*, November 3, 1972, p. 4-A.

"Policewoman Seals Teenage Drug Case." *Corpus Christi (TX) Times*, May 20, 1959, p. 9-C.

"Policewoman Serves as 10-Minute Chief." *Paris (TX) News*, September 11, 1958, p. 4.

"Policewoman Tells How She Made False Love to Sinatra." *El Paso Herald-Post*, March 8, 1957, p. 40.

"Policewoman Uses Scientific Routine in Sleuthing Job." *Charleston (WV) Gazette*, April 12, 1953, p. 37.

"Policewoman Who 'Joined' CP Names Teacher as Communist." *Hornell (NY) Evening Tribune*, October 3, 1950, p. 1.

"Policewoman Wins Honors." *Troy (NY) Record*, July 9, 1959, p. 23.

"Policewoman's Charge of Sex Discrimination Is Upheld." *Modesto Bee,* February 14, 1966, p. A-12.

"Policewomen Ask Equal Pay, Cite Discrimination." *Cedar Rapids (IA) Gazette*, June 18, 1969, p. 12B.

"Policewomen Speak." *Syracuse (NY) Herald-American*, December 19, 1965, p. 35.

Robles, Rosalie. "She's a Trim Pert Lady Cop." *Tucson Daily Citizen*, June 23, 1960, p. 28.

"Rookie Cops Net Dope Peddlers." *Bridgeport (CT) Post*, January 24, 1967, p. 11.

Ross, Sid, and Ed Kiester. "Tomboys with Knives: A New National Problem." *Parade*, April 17, 1955, pp. 10–11, 13.

Shearer, Lloyd. "The Two Worlds of a Policewoman." *Parade*, March 16, 1969, pp. 7–9.

" 'She's Important,' Says Sheriff of Policewoman." *Daily Northwestern*, February 3, 1968, p. 8.

"Shoplifting Gang of Girls Broken Up." *Bridgeport (CT) Telegram*, December 29, 1956, p. 7.

"Singing Star Held on Dope Charge." *Eau Claire (WI) Daily Telegram*, March 17, 1953, p. 9.

Stevens, Boyd. "Question-Aires." *Dunkirk (NY) Evening Observer*, January 19, 1963, p. 2.

"Stockton Policewoman Who Helped Break Up Dope Ring Gets Threat." *Modesto Bee*, February 3, 1958, p. 16.

"Strengthening the Police Force." *Jefferson City (MO) Post-Tribune*, October 9, 1953, p. 10.

"Three Cops Quit as Woman Joins Force." *Paris (TX) News*, November 14, 1957, p. 1.

"Throw 'Book' at Youth." *Hammond (IN) Times*, December 12, 1956, p. B-3.

Toomey, Elizabeth. "Housework Builds Power to Pass Policewoman Test." *Elyria (OH) Chronicle-Telegram*, August 27, 1954, p. 13.

"Top Cop Draws Whistles." *Jefferson City (MO) Daily Capital News*, November 4, 1972, p. 15.

"Two Women Seek Vice Presidency." *Billings (MT) Gazette*, July 20, 1952, p. 18.

"University Instructor's Wife Is First City Policewoman." *Albuquerque Journal*, May 3, 1954, p. 18.

Vernon, Terry. "Tele-Vues: *Policewoman U.S.A.*" *Long Beach (CA) Independent*, January 17, 1951, p. 28.

Walters, Fred. "The Philadelphia Story: Undercover Agents Trap Dope Peddlers." *Cedar Rapids (IA) Gazette*, December 18, 1955, p. 14.

"The Weaker Sex?" *Sheboygan (WI) Press*, August 20, 1956, p. 24.

Wearsch, Irene. "Her Job Is Most Important Thing to Amherst's Only Policewoman." *Elyria (OH) Chronicle-Telegram*, March 2, 1962.

"Woman Accused of Hair-Pulling to be Arraigned." *Albuquerque Journal*, February 28, 1969, p. A-6.

"Women Get Wild Ride." *Southern Illinoisian*, July 26, 1968, p. 17.

"Women on the Rise on City's Police Force." *Indianapolis Business Journal*, September 28, 1998.

Wood, Betty. "Women in the News: Barbara Fitzimmons." *Andersonville (IL) Herald*, October 6, 1968, 16.

Wood, Ray. "Former L.A. Policewoman Now Hangtown Housewife." *Placerville (CA) Times*, December 6, 1962.

"Young Policewoman, Teenager Team." *San Antonio Express*, September 15, 1959, p. 1.

Chapter 5

"Angie Dickinson Cops Police Role." *San Antonio Express*, March 25, 1974, p. 10.

Arnold, Roxanne. "'Calamity Jane': Rotten Luck Is Officer's Beat." *Los Angeles Times*, December 24, 1986, p. OC12.

"Arresting Preconceptions." *Time*, May 27, 1974.

"Austin Gets 1st Women." *Austin (TX) American-Statesman*, March 2, 1976.

Baldwin, Tom. "State Police-Woman Quits Force, Charges Harassment." *Dubois (PA) Courier-Express*, June 14, 1974, p. 1.

"Barger Tried to Fashion Reputation as Reformer." *Oil City (PA) Derrick*, January 14, 1976, p. 2.

"Being Chicago's First Mounted Policewoman Has Its Advantages, Too." *Jefferson City (MO) News Tribune*, August 24, 1975.

Berls, Jodi. "'I Am the MoPac Rapist,' Man Says; Policewoman's 3-Week Search of Database Led to Suspect's Arrest." *Austin (TX) American-Statesman*, September 2, 1996, p. A1.

"Black Policewoman Finished in Flint?" *Benton Harbor–St. Joseph (MI) Herald-Palladium*, October 22, 1977, p. 14.

Breslau, Karen. "A New Team in Town." *Newsweek*, October 24, 2005, p. 64.

Brown, Peter. "SF's Lady Cops—Far from TV." *New Mexican*, April 30, 1976, p. A8.

Buck, Jerry. "Actress Favors Sex Appeal in Screen Realism of Today." *Lumberton (NC) Tobesonian*, November 18, 1974, p. 5.

Burnett, Sara. "Challenge Tempts Political Novice." *Alton (IL) Telegraph*, January 24, 1995, p. 1.

Carlson, Brad. "State Police Plan $2M Regional Office Near Jerome." *Idaho Business Review*, September 11, 2001.

Casey, Phil. "Women Seeking Jobs That Were Once Considered Strictly Male." *Greeley (CO) Tribune*, August 22, 1969, p. 26.

Chang, Cindy. "Edward M. Davis, 89, Ex-Police Chief, Dies." *New York Times*, April 26, 2006.

Cheshire, Ashley. "Policewoman Prove Capabilities on Patrol Duty." *Tucson Daily Citizen*, August 16, 1972, p. 15.

"Chief Frank's 'Girl Friday,'" *Sheboygan (WI) Journal*, November 18, 1972, p. 34.

Crane, Tricia. "Lady Cop Cashes In on Capers." *Valley News*, October 20, 1977, p. 3.

"Crime Stopper Causes Traffic Jam." *Columbus (NE) Telegram*, April 30, 1976, p. 2.

"Department Doesn't Support Firing." *Ironwood (MI) Daily Globe*, May 30, 1980, p. 6.

"Detroit Policewoman Regains Job." *Alton (IL) Telegraph*, June 12, 1980, p. B-9.

"Discrimination Suit Settled in Peterboro." *Nashua (NH) Telegraph*, February 14, 1978, p. 13.

"Drug Dealer Says He Paid Former Policewoman for Information." *Florence (SC) Morning News*, October 17, 2008.

Durbak, Meghan. "Mom on the Force." *Kokomo (IN) Tribune*, May 11, 2008, p. A6.

Dwyer, Jim. "A Policewoman Looks Back on the Craziest of Love Duets." *New York Times*, May 23, 2007.

Edmonds, Richard. "Chief Stops Porno Film; Policewoman Had Role." *Des Moines Register*, August 23, 1977, p. 2B.

Eisenberg, Adam C. "The First Nine: Lure of Equal Pay Changed SPD Culture Forever." *Seattle Post Intelligencer*, October 28, 2001, p. D-4.

"Experts Debate Bulletproof Vests." *Gettysburg (PA) Tribune*, January 4, 1996, p. A5.

Evans-Nash, Vickie. "Deborah Montgomery Seeks to Retain St. Paul Ward 1 Seat." *Minnesota Spokesman-Record*, March 3, 2007.

"Fired Cop Who Had Sex Change Wants Job Back." *Chicago Daily Herald*, August 28, 1982, p. 5.

"First Black Policewoman Named to Oakland Force." *Oxnard (CA) Press-Courier*, December 16, 1970, p. 3.

"Flatfoot Floozies." *Time*, May 18, 1970.

Fogg, Susan. "Women Make Good Cops." *Beckley (WV) Post-Herald and Register*, May 26, 1974, p. 8.

"Former Model Discusses First Duty as Oakland Policewoman." *Ukiah (CA) Daily Journal*, June 27, 1978, p. 8.

"Former Nun Is Prostitute for Police." *Lincoln (NE) Star*, August 23, 1976, p. 3.

"Gunshot Scares Crowd at Trial of Policewoman." *St. Joseph (MI) Herald-Palladium*, June 3, 1976, p. 8.

"Hire Woman, Judge Tells Police Force." *Ogden (UT) Standard-Examiner*, May 15, 1974, p. 8A.

"Hooker Real Crime Stopper," *Brownsville (TX) Herald*, April 30, 1976, p. 16.

Ingersoll, Brenda. "Pioneer Female Officers Honored." *Wisconsin State Journal*, February 17, 1999, p. 1C.

Jones, James and Jason Cherkis. "Cathy Lanier's On-the-Job Training." *Washington City Paper*, November 29, 2006. http://www.washingtoncitypaper. com/lips/2006/lips1201.html.

Kaleina, Georgene. "Police Decoy: Learning to Act Like a Prostitute Rough." *Frederick (MD) News*, August 14, 1978, p. B-5.

Keener, Avery. "'Bull's-Eye Betty' Is Top Policewoman." *Aiken (SC) Standard*, December 3, 1970, p. 5-B.

Kerr, Adelaide. "That Glamor Girl May Be a Lady Cop." *Uniontown (PA) Morning Herald*, September 19, 1947, p. 7.

Kucmierz, Ginny. "Clerk Dons Police Garb." *Roselle (IL) Register*, December 9, 1978, p. 1.

"Lady Cop Centerfold: Everyone Wants a Peek." *Elyria (OH) Chronicle-Telegram*, April 1, 1982, p. A-4.

"Lady Cop Killed on Duty." *Florence (SC) Morning News*, September 21, 1974, p. 8-C.

"Lady Cop Reinstated After 'Stripped' of Job." *Elyria (OH) Chronicle-Telegram*, April 10, 1985, p. D-3.

"Life on the Run Ends for *Playboy* Waitress." *Aiken (OH) Standard*, October 18, 1990, p. 2A.

Macht, Maury. "There's a Woman on City Police Beat." *Hagerstown (MD) Daily Mail*, April 1, 1977, p. 13.

"Madeline Fletcher Gets Police Job Back and $7,000." *Jet*, October 1976, p. 28.

"Man Arrested, Charged in Policewoman's Killing." *Sunday Intelligencer/ Montgomery County (MD) Record*, September 23, 1984, p. A-6.

McDowell, Jeanne. "Are Women Better Cops?" *Time*, February 17, 1992, p. 70.

McKinney, Joan. "Saundra Scores a Police First." *Oakland Tribune*, December 14, 1970, p. 28.

Mermigas, Diane. "Angie Objects to Pepper's Use of Spice to Lure Bad Guys, Audience." *Arlington Heights (IL) Daily Herald*, March 10, 1978, pp. 4–7.

Montgomery, Deborah Gilbreath. Interview with Kate Cavett, July 11, 2005. http://www.oralhistorian.org/SPPD___Montgomery.htm.

"Moral: Never Kiss a Policewoman." *Long Beach (CA) Press-Telegram*, December 12, 1977, p. A-10.

"Not 'Out to Lunch,' But 'Out to Sex.'" *Moberly (MO) Monitor-Index*, October 25, 1972, p. 19.

"NYC Policewoman Files Harassment Suit." *Albany (NY) Times Union*, August 16, 1994, p. B2.

O'Brien, Matt. "Female Employees Sue Hayward Police Department." *Oakland Tribune*, November 14, 2007.

"Officer Is Awarded Back Pay." *New York Times*, November 10, 1985.

"Officer Testifies Against Moses." *Logansport (IN) Pharos-Tribune*, February 13, 1985, p. 14.

"Pantsuits for Policewomen Given Go-Ahead by Nichols." *Detroit News*, c. 1971, issue data unavailable, via Criminal Justice and Law Center, Lansing Community College.

Parker, John. "Policewoman Fatally Shoots Man." *Albuquerque Tribune*, March 19, 1976, p. 1.

Pauley, Gay. "Policewomen Performing the Same Duties as Policemen." *Brownsville (TX) Herald*, April 7, 1974, p. 7-C.

___. "This Nun Is Policewoman and Carries a Gun in D.C." *Bridgeport (CT) Post*, May 25, 1970, p. 26.

"Police Biased Against Women." *Jefferson City (MO) Post-Tribune*, April 12, 1972, p. 13.

"Policewoman Doesn't See Sense in her Reassignment." *Lincoln (NE) Star*, April 1, 1977, p. 12.

"Policewoman Files Discrimination Suit." *Tyrone (PA) Daily Herald*, February 11, 1976, p. 8.

"Policewoman, 51, Surrenders Star to Become Nun." *Cedar Rapids (IA) Gazette*, August 30, 1964, p. 8-C.

"Policewoman Finds Decoy Role Boring." *Lima (OH) News*, July 27, 1974, p. 8.

"Policewoman Given $100,000." *Alton (IL) Telegraph*, March 31, 1987, p. A-4.

"Policewoman Gunned Down." *Ironwood (MI) Daily Globe*, September 22, 1984, p. 7.

"Policewoman Has No Regrets over Photographs in *Playboy*." *Marysville (OH) Journal-Tribune*, March 30, 1982, p. 4.

"Policewoman Is Back in School." *St. Joseph (MI) Herald-Palladium*, October 12, 1976, p. 9.

"Policewoman Is Fired by Board." *Holland (MI) Evening Sentinel*, July 21, 1971, p. 22.

"Policewoman Nabs Airport Gunman." *Mexico (MO) Ledger*, January 20, 1973, p. 1.

"Policewoman Nabs Cop in Assault Case." *Tyrone (PA) Daily Herald*, June 8, 1979, p. 4.

"Policewoman Quits—for Two Reasons." *Tucson Daily Citizen*, November 13, 1970, p. 30.

"Policewoman Receives High Rank." *Cedar Rapids (IA) Gazette*, January 24, 1972, p. 12.

"Policewoman Sees Different World at Job." *Abilene (TX) Reporter-News*, August 23, 1976, p. 12-A.

"Policewoman's Sex Bias Complaint Rejected By State." *Sheboygan (WI) Press*, December 29, 1976, p. 3.

"Policewoman Suggests Women on Patrol Duty." *Albuquerque Journal*, December 10, 1971, p. E-9.

"Policewoman to Continue Fight in Sex Battle." *Connellsville (PA) Daily Courier*, March 8, 1976, p. 4.

"Policewoman to Head Street Patrol Group." *Panama City (FL) News-Herald*, July 5, 1971, p. 9A.

"Policewomen Fine on Patrol." *Bucks County (PA) Courier Times*, May 20, 1974, p. 5.

"Policewomen to Appeal Firings for Cowardice." *Alton (IL) Telegraph*, March 19, 1980, p. A-7.

"Policewomen to Get Tougher Duty." *Oshkosh (WI) Daily Northwestern*, June 10, 1974, p. 20.

"A Pregnant Policewoman Files Suit." *Fresno Bee*, January 5, 1977, p. B8.

Reinhold, Robert. "Policewoman in Denim Is Betty Grable of Gulf." *Provo Journal*, February 15, 1991.

Scharper, Julie. "Annapolis Force's First Woman Retires." *Baltimore Sun*, September 11, 2008.

Schuetz, Lisa. "Retired Cop Recalls Blazing a Couple Trails." *Wisconsin State Journal*, October 2, 2004, p. B1.

Schulz, Dorothy Moses. "A More Level Playing Field." *Law Enforcement News*, September 30, 2000.

"Sex Discrimination Case Goes to Court." *Gettysburg (PA) Times*, January 5, 1972, p. 6.

Sharbutt, Eve. "Policewoman on Beat Carries Nightstick as Well as Lipstick." *Oxnard (CA) Press-Courier*, November 28, 1972, p. 9.

Siegel, Micki. "Undercover Cop Kathy Burke: She Flirts with Danger." *Parade*, October 17, 1976, p. 8.

Simms, Gregory. "Race and Sex: Keys to Lady Cop's Case in Police Shootout." *Jet*, March 25, 1976, pp. 24–27.

"Sue Ane Langdon's Ideas on a Policewoman's Life." *TV Times*, November 10, 1973, p. 7.

"Suspended Policewoman Sues for $1 Million." *Galveston Daily News*, April 27, 1982, p. 5-B.

"Task Described as 'Immoral.'" *Victoria (TX) Advocate*, May 21, 1970, p. 7B.

Terry, Mary. "Officer Finds Work a Challenge." *Columbia (SC) State*, December 20, 1973, p. D1.

Thomas, Phil. "Lady Cop Turns Writer." *Jefferson City (MO) Post Tribune*, June 13, 1973, p. 10.

"Title VII Bars Physical Test for Police Women." *Juvenile Justice Digest* 31 (December 2005), p. 2.

"Vice Officers Try to Arrest Each Other." *Chillicothe (OH) Constitution-Tribune*, June 22, 1982, p. 6.

"Virginia Policewoman Shoots, Wounds Man." *High Point (NC) Enterprise*, March 9, 1976, p. 1.

"Wanted: One Uniform to Make 123 Officers Look Great." *Detroit News*, February 20, 1974, via Criminal Justice and Law Center, Lansing Community College.

Westfeldt, Amy. "Female Police Officer Shot, Killed During Bank Robbery." *Indiana Gazette*, January 3, 1996, p. 3.

White, Ron. "San Antonio's Lady Cops." *San Antonio Light*, February 15, 1970, p. 9.

Witt, Linda. "The Force Says It's with Them, but Detroit's Women Cops Have Had to Fight for Acceptance." *People*, October 6, 1980.

"Woman, 22, Bans Pusher of Drugs." *Pasadena (CA) Star-News*, December 9, 1971, p. C-2.

"Woman Helps Vice Squads." *Idaho Free Press & News-Tribune*, July 15, 1974, p. 11.

"The Women in Blue." *Time*, May 1, 1972.

"Young Lady Keeps Fighting to Become Police Officer." *Lebanon (PA) Daily News*, June 25, 1970, p. 34.

Chapter 6

Arnold, Roxane. "'Calamity Jane': Rotten Luck Is Officer's Beat." *Los Angeles Times*, December 24, 1986, p. OC12.

Arnold, Roxane. "Injury-Prone Officer Falls Prey Again." *Los Angeles Times*, December 25, 1986, p. A4.

Baker, Al. "911 Dispatchers Still Haunted by Voices of September 11th Attacks." *Indiana Gazette,* April 17, 2002, p. 9.

Lisa Belkin, "Woman Named Police Chief of Houston." *New York Times,* January 20, 1990.

Blackburn, Daniel. "A Penny for His Thoughts." *New Times,* August 25, 2004. http://archive.newtimesslo.com/archive/2004-08-25/archives/cov_stories_2004/cov_05052004.htm.

Breslau, Karen. "A New Team in Town." *Newsweek,* October 24, 2005, p. 64.

Cain, Brad. "Oregon's Gary-Marriage Foes Submit Record Signatures." *Seattle Times,* July 1, 2004.

Coddington, Brian. "Memorial Planned for Slain ISP Officer." *Spokane (WA) Spokesman-Review,* June 21, 1998.

Cole, Wendy. "To Each Her Own: Combining Talent and Drive, Ten Tough-Minded Women Create Individual Rules for Success." *Time,* November 8, 1990, 46.

"Controversial Policewoman to Appeal Firing." *Benton Harbor-St. Joseph (MI) Herald-Palladium,* November 12, 1976, p. 9.

"Cop Poses in *Playboy.*" *Extra Spin,* May 30, 2001. http://telepixtvcgi.warnerbros.com/reframe.html?http://telepixtvcgi.warnerbros.com/dailynews/extraspin/05_01/05_30a.html.

De La Cruz, Donna. "Remains of Only Policewoman Killed in WTC Attack Found." *Clute (TX) Facts,* March 22, 2002, p. 12A.

Delaney, Sean. "Discrimination Lawsuits Filed by 3 Dearborn Female Police Officers Continue to Generate Controversy." *Press and Guide,* January 6, 2008.

Egan, Timothy. "Chief of Police Becomes the Target in an Oregon Anti-Gay Campaign." *New York Times,* October 4, 1992.

Fahrenthold, Laura, Alice McQuillan, and Michael Lewittes. "Under Covers Cop Another Nudie Run for NYPD." *New York Daily News,* March 29, 1995.

Fernandez, A.M. "Rewind: Retired Raleigh Officer Polly Davis Denton." *Behind the Badge: Newsletter of the Raleigh Police Department,* February 2008.

"Field Day for Looters: 'If You See Something, You Take It.'" *Alton (IL) Telegraph,* May 1, 1992, p. C-3.

Fried, Joseph P. "Following Up: The 'N.Y.P.D. Nude' Enjoys Work Again." *New York Times*, August 8, 2004.

Harriston, Keith A., and Mary Pat Flaherty. "D.C. Police Paying for Hiring Binge." *Washington Post*, August 28, 1994, p. A-1.

Ho, Vanessa. "Same-Sex Marriages Voided in Oregon." *Seattle Post-Intelligencer*, April 15, 2005.

Hobson, Mafara. "Mayor-Elect Adrian Fenty Names Pick for D.C. Police Chief." News release, November 20, 2006.

Horne, Peter. "Policewomen: Their First Century and the New Era." *Police Chief*, September 2006. http://www.policechiefmagazine.org/magazine/ index.cfm?fuseaction=display_arch&article_id=1000&issue_id=92006.

"Idaho State Trooper Killed in Parking-Lot Shootout." *Seattle Times*, June 18, 1998.

James, George. "Police Officer in *Playboy*; This Time, Official Yawns." *New York Times,* June 27, 1994.

Johnson, Allen, Jr. "The Legacy of Officer Cotton." *New Orleans Magazine*, April 2008.

Johnson, Mike. "Pewaukee Officials Have Recordings of Police Chief." *Milwaukee Journal Sentinel*, September 23, 2007.

Kershaw, Sarah. "Oregon Supreme Court Invalidates Same-Sex Marriages." *New York Times*, April 15, 2005.

Knickerbocker, Brad. "Tug of War Intensifies on Gay-Marriage Issue." *Christian Science Monitor*, May 5, 2005.

Kutz, Martin. "LAPD Officer Bares All in Playboy Spread." *Los Angeles Daily News*, May 30, 2001.

Leusner, Jim. "Orlando's New Police Chief Brings Take-Charge Attitude to Job." *Orlando Sentinel,* November 28, 2007.

Lonsway, Kim. "Law and Order Roundtable Discussions: Police Women and the Use of Force." *Law and Order Magazine*, July 2001, pp. 109–14.

Los Angeles Police Department, "First Female Officer Promoted to Deputy Chief." *Los Angeles Police Beat Newsletter,* July 2000.

McLellan, Dennis. "Old Ties Unbound." *Los Angeles Times*, October 22, 1997, E-1.

McPhee, Michele. "Cop Left to Raise Daughter Coping with Loss." *Southern Illinoisian*, September 12, 2002, p. 3.

Meinke, Samantha. "Police Work Runs in Family." *Greater Lansing Woman*, December 2007, p. 70.

Munoz, Hilda. "Working to Get More Female Police Officers." *Los Angeles Times*, May 30, 2003, p. B-2.

O'Brien, Matt. "Female Employees Sue Hayward Police Department." *Oakland Tribune*, 14 November 2007.

"Officer Is Awarded Back Pay." *New York Times*, November 10, 1985.

"Officer's Harassment Suit." *New York Times*, August 16, 1994.

Phoenix Police Department. "Arizona Police Officer Jennifer Moore Inducted Into IACP/DuPont Kevlar Survivors' Club." Press release, November 12, 2008.

Pierson, David. "LAPD Officer Leaves Uniform Off for *Playboy*." *Los Angeles Times*, May 30, 2001, p. B-3.

"Policewoman Fired After Posing in Nude." *Daily Sitka (AK) Sentinel*, March 8, 1995, p. 10.

"Policewoman's Remains Found at WTC." *St. Petersburg (FL) Times*, March 21, 2002, p. 12A.

"Pregnancy and the Chief: Houston Chief of Police Elizabeth M. Watson Is Pregnant." *Time*, June 18, 1990, p. 23.

Reed, Susan. "Nicknamed 'Calamity Jane,' Rookie Cop Anita McKeown Gets Nothing but Bad Breaks." *People*, August 12, 1985.

Reinhold, Robert. "Policewoman in Denim Is Betty Grable of Gulf." *New York Times*, February 15, 1991.

"Rookie Cop Fatally Shot 4 Days After Graduation." *Arlington Heights (IL) Daily Herald*, February 24, 1994, p. 19.

Scarborough, Senta. "Phoenix Officer Is Shot During Routine Stop." *Arizona Republic*, June 30, 2008.

Schmitt, Ben. "City Officials May Be Tried for Allegedly Slandering Police." *Detroit Free Press*, January 24, 2008.

—, and Naomi R. Patton. "Bully-Cummings Retires Right After Mayor's Plea." *Detroit Free Press*, September 4, 2008.

Shapiro, Walter. "Reforming Our Image of a Chief." *Time*, November 26, 1990, pp. 80–82.

Shuster, Beth. "First She Sued County as Plaintiff, Now as Lawyer." *Los Angeles Times*, October 16, 2000, p. A-16.

__. "Sheriff's Dept. in Belated Effort to End Gender Bias." *Los Angeles Times*, October 16, 2000, p. A-1.

Spikol, Liz. "CSI: The Spikol Chronicles." *Philadelphia Weekly*, March 30, 2006, http://trouble.pwblogs.com/2006/03/30/csi-the-spikol-chronicles.

Spillar, Katherine, and Penny Harrington. "This Is What You Get When Men Rule Roost." *Los Angeles Times*, January 18, 2000, p. B-9.

Suro, Roberto. "Houston Mayor Removes Female Police Chief." *New York Times*, February 18, 1992.

Tearman, Margaret. "Cathy Lanier's Long Climb." *Bay Weekly*, January 25–31, 2007. http://www.bayweekly.com/year07/issuexv4/leadxv4_1.html.

"Top Cop in Buff Huff, Wants Play Time Over." *New York Daily News*, March 9, 1995.

"Topics: On the Street Police Story." *New York Times*, August 2, 1985.

"Trooper Says She Feared Heckling If She Helped King." *Elyria (OH) Chronicle-Telegram*, March 30, 1993, p. A-6.

Valdez, Angela. "Feeling Blue." *Washington City Paper*, May 2, 2007. http://www.washingtoncitypaper.com/display.php?id=1397.

"Women Cops on the Beat." *Time*, March 10, 1980.

Chapter 7

Shapiro, Walter. "Reforming Our Image of a Chief." *Time*, November 26, 1990, p. 80.

OTHER SOURCES

Albiston, Barbara. "Crime Fighting 'Mothers': A History of Female Law Enforcement Officers." *Bulletin of the Idaho Peace Officer Standards & Training Academy*, March 2001.

Baker, Lynda M. "The Information Needs of Female Police Officers Involved in Undercover Prostitution Work." *Information Research*, October 2004, http://informationr.net/ir/10-1/paper209.html.

Blake, Fanchon, et al., Plaintiffs-Appellants, v. City of Los Angeles et al., Defendants-Appellees, 595 F.2d 1367 (9th Cir. 1979). Federal Circuits, 9th Circuit. Docket number 77-3595,77-3601, May 2, 1979.

Bouman v. Block, 940 F.2d 1211 (9th Cir., 1991).

Bureau of Transportation Statistics, Research and Innovative Technology Administration. "Table 1-11: Number of U.S. Aircraft, Vehicles, Vessels, and Other Conveyances." http://www.bts.gov/publications/national_transportation_statistics/html/table_01_11.htm.

"D.C.'s First Female Police Chief Not Afraid of a Challenge." *CNN: People You Should Know,* May 8, 2007. http://www.cnn.com/2007/US/05/08/pysk.lanier/index.html.

Fletcher, Connie. "The 250-Pound Man in an Alley: Police Storytelling." *Journal of Organizational Change Management* 9, no. 5 (1996), pp. 36–42.

Grant, Susan. "Does TV Degrade Female Officers?" Officer.com. http://www.officer.com/web/online/Police-Life/Does-TV-Degrade-Female-Officers/17$34717.

Hickman, Kenneth G. "Measuring Job Performance Success for Female Officers of the Los Angeles Police Department." Ph.D. dissertation submitted to the faculty of the Department of Criminal Justice, Claremont Graduate University, Claremont, CA. 1983.

Horne, Peter. "The Role of Women in Law Enforcement." Thesis presented to the faculty of the Department of Police Science, California State University, Los Angeles. 1972.

Jones, Robin. "Recruiting Women." *Police Chief,* April 2004.

Kelly, Don. "History of the Baton Rouge Police Department." E-mail to author, November 21, 2008.

Lonsway, Kim. "Police Women and the Use-of-Force." *Law & Order,* July 2001, pp. 109–14.

Los Angeles Police Department. *Affirmative Action Program.* LAPD, 1992.

Lunneborg, Patricia Wells, and Roberta Wells Ryan. "Fictional Women Police: How Close to the Facts?" *Women Police* 35, no. 4 (Winter 2001), p. 16.

Marzuk, Peter M.; Matthew K. Nock; Andrew C. Leon; Laura Portera; and Kenneth Tardiff. "Suicide Among New York City Police Officers, 1977–1996." *American Journal of Psychiatry*, December 2002, pp. 2069–71.

New York City Police Museum. "Women in Policing." http://www.nycpolice-museum.org/html/tour/wip_web.htm.

Nixon, Richard. *Statement About Signing the Equal Employment Opportunity Act of 1972*. March 25, 1972. http://www.presidency.ucsb.edu/ws/index.php?pid=3358.

Officer Down Memorial Page. "Police Officer Moira Smith." http://www.odmp.org/officer/15104-state-trooper-linda-carol-huff.htm.

___. "State Trooper Linda Carol Huff." http://www.odmp.org/officer/15818-police-officer-moira-smith.

Orlov, Rick. "Event Honors Department's First Female Officers." *Los Angeles Daily News*, November 23, 1996.

"Person of the Week: Ella Bully-Cummings." *ABC World News Tonight*, November 14, 2003. http://www.abcnews.go.com/WNT/personofweek/story?id=131845.

Police Foundation. "About the Police Foundation." http://www.policefoundation.org/docs/history.html.

Portsmouth Police Department, "Portsmouth Police Department History." http://www.cityofportsmouth.com/Police/depart-history.htm.

Powell, George W. "Report of [the] Superintendent of Police," *City of Indianapolis Annual Report for 1894*. January 1, 1895. http://edit.indygov.org/NR/rdonlyres/8D5B8B80-97C1-41B8-A097-E7C016B2BB17/0/1894AnnualReport.pdf.

Ryan, Gail. "Legendary Ladies of the LAPD." Los Angeles Women Police Officers and Associates, 2007. http://www.lawpoa.org/history.htm.

Sichel, Joyce L.; Lucy N. Friedman; Janet C. Quint; and Michael E. Smith. *Women on Patrol: A Pilot Study of Police Performance in New York City*. Washington, D.C.: National Institute of Law Enforcement and Criminal Justice, Law Enforcement Assistance Administration, U.S. Department of Justice, January 1978.

Tapper, Jake, and Max Culhane. "She's the Chief: From High School Dropout to the Capital's First Female Police Chief." *ABC News*, January 29, 2007. http://abcnews.go.com/Nightline/story?id=2821100&page=1.

U.S. Congress. House of Representatives. Committee on Un-American Activities. *Testimony of Miss Stephanie Horvath, New York City Police.* 84th Cong., 2nd sess., June 14, 1956.

——. Senate. Permanent Subcommittee on Investigation of the Committee on Government Operations. *Testimony of Miss Ruth Eagle, New York City Police.* 83rd Cong., 2nd sess., pursuant to S. Res. 189, September 28, 1953.

——. Senate. Subcommittee to Investigate the Administration of the Internal Security Act and Other Internal Security Laws of the Committee on the Judiciary. *Testimony of Stephanie Horvath, Detective, New York City Police Department. Scope of Soviet Activity in the United States.* 85th Cong., 1st sess., August 14, 1957.

U.S. Department of Justice, Office of Justice Programs, Bureau of Justice Statistics. "Law Enforcement Statistics." http://www.ojp.usdoj.gov/bjs/lawenf. htm.

U.S. Department of Labor, Women's Bureau. "Quick Stats 2007." http://www. dol.gov/wb/stats/main.htm.

U.S. District Court for the District of Columbia. *Deposition of Sgt. Cathy Lynn Lanier.* Civil Action No. 95-1297 (SS), Washington, D.C., April 16, 1996.

Vaughan, Michele. "History of Women in the Ohio State Highway Patrol." Ohio State Highway Patrol. http://statepatrol.ohio.gov/recruitment/ FemaleMinority/historywomen.htm.

INTERVIEWS

The author conducted interviews with the following people from August 2008 through February 2009.

Abner, Roberta—Los Angeles County Sheriff's Department
Aguinaga, Veneza—Austin, (TX), Police Department

Bailor, Christine—Richmond (VA) Police Department

Bacus, Donna—Iowa State Patrol

Baker, Marilyn—Los Angeles Sheriff's Department

Burrascano, Lucille—New York Police Department

Bradbury, Beth—Idaho State Police

Castro, Lynda—Los Angeles County Sheriff's Department

Cotten, Michelle—Virginia State Police

Crews-Carey, Jennifer—Annapolis (MD) Police Department

Couper, David—Madison (WI) Police Department

Darbonne (Howard), Juanita—Oakland (CA) Police Department

Desimini, Lisa—Author/Artist

Diké (Greene), Ethel—Columbia (SC) Police Department

Downing, M. Rebecca—York County (PA) Police Department

Fleming, Rhonda—Texas Highway Patrol

Fogt, Virginia—Ohio State Highway Patrol

Fox, Peggy—Topeka (KS) Police Department

Fry, Lora Lee (Lori)—Madison (WI) Police Department

Gerhardt, Judy—Los Angeles County Sheriff's Department

Greear, Jonelle—Idaho State Highway Patrol

Grimes, Julia—Alaska State Troopers

Halloran, Joan—Chicago Police Department

Jaramillo, Bernadette—New Mexico State Patrol

Jaramillo, Sara—Los Angeles Police Department

McGrath, Lori—Nevada Highway Patrol

Myer, Julie—Wisconsin State Police

Perry, Geraldine—Chicago Police Department

Rice, Jill—Indiana State Police

Robinson, Elizabeth—Indianapolis Police Department

Sanchez, Sheila—Los Angeles County Sheriff's Department

Sanders, Cheryl—Tennessee Highway Patrol

Scott, Alice—Los Angeles County Sheriff's Department

Spreckelmeyer, Shannon—Indiana State Police

Whitfield, Elizabeth—New Mexico State Police

Zangar, Kim—Washington State Patrol

ENDNOTES

CHAPTER I

1   New York City Police Museum, "Women in Policing," www.nycpolice-museum.org/html/tour/wip_web.htm.

2   Nell Irvin Painter, *Standing at Armageddon: The United States, 1877–1919* (New York: W. W. Norton, 1987), p. 231.

3   Mary Jenks, *Behind the Bars; or, Ten Years of the Life of a Police Matron* (Pawtucket, RI: Salisbury Manufacturing Company, 1902), p. 54.

4   "Managed by Women: They Preserve Model Discipline in the Prison for Women at Auburn," *Waterloo (IA) Courier*, February 5, 1896, p. 2.

5   "Matron Campbell Dead," *New York Times*, June 3, 1907, p. 7.

6   Joseph Howard, "About Two Women: Prison Matron Foster and Prima Donna Patti," *Syracuse (NY) Herald*, February 7, 1892, p. 7.

7   Joanne Belknap, *The Invisible Woman: Gender, Crime, and Justice* (Belmont, CA: Wadsworth/Thomson Learning, 2001), p. 160.

8   "Inspecting Prison Work: A Visit to the Kings County Penitentiary," *New York Times*, January 5, 1883, p. 8.

9   "A Police Matron: Influence of a Womanly Woman over a Despised and Hardened Outcast," *Lima (OH) Daily Times*, July 29, 1891, p. 2.

10 "A Month of Bourbon Rule: Making and Grabbing Offices Under Gov. Cleveland," *New York Times*, February 5, 1883, p. 1.

11 Editorial, *Fitchburg (MA) Sentinel*, August 11, 1887, p. 2.

12 "Brevities," *Davenport (IA) Tribune*, July 3, 1889, p. 2.

13 "The House of Detention," *Davenport (IA) Tribune*, March 7, 1891, p. 2.

14 "A Police Matron," *Decatur (IL) Morning Review*, September 17, 1890, p. 3.

15 New York City Police Museum, "Women in Policing."

16 Ibid.

17 "The First Municipal Woman Detective in the World," *New York Times*, March 3, 1912, p. SM1.

18 George W. Powell, "Report of [the] Superintendent of Police," *City of Indianapolis Annual Report for 1894*, January 1, 1895, 206, http://edit.indygov.org/NR/rdonlyres/8D5B8B80-97C1-41B8-A097-E7C016B2BB17/0/1894AnnualReport.pdf.

19 Jenks, *Behind the Bars*, p. vi.

20 Ibid., pp. 10–11.

21 Ibid., p. 11.

22 Ibid., pp. 31–32.

CHAPTER 2

23 "Policewoman Rides Horse: New Guardian of Cleveland Parks Will Make Young Men Behave," *New York Times*, June 7, 1914, p. 12.

24 "Policewomen," *New York Times*, March 31, 1880, p. 4.

25 "Tells Why Police Women Are Needed: Intelligent Handling of Social Evil Demands Them, Says Miss Milholland," *New York Times*, March 7, 1913, p. 20.

26 Ibid.

27 Ibid.

28 "The Only Policewoman," *Iowa State Press*, May 3, 1899, p. 7.

29 "Work of Policewomen: Miss Bixby Tells of Duties," *Indianapolis Star*, December 4, 1910, p. 39.

30 Ibid.

31 "Women Police Needed in Harlem, Declares Woman 'Cop,'" *Syracuse (NY) Herald*, January 23, 1910, p. 65.

32 "Why I Want to Be a Policewoman," *Oakland Tribune*, May 5, 1907.

33 "Call for Policewomen to Protect the Boys: Why Not? Asks Mrs. Goldzier, 'Clubwoman' of Bayonne," *New York Times*, March 7, 1907, p. 9.

34 "Police Women on View," *New York Times*, April 6, 1909, p. 6.

35 "Bayonne's Policewoman: When Mayor Appointed R. McAdie He Didn't Know Applicant's Sex," *New York Times*, April 25, 1914, p. 6.

36 "Woman Refuses to Stop Spooners," *New Castle (PA) News*, July 13, 1914, p. 8.

37 "Policewoman's Service," *Kansas City Journal* via *Indianapolis Star*, March 3, 1911, p. 8.

38 "Arrest by Policeman: Exhibition in Madison Square Garden Enlivened by Bluecoat in Skirts," *New York Times*, October 8, 1902, p. 9.

39 "Chicago's Policewoman," *Frederick (MD) Daily News*, December 6, 1907, p. 3.

40 "Female Copper Was Humiliated," *Longsport (IN) Daily Reporter*, May 12, 1909, p. 6.

41 "Girls Are Gaining," *Emporia (KS) Gazette*, May 13, 1909, p. 1.

42 "Husky Women Sought for the Police Force," *Atlanta Constitution*, July 10, 1913, p. 2.

43 "First Arrest by New Policewomen," *Fort Wayne (IN) Sentinel*, August 8, 1913, p. 6.

44 "The Policewoman," *Middletown (NY) Daily Times-Press*, August 12, 1913, p. 4.

45 "Police Woman on Motorcycle," *Ogden (UT) Evening Standard*, December 7, 1912, p. 14.

46 "Policewoman Rides Horse."

47 Lola Baldwin, "Our Policewomen," *Oregonian*, May 1953.

48 "Police Woman and Her Duty," *Oshkosh (WI) Daily Northwestern*, May 18, 1915, p. 9.

49 Alice Stebbins Wells, "Personal History of Los Angeles' First Policewoman," *Los Angeles Police Associations Bulletin*, October 1940, p. 5.

50 "Have Appointed 'Policewoman,'" *Cedar Rapids (IA) Evening Gazette*, August 5, 1910, p. 1.

51 Peter Horne, "The Role of Women in Law Enforcement" (thesis presented to the faculty of the Department of Police Science, California State University, Los Angeles, 1972), p. 26.

52 Larry Harnisch, "The Vexations of Research: Alice Stebbins Wells," *Los*

Angeles Times, August 19, 2007, http://latimesblogs.latimes.com/thedailymirror/2007/08/the-vexations-o.html.

53 Horne, "The Role of Women in Law Enforcement," p. 26.

54 "The Mother Police," *Washington Post*, July 30, 1916, p. 8.

55 "Policewoman Doing Satisfactory Work," *Salt Lake Tribune*, May 4, 1916, p. 12.

56 "Proper Policewoman," *Washington Post* via *Rochester Herald*, July 16, 1910, p. 4.

57 "Persecution Drove Policewoman from Racine, She Claims," *La Crosse (WI) Tribune and Leader-Press*, October 16, 1922, p. 6.

58 "Policewoman Is a Sphinx," *Stevens Point (WI) Daily Journal*, August 11, 1910, p. 3.

59 "Two of Police Women Refuse to Surrender," *San Antonio Light*, February 1, 1919, p. 3.

60 Ibid.

61 "Young Policewoman, Fired for Efficiency, Is Now Back on the Job," *Fort Wayne (IN) Sentinel* , May 27, 1913, p. 8.

62 Portsmouth Police Department, "Portsmouth Police Department History," http://www.cityofportsmouth.com/Police/depart-history.htm.

63 "Women to Be Cops," *Syracuse (NY) Herald*, September 19, 1911, p. 10.

64 Ibid.

65 Ella Wilson, "A Woman Tells Some of Her Interesting Experiences as Mayor of a City," *New York Times*, September 24, 1911, p. SM8.

66 "Policewoman at Movies," *New York Times*, June 19, 1914, p. 4.

67 "Policewoman to Sterilize Music," *La Crosse (WI) Tribune*, December 2, 1912, p. 1.

68 "Woman Wants Police Job: Mrs. O'Shea, Who Fought 'Spooning' in Ossining, Would Come Here," *New York Times*, November 12, 1921, p. 13.

69 "Puts Ban on Tango," *Oelwein (IA) Daily Register*, January 13, 1914, p. 2.

70 "Policewoman Follows Up Violations," *Olean (NY) Evening Herald*, February 18, 1919, p. 5.

71 "Pinch for a Pinch," *Logansport (IN) Pharos-Reporter*, March 5, 1919, p. 9.

72 "Lady Coppers in Quaker City," *Fond du Lac (WI) Daily Commonwealth*, February 5, 1913, p. 2.

73 "Keep Back Men! Hoseless Bath Suits Upheld," *Oakland Tribune*, August 17, 1919, p. B-5.

74 Barbara Craydon, "High Jinks in the English Surf," *Fort Wayne (IN) Sentinel*, August 16, 1919, p. 10.

75 "Policewomen Wash Rouged Girls' Faces," *New York Times*, November 30, 1918, p. 4.

76 "Police Recovered Thirty-One Cars Stolen in 1923, Report Says," *Appleton (WI) Post-Crescent*, February 19, 1924, p. 7.

77 "Healer Lays Curse on Police Woman: Anathema Against Miss Preiss Published in 'Ram's Horn,' Schlatter's Paper," *New York Times*, June 14, 1916, p. 6.

78 "Loiterers to Workhouse," *New York Times*, November 12, 1913, p. 3.

79 "Slave Ring Is Investigated by Policewoman," *Des Moines News*, April 28, 1916, p. 10.

80 "What One Woman Did to Become a Policewoman," *Hamilton (OH) Daily Republican-News*, July 15, 1914, p. 1.

81 "Postpone Policewoman Exams for Age 'Errors,'" *Oakland Tribune*, November 16, 1913, p. 2.

82 James Walter Smith, "Enter the Lady Cops of Gotham," *Boston Evening Transcript*, May 18, 1918, http://www.sameshield.com/press/sspress09aa.html.

83 "Policewoman Subdues Man: Pulls Fighter from a Chicago Street Car and Arrests Him," *New York Times*, December 27, 1913, p. 4.

84 "Policewoman, Not Scared, Says 'Rest Easy, I Pack a Gun,'" *New York Times*, May 17, 1922, p. 18.

85 "Woman Cop Cures Man of Flirting," *Logansport (IN) Pharos-Reporter*, May 17, 1919, p. 9.

86 "This Female Sampson [*sic*] to Guard Visitors at the Panama Expo," *Bismarck (ND) Daily Tribune*, February 19, 1915, p. 1.

87 Richard Feiner, "Blanche Payson," http://www.laurelandhardyarchive.com/stills/1-laurel-hardy/379-46-l32-07/associated/people/all/item/26-blanche-payson.

88 "Should Policewoman Wear Uniform? Delegates at Sea," *Indianapolis Star*, May 11, 1916, p. 4.

89 "A Gun? Too Heavy to Lug, Says Police Woman," *Lima (OH) Sunday News*, December 12, 1926, p. 11.

90 "Butte's Woman Officer Authorized to Carry Gun," *Anaconda (MT) Standard*, December 3, 1913, p. 7.

91 "Warren's Police Woman Success," *New Castle (PA) News*, September 11, 1917, p. 6.

92 "Police Women Not a Failure," *La Crosse (WI) Tribune*, April 7, 1914, p. 1.

93 "Suzanne Frances Napton Is Appointed W.C.T.U. Policewoman for Missouri," *Chillicothe (MO) Constitution*, September 24, 1915, p. 5.

94 Ibid.

95 Frederic J. Haskin, "Police Women in Washington," *Fitchburg (MA) Daily Sentinel*, December 27, 1918, p. 4.

96 "More Skirted Cops: Colored Women to Be Appointed with Full Police Power," *Washington Post*, August 2, 1918, p. 1.

97 Frederic J. Haskin, "Police Women in Washington," *Fitchburg (MA) Daily Sentinel*, December 27, 1918, p. 4.

98 Ibid.

99 "The Port of Missing Girls," *San Antonio Light*, July 25, 1920, p. 10-C.

100 Ibid.

101 Ibid.

102 Louise Egan Steele, "Policewoman's Lot Not an Ordinary One," *Pasadena (CA) Star-News*, July 28, 1977, p. B-2.

103 Ibid.

104 "More Skirted Cops."

105 "Woman Policemen to Protect Women," *Bismarck (ND) Tribune*, December 5, 1923, p. 7.

106 "Washington's Valiant Policewoman," *Brownsville (TX) Daily Herald*, November 15, 1923, p. 4.

107 "More Skirted Cops."

108 Appier, *Policing Women*, p. 34.

109 "Washington's Interesting Policewoman," *Mexia (TX) Evening News*, April 18, 1922, p. 5.

110 "Truck Injures Policewoman," *Washington Post*, November 12, 1918, p. 18.

111 "Take Suffragists at the Capital," *Stevens Point (WI) Journal*, June 23, 1917, p. 4.

112 Ibid.

113 Smith, "Enter the Lady Cops of Gotham."

114 "R. Wanamaker Made a Police Deputy," *New York Times*, February 26, 1918.

115 "Women's Auxiliary for Police Reserve," *New York Times*, May 10, 1918, p. 11.

116 Smith, "Enter the Lady Cops of Gotham."

117 Ibid.

118 "Duties of Women Police," *New York Times*, July 28, 1918, p. 31.

119 Ibid.

120 Ibid.

121 Ibid.

122 "How New York's Policewomen 'Spot' German Spies," *Washington Post*, September 15, 1918, p. 1.

123 Ibid.

124 Ibid.

125 E. M. Thierry, "N.Y. Policewoman Sets Off Bomb," *Wisconsin State Journal*, December 19, 1920.

126 Ibid.

127 "Policewoman Takes Rap at Those Prohibitionists," *Des Moines (IA) National-Democrat*, June 1, 1916, p. 4.

128 Ibid.

CHAPTER 3

129 Adelaide Kerr, "Women at Their Work, Lady Cop Likes Job," *Council Bluffs (IA) Nonapreil*, June 11, 1946, p. 6.

130 "The Girl Who Always Wanted to Be a Cop," *Syracuse (NY) Herald*, October 5, 1924, magazine section.

131 Phillip D. Schertzing, *Preserve, Protect and Defend: An Illustrated History of the Michigan State Police in the Twentieth Century* (Paducah, KY: Turner, 2002).

132 "Chief Opposed to Policewoman," *Hagerstown (MD) Daily Mail*, January 21, 1947, p. 1.

133 "Policewoman Proves Need, Official Says," *Blytheville (AR) Courier News*, August 16, 1928, p. 3.

134 "Washington Police Jobs Are Offered to Charleston Women," *Charleston (WV) Gazette*, November 11, 1928, p. 8.

135 Civil service advertisement, *Benton Harbor (MI) News-Palladium*, October 9, 1947, p. 13.

136 "Policewoman Exams to Be Held July 25," *Fayetteville (AR) Democrat*, July 11, 1923, p. 2.

137 "The Girl Who Always Wanted to Be a Cop," *Syracuse (NY) Herald*, October 5, 1924, magazine section.

138 Doris Scharfenberg, " 'The Division Has Become a Necessity,' " *Michigan History Magazine*, November–December 2002, p. 76.

139 "Webs to Catch the Broadway Butterflies," *Oakland Tribune*, April 13, 1930, p. 59.

140 Scharfenberg, " 'The Division Has Become a Necessity,' " p. 76.

141 "Crime Is a Medical Problem," *Elyria (OH) Chronicle-Telegram*, October 4, 1924, p. 10.

142 "Women Sherlocks Making Good in New York City," *San Antonio Express*, April 27, 1924, p. B-5.

143 "Learn Jiu-Jitsu, Advice of Veteran Policewoman," *Monesson (PA) Daily Independent*, March 13, 1936, p. 2.

144 "Scratch 'Em First; Then Pinch," *Lincoln (NE) Star*, March 21, 1924, p. 16.

145 "My Most Thrilling Moment: Mary E. Hamilton." *Oakland Tribune*, February 28, 1926.

146 Carol Bird, "Policewomen's School," *New York Times*, July 31, 1921, p. 74.

147 "Police Prepare to Protect N.Y. Visitors from Crooks," *Zanesville (OH) Times-Signal*, June 22, 1924, p. 6.

148 Mary E. Hamilton, "Identify Yourself," *Billings (MT) Gazette*, October 1, 1933, pp. 3, 13.

149 Kerr, "Women at Their Work," p. 6.

150 Mary Elizabeth Plummer, "Women Cops Varied Lot," *San Antonio Express*, May 4, 1941, p. 11.

151 Kerr, "Women at Their Work," p. 6.

152 Unsigned review of *My Double Life*, by Mary Sullivan, *Time*, July 11, 1938.

153 "In New York," *Fitchburg (MA) Sentinel*, November 17, 1924, p. 14.

154 "Very Few Women Are Bootleggers, Policewoman Says," *Bridgeport (CT) Telegram*, November 18, 1926, p. 16.

155 Ibid.

156 Joseph Barber, "Get Tough, Lady, If Molested, Says Policewoman in Salt Lake," *Ogden Standard-Examiner*, March 5, 1943, p. 1.

157 Larry Boardman, "Automobile and Liquor Termed Foes to Morals," *Ogden (UT) Standard-Examiner*, July 17, 1925, p. 1.

158 Ibid.

159 "Birth Control Raid," *Time*, April 29, 1929.

160 "Women Hoot, Jeer; Put Out of Courtroom," *Sioux City (IA) Journal*, April 25, 1929, p. 1.

161 "Masher Tries to Flirt with Wrong Woman," *Estherville (IA) Daily News*, September 12, 1946, p. 1.

162 Joseph Barber, "Get Tough, Lady, If Molested, Says Policewoman in Salt Lake," *Ogden (UT)Standard-Examiner*, March 5, 1943, p. 1.

163 "Policewoman Defends Sally [Rand] in Nude Dance," *Oakland Tribune*, September 26, 1933, p. B-10.

164 Ione Quinby, "University Town Puts 'O.K.' on Fan Dance Chicago Barred," *Massillon (OH) Evening Independent*, October 13, 1933, p. 7.

165 Arthur V. Deck, "Fan Dance Is Art; Jury Frees Girl," *Oakland Tribune*, June 8, 1935, p. C-2.

166 Ibid.

167 "Fan Dancer Says Act Is Art," *Zanesville (OH) Times Recorder*, November 14, 1946, p. 2.

168 "Sally Rand Still Says She's Artistic," *Idaho Falls Post-Register*, July 16, 1950, p. 6.

169 "State Is Closing Against Pantages," *Galveston (TX) Daily News*, October 15, 1929, p. 1.

170 "Nice Work If You Can Get It! But Beauty Contest Ends in Court," *Nevada State Journal*, May 7, 1938, p. 1.

171 Ibid.

172 "Four Little Boys Found Left Without Food, Fire or Sufficient Clothing," *Syracuse (NY) Herald*, January 14, 1936, p. 3.

173 "Crime Is a Medical Problem."

174 "Appleton's New Policewoman," *Appleton (WI) Post-Crescent*, April 6, 1922, p. 9.

175 "Most Girls Picked Up by Vice Squad Are Juveniles," *Corpus Christi (TX) Tribune*, July 16, 1947, p. B-1.

176 Gail Ryan, "Legendary Ladies of the LAPD," Los Angeles Women Police Officers and Associates, 2007, http://www.lawpoa.org/history.htm.

177 American Social Hygiene Association, *Journal of Social Hygiene, Volume I* (New York: Waverly Press, 1916), pp. 494–95.

178 "Score Taken in Raids on Slave Rings," *Helena (MT) Independent*, January 27, 1938, p. 1.

179 "Policewoman Blames Parents for Delinquency," *Syracuse (NY) Herald*, June 26, 1922, p. 10.

180 "Parents to Blame for Runaway Girls, Says Policewoman," *Wichita Daily Times*, May 16, 1921, p. 8.

181 "Woman Dies to Save 3 Children," *San Antonio Express*, March 14, 1930, p. 4.

182 Anna M. Brice, "Must Eliminate Politics in Chester to Cope with Crime, Policewoman Says." *Chester (PA) Times*, July 27, 1945, p. 1.

183 "Vamps Who Oggle Auto Drivers to Be Caught in Chicago Grill Drive," *Modesto Evening News*, July 27, 1922, p. 1.

184 "Lack of Courtesy Disturbs Women Who Drive Cars," *Montana Standard*, April 14, 1929, p. 7.

185 "Police Are Called, Not Undertaker," *Ogden (UT) Standard-Examiner*, December 30, 1928, p. 7.

186 "Policewoman Just Puts Gun on Them And . . . ," *Uniontown (PA) Morning Herald*, October 8, 1932, p. 5.

187 Mary Elizabeth Plummer, "Nurses, Pianists, Lawyers Hold Jobs on Force." *Nebraska State Journal*, April 25, 1941, p. 2.

188 Mary Elizabeth Plummer, "Women Invade Police Ranks," *Mansfield (OH) News-Journal*, August 27, 1950, p. 7.

189 "Downey Offers Motorcycles for Use of Policewomen," *Lowell (MA) Sun*, February 21, 1929, p. 1.

190 Plummer, "Women Cops Varied Lot."

191 Plummer, "Nurses, Pianists, Lawyers."

192 "Jobs Seeking Graduates as Result of War," *Tucson Daily Citizen*, July 14, 1943, p. 9.

193 "Woman Guards GI Equipment, with a Ready .45 at Her Hand," *Wisconsin State Journal*, July 10, 1944, p. 14.

194 Eleanor Ragsdale, "Capital's Juvenile Deliquency No. 1 Policewoman Headache," *Kingsport (LA) Times*, July 17, 1942, p. 2.

195 "Policewoman's Job Unchanged by War, Declares Mrs. Dukes," *New Castle (PA) News*, May 4, 1945, p. 11.

196 "High Wages Blamed for Delinquency," *Chicago (IL) Southtown Economist*, July 21, 1943, p. 1.

197 "Fresno Teacher Is Named City Policewoman," *Fresno Bee*, July 4, 1944, p. 1.

198 "Woman Dressed 'Coast Style' is Arrested," *El Paso Herald*, July 7, 1945, p. 1.

199 "Madison Not Jeep Track, Judge Rules," *Wisconsin State Journal*, June 4, 1943, p. 18.

200 "Mrs. Reese to Resign Police Job," *Wisconsin State Journal*, February 5, 1944, p. 1.

201 "Chief Asks Council to Exonerate Police in Beating of Wife," *El Paso Herald-Post*, November 28, 1944, p. 1.

202 "Chief Considering Moving Policewoman from Military Work," *El Paso Herald-Post*, December 1, 1944, p. 1.

203 Bessie Simpson, "Great-Grandmother of Eight Feted as 'Mother of the Year,'" *El Paso Herald-Post*, May 11, 1963, p. 8.

204 Ruth Millett, "We, the Women: Mary Shanley," *Wisconsin Rapids Daily Tribune*, February 1, 1939, p. 3.

205 James Lardner and Thomas Reppetto, *NYPD: A City and Its Police* (New York: Holt, 2001), p. 223.

206 New York City Police Museum, "Women in Policing," New York City Police Museum, http://www.nycpolicemuseum.org/html/tour/wip_web.htm.

207 "Policewomen Don Navy Blue Dress," *Detroit News*, July 29, 1942, via Criminal Justice and Law Center, Lansing Community College.

208 "Lady Cops Shriek 'No!' as Toy Unveils Uniform," *Detroit Free Press*, May 3, 1949, via Criminal Justice and Law Center, Lansing Community College.

CHAPTER 4

209 "Policewoman Defends the Female Cruiser Partner," *Cedar Rapids (IA) Gazette*, September 25, 1968, p. 12B.

210 Bureau of Transportation Statistics, Research and Innovative Technology Administration, "Table 1-11: Number of U.S. Aircraft, Vehicles, Vessels, and Other Conveyances," http://www.bts.gov/publications/national_transportation_statistics/html/table_01_11.htm.

211 Marion E. Gold, *Top Cops: Profiles of Women in Command* (Chicago: Brittany, 1999), p. 20.

212 "Strengthening the Police Force," *Jefferson City (MO) Post-Tribune*, October 9, 1953, p. 10.

213 Elizabeth Toomey, "Housework Builds Power to Pass Policewoman Test," *Elyria (OH) Chronicle-Telegram*, August 27, 1954, p. 13.

214 "The Weaker Sex?" *Sheboygan (WI) Press*, August 20, 1956, p. 24.

215 Ray Wood, "Former L.A. Policewoman Now Hangtown Housewife," *Placerville (CA) Times*, December 6, 1962.

216 Martha Schnabel, *Officer Mama* (San Antonio, TX: Naylor, 1973), p. 16.

217 Ibid., p. 21.

218 Sid Ross and Ed Kiester, "Tomboys with Knives: A New National Problem," *Parade Magazine*, April 17, 1955, pp. 10–11.

219 Ibid., p. 12.

220 "'Girl Gangs' Rivaling Boys in Philadelphia," *Monessen (PA) Daily Independent*, November 24, 1953, p. 1.

221 "Most of New Drug Addicts Juveniles, Policewoman Says," *Corpus Christi (TX) Times*, March 21, 1957, p. 7.

222 Schnabel, *Officer Mama*, p. 25.

223 Mary Elizabeth Plummer, "Women Invade Police Ranks," *Mansfield (OH) News-Journal*, August 27, 1950, p. 7.

224 "Young Policewoman, Teenager Team," *San Antonio Express*, September 15, 1959, p. 1.

225 "Dope-User Suspects Lured into Arrest," *Arizona Republic*, December 15, 1959, p. 14.

226 Rosalie Robles, "She's a Trim Pert Lady Cop," *Tucson Daily Citizen*, June 23, 1960, p. 28.

227 "LSD, Heroin Easy to Get in Portland," *Pasco, Kennewick, Richland (WA) Tri-City Herald*, January 19, 1968, p. 24.

228 "Women Get Wild Ride," *Southern Illinoisian*, July 26, 1968, p. 17.

229 Joan Halloran and Geraldine Perry, Chicago Police Department, interview with author.

230 Phil Gunby, "Champs Rarely Come Prettier," *Billings (MT) Gazette*, October 17, 1963, p. 14.

231 Karl Kidder, "Fresno Policewomen Find Job Rough on Complexion," *Fresno Bee*, July 21, 1953.

232 "Mother's a Cop on Night Shift," *Long Beach (CA) Independent-Press-Telegram*, November 22, 1959, p. A-12.

233 "Policewoman Earns Badge, Makes Uniform," *Hammond (IN) Times*, July 3, 1966, p. 1.

234 "Grilling Is Man's Job, Boy Insists," *Lubbock (TX) Avalanche*, April 13, 1954, p. 9.

235 "Policewoman Quits, Accuses Chief of Making Advances," *Wisconsin State Journal*, July 18, 1953.

236 "Three Cops Quit as Woman Joins Force," *Paris (TX) News*, November 14, 1957, p. 1.

237 "Policewoman Quits in Huff at St. Louis," *Chillicothe (MO) Constitution-Tribune*, August 3, 1954, p. 3.

238 "Policewoman Quits Before Demotion Hits," *Jefferson City (MO) Sunday News and Tribune*, April 27, 1958, p. 16.

239 "Peephole-Drilling Milkman Meets Chicago Policewoman Eye to Eye," *Terre Haute (IN) Star*, January 12, 1950, p. 1.

240 "Masquerading Fugitive Seized By Policewoman," *Zanesville (OH) Times Recorder*, June 27, 1953, p. 1.

241 Jack French, *Private Eyelashes: Radio's Lady Detectives* (Albany, GA: Bearmanor Media, 2004).

242 James Padgitt, "Around Hollywood." *New Castle (PA) News*, July 17, 1950, p. 9.

243 Terry Vernon, "Tele-Vues: *Policewoman U.S.A*," *Long Beach (CA) Independent*, January 17, 1951, p. 28.

244 Erskine Johnson, "Female Friday Will Prowl," *Rhinelander (WI) Daily News*, September 26, 1957, p. 6.

245 "N.Y. Policewoman Spurned Quiz Spot," *Syracuse (NY) Herald-Journal*, November 4, 1959.

246 Boyd Stevens, "Question-Aires," *Dunkirk (NY) Evening Observer*, January 19, 1963, p. 2.

247 "One Man's Army," *Time*, March 1, 1954.

248 U.S. Senate, Subcommittee to Investigate the Administration of the Internal Security Act and Other Internal Security Laws of the Committee on the Judiciary, *Testimony of Stephanie Horvath, Detective, New York City Police Department, Scope of Soviet Activity in the United States,* 85th Cong., 1st sess., August 14, 1957.

249 "Policewoman Fired as Red," *Troy (NY) Times Record*, January 27, 1954, p. 19.

250 "Eleven-Year-Old Girl Says Parents Sold Her for Five Dollars and Tankful of Gas," *Lowell (MA) Sun*, January 30, 1951, p. 18.

251 Grant V. Messerly, "Daughter for Car? Pair Held," *Salt Lake Tribune*, November 9, 1961, p. B1.

252 "Belly Dancer Convincing Witness," *Long Beach (CA) Press-Telegram*, May 14, 1960, p. 1.

253 Lloyd Shearer, "The Two Worlds of a Policewoman," *Parade*, March 16, 1969, p. 7.

254 Ibid.

255 "Grand Rapids Policewoman Describes Her Activities," *Holland (MI) Evening Sentinel*, October 26, 1967, p. 7.

256 "Policewoman in Nun's Habit Halts Shakedown Plot," *Cedar Rapids (IA) Gazette*, March 4, 1969, p. 11A.

257 William H. Honan, "Felicia Shpritzer Dies at 87; Broke Police Gender Barrier," *New York Times*, December 31, 2000.

258 Adam Heilman, "Focus: Women in Blue," *Daily Pennsylvanian*, February 24, 1992.

259 "Court Spurns Policewoman Claim of Discrimination," *Kittanning (PA) Leader-Times*, May 9, 1967, p. 3.

260 Gold, *Top Cops*, p. 21.

261 "Policewomen Ask Equal Pay, Cite Discrimination," *Cedar Rapids (IA) Gazette*, June 18, 1969, p. 12B.

262 John McLoughlin, "Mrs. Barnes Wins Suit but Resigns as Cohoes Policewoman," *Troy (NY) Times-Record*, February 14, 1966, p. 1.

263 Ibid.

264 "Policewoman Does Routine Patrol Duty," *Troy (NY) Record*, November 29, 1969, p. B-22.

265 "Policewoman Says Calls for Aid Bring Help Fast," *San Antonio Express*, November 3, 1972, p. 4-A.

266 "Top Cop Draws Whistles," *Jefferson City (MO) Daily Capital News*, November 4, 1972, p. 15.

267 "New Program: Women Placed in Patrol Cars," *Morgantown (WV) Dominion News*, September 25, 1968, p. 9-B.

268 "Policewoman Defends the Female Cruiser Partner," *Cedar Rapids (IA) Gazette*, September 25, 1968, p. 12B.

269 "Women on the Rise on City's Police Force," *Indianapolis Business Journal*, September 28, 1998.

270 Dorothy Moses Schulz, *From Social Worker to Crimefighter: Women in United States Municipal Policing* (Westport, CT: Praeger, 1995), 5, as quoted in Joanne Belknap, *The Invisible Woman: Gender, Crime, and Justice* (Belmont, CA: Wadsworth/Thomson Learning, 2001), p. 349.

271 "Policewomen Speak," *Syracuse (NY) Herald-American*, December 19, 1965, p. 35.

272 Gayleen Hays with Kathleen Moloney, *Policewoman One: My Twenty Years on the LAPD* (New York: Willard Books, 1992), p. 8.

273 Paul Hospodar, "Speaking About L.A. Police Job Opportunities," *Van Nuys (CA) News*, November 14, 1968, p. 2-A.

274 Don Maddock, "Policewoman Still Typical Women," *Long Beach (CA) Independent-Press-Telegram*, March 31, 1963, p. A-3.

275 Shearer, "The Two Worlds of a Policewoman."

276 Earl Griswold, "Women Gains in Police Jobs Told," *Long Beach (CA) Press-Telegram*, October 29, 1968, p. A-15.

CHAPTER 5

277 Tricia Crane, "Lady Cop Cashes In on Capers," *Van Nuys (CA) Valley News*, October 20, 1977, p. 3.

278 Joan McKinney, "Saundra Scores a Police First," *Oakland Tribune*, December 14, 1970, p. 28.

279 Kim Zangar, Washington State Patrol, interview with author.

280 "The Women in Blue," *Time*, May 1, 1972.

281 "Hire Woman, Judge Tells Police Force," *Ogden (UT) Standard-Examiner*, May 15, 1974, p. 8A.

282 Lora Lee (Lori) Fry, Madison (WI) Police Department, interview with author.

283 Donna Bacus, Iowa State Patrol, interview with author.

284 Jill Rice, Indiana State Police, interview with author.

285 Norma Jean Almodovar, *Cop to Call Girl: Why I Left the LAPD to Make an Honest Living as a Beverly Hills Prostitute* (New York: Simon & Schuster, 1993), p. 14.

286 Julie Scharper, "Annapolis Force's First Woman Retires," *Baltimore Sun*, September 11, 2008.

287 Adam C. Eisenberg, "The First Nine: Lure of Equal Pay Changed SPD Culture Forever," *Seattle Post Intelligencer*, October 28, 2001, p. D-4.

288 Ibid.

289 Ibid.

290 McKinney, "Saundra Scores a Police First."

291 "First Black Policewoman Named to Oakland Force," *Oxnard (CA) Press-Courier*, December 16, 1970, p. 3.

292 McKinney, "Saundra Scores a Police First."

293 Lisa Schuetz, "Retired Cop Recalls Blazing a Couple Trails," *Wisconsin State Journal,* October 2, 2004, p. B1.

294 Ibid.

295 Ibid.

296 The Police Foundation, "About the Police Foundation," http://www.policefoundation.org/docs/history.html.

297 "Police Biased Against Women," *Jefferson City (MO) Post-Tribune*, April 12, 1972, p. 13.

298 Richard Nixon, "Statement About Signing the Equal Employment Opportunity Act of 1972," March 25, 1972, American Presidency Project, http://www.presidency.ucsb.edu/ws/index.php?pid=3358.

299 Michele Vaughan, "History of Women in the Ohio State Highway Patrol," Ohio State Highway Patrol. http://statepatrol.ohio.gov/recruitment/FemaleMinority/historywomen.htm.

300 Eisenberg, "The First Nine."

301 "Policewoman Files Discrimination Suit," *Tyrone (PA) Daily Herald*, February 11, 1976, p. 8.

302 "Policewoman to Continue Fight in Sex Battle," *Connellsville (PA) Daily Courier*, March 8, 1976, p. 4.

303 Ibid.

304 "Policewoman's Sex Bias Complaint Rejected By State," *Sheboygan (WI) Press*, December 29, 1976, p. 3.

305 "Chief Frank's 'Girl Friday,'" *Sheboygan (WI) Journal*, November 18, 1972, p. 34.

306 M. Rebecca Downing, York County (PA) Police Department, interview with author.

307 Tom Baldwin, "State Police-Woman Quits Force, Charges Harrassment," *Dubois (PA) Courier-Express*, June 14, 1974, p. 1.

308 "Barger Tried to Fashion Reputation as Reformer," *Oil City (PA) Derrick*, January 14, 1976, p. 2.

309 Virginia Fogt, Ohio State Highway Patrol, interview with author.

310 Eisenberg, "The First Nine."

311   Zangar, interview.

312   Katherine Martin, *Women of Courage: Inspiring Stories from the Women Who Lived Them* (Novato, CA: New World Library, 1999), pp. 213–14.

313   Ibid.

314   Gregory Simms, "Race and Sex: Keys to Lady Cop's Case in Police Shoot-out," *Jet*, March 25, 1976, pp. 24–27.

315   "Madeline Fletcher Gets Police Job Back and $7,000," *Jet*, October 1976, p. 28.

316   "Black Policewoman Finished in Flint?" *Benton Harbor–St. Joseph (MI) Herald-Palladium*, October 22, 1977, p. 14.

317   "Policewomen to Appeal Firings for Cowardice," *Alton (IL) Telegraph*, March 19, 1980, p. A-7.

318   "Department Doesn't Support Firing," *Ironwood (MI) Daily Globe*, May 30, 1980, p. 6.

319   Linda Witt, "The Force Says It's with Them, but Detroit's Women Cops Have Had to Fight for Acceptance," *People*, October 6, 1980.

320   Micki Siegel, "Undercover Cop Kathy Burke—She Flirts with Danger," *Parade*, October 17, 1976, p. 8.

321   Ibid.

322   Georgene Kaleina, "Police Decoy: Learning to Act Like a Prostitute Rough," *Frederick (MD) News*, August 14, 1978, p. B-5.

323   "Woman, 22, Bans Pusher of Drugs," *Pasadena Star-News*, December 9, 1971, p. C-2.

324   "Policewoman Nabs Cop in Assault Case," *Tyrone (PA) Daily Herald*, June 8, 1979, p. 4.

325   "Hooker Real Crime Stopper," *Brownsville (TX) Herald*, April 30, 1976, p. 16.

326   "Not 'Out to Lunch,' but 'Out to Sex,'" *Moberly (MO) Monitor-Index*, October 25, 1972, p. 19.

327   "Flatfoot Floozies," *Time*, May 18, 1970.

328   "Former Nun Is Prostitute for Police," *Lincoln (NE) Star*, August 23, 1976, p. 3.

329   "Policewoman Finds Decoy Role Boring," *Lima (OH) News*, July 27, 1974, p. 8.

330 "Task Described as 'Immoral,'" *Victoria (TX) Advocate*, May 21, 1970, p. 7B.

331 "Woman Helps Vice Squads," *Idaho Free Press & News-Tribune*, July 15, 1974, p. 11.

332 Gay Pauley, "This Nun Is Policewoman and Carries a Gun in D.C.," *Bridgeport (CT) Post*, May 25, 1970, p. 26.

333 "Policewoman, 51, Surrenders Star to Become Nun," *Cedar Rapids (IA) Gazette*, August 30, 1964, p. 8-C.

334 "Young Lady Keeps Fighting to Become Police Officer," *Lebanon (PA) Daily News*, June 25, 1970, p. 34.

335 Phil Casey, "Women Seeking Jobs That Were Once Considered Strictly Male," *Greeley (CO) Tribune*, August 22, 1969, p. 26.

336 "Young Lady Keeps Fighting."

337 Ibid.

338 "Being Chicago's First Mounted Policewoman Has Its Advantages, Too," *Jefferson City, (MO) News Tribune*, August 24, 1975.

339 "Policewoman Doesn't See Sense in Her Reassignment," *Lincoln (NE) Star*, April 1, 1977, 12.

340 Maury Macht, "There's a Woman on City Police Beat," *Hagerstown (MD) Daily Mail*, April 1, 1977, p. 13.

341 Ibid. p. 340.

342 Mary Terry, "Officer Finds Work a Challenge," *Columbia (SC) State*, December 20, 1973, p. D1.

343 "Former Model Discusses First Duty as Oakland Policewoman," *Ukiah (CA) Daily Journal*, June 27, 1978, p. 8.

344 "Pantsuits for Policewomen Given Go-Ahead by Nichols," *Detroit News*, c. 1971, issue data unavailable, via Criminal Justice and Law Center, Lansing Community College.

345 Alice Scott, Los Angeles County Sheriff's Department, interview with author.

346 Gay Pauley, "Policewomen Performing the Same Duties as Policemen," *Brownsville (TX) Herald*, April 7, 1974, p. 7-C.

347 Ashley Cheshire, "Policewoman Prove Capabilities on Patrol Duty," *Tucson Daily Citizen*, August 16, 1972, p. 15.

348 Deborah Gilbreath Montgomery, interview with Kate Cavett, July 11, 2005, http://www.oralhistorian.org/SPPD__Montgomery.htm.

349 Lynda Castro, Los Angeles County Sheriff's Department, interview with author.

350 Eve Sharbutt, "Policewoman on Beat Carries Nightstick as Well as Lipstick," *Oxnard (CA) Press-Courier*, November 28, 1972, p. 9.

351 Lucille Burrascano, New York Police Department, interview with author.

352 "Policewoman Receives High Rank," *Cedar Rapids Gazette*, January 24, 1972, p. 12.

353 "Policewoman Suggests Women on Patrol Duty," *Albuquerque Journal*, December 10, 1971, p. E-9.

354 Veneza Aguinaga, Los Angeles County Sheriff's Department, interview with author.

355 Avery Keener, "'Bull's-Eye Betty' Is Top Policewoman." *Aiken (SC) Standard*, December 3, 1970, p. 5-B.

356 Roberta Abner, Los Angeles County Sheriff's Department, interview with author.

357 Bernadette Jaramillo, New Mexico State Patrol, interview with author.

358 Crane, "Lady Cop Cashes In."

359 Phil Thomas, "Lady Cop Turns Writer," *Jefferson City (MO) Post Tribune*, June 13, 1973, p. 10.

360 Crane, "Lady Cop Cashes In."

361 "Sue Ane Langdon's Ideas on a Policewoman's Life," *TV Times*, November 10, 1973, p. 7.

362 "Angie Dickinson Cops Police Role," *San Antonio Express*, March 25, 1974, p. 10.

363 Jerry Buck, "Actress Favors Sex Appeal in Screen Realism of Today," *Lumberton (NC) Robesonian*, November 18, 1974, p. 5.

364 Diane Mermigas, "Angie Objects to Pepper's Use of Spice to Lure Bad Guys, Audience," *Arlington Heights (IL) Daily Herald*, March 10, 1978, pp. 4–7.

CHAPTER 6

365 Kim Lonsway, "Law and Order Roundtable Discussions: Police Women and the Use of Force," *Law and Order Magazine*, July 2001, pp. 109-114.

366 Shannon Spreckelmeyer, Indiana State Police, interview with author.

367 Judy Gerhardt, Los Angeles County Sheriff's Department, interview with author.

368 Speckelmeyer, interview.

369 Julie Myer, Wisconsin State Police, interview with author.

370 Elizabeth Whitfield, New Mexico State Police, interview with author.

371 Marilyn Baker, Los Angeles Sheriff's Department, interview with author.

372 Mona Ruiz with Geoff Boucher, *Two Badges: The Lives of Mona Ruiz* (Houston, TX: Arte Público Press, 1997). p. 228.

373 Lora Lee (Lori) Fry, Madison (WI) Police Department, interview with author.

374 Lori McGrath, Nevada Highway Patrol, interview with author.

375 Rhonda Fleming, Texas Highway Patrol, interview with author.

376 Spreckelmeyer, interview.

377 Lynda Castro, Los Angeles County Sheriff's Department, itnerview with author.

378 Julia Grimes, Alaska State Troopers, interview with author.

379 Peggy Fox, Topeka (KS) Police Department, interview with author.

380 Fry, interview.

381 Beth Bradbury, Idaho State Police, interview with author.

382 Fry, interview.

383 Bradbury, interview.

384 *Bouman v. Block*, 940 F.2d 1211 (9th Cir., 1991).

385 Beth Shuster, "Sheriff's Dept. in Belated Effort to End Gender Bias," *Los Angeles Times*, October 16, 2000, p. A-1.

386 Ibid.

387 Roberta Abner, Los Angeles County Seriff's Department, interview with author.

388 Sheila Sanchez, Los Angeles County Sheriff's Department, interview with author.

389 Timothy Egan, "Chief of Police Becomes the Target in an Oregon Anti-Gay Campaign," *New York Times*, October 4, 1992.

390 Brad Cain, "Oregon's Gay-Marriage Foes Submit Record Signatures," *Seattle Times*, July 1, 2004.

391 Sarah Kershaw, "Oregon Supreme Court Invalidates Same-Sex Marriages," *New York Times*, April 15, 2005.

392 Brad Knickerbocker, "Tug of War Intensifies on Gay-Marriage Issue," *Christian Science Monitor*, May 5, 2005.

393 Sara Jaramillo, Los Angeles Police Department, interview with author.

394 "Field Day for Looters: 'If You See Something, You Take It,'" *Alton (IL) Telegraph*, May 1, 1992, p. C-3.

395 Ibid.

396 "Trooper Says She Feared Heckling If She Helped King," *Elyria (OH) Chronicle-Telegram*, March 30, 1993, p. A-6.

397 Grimes, interview.

398 Jennifer Crews-Carey, Annapolis (MD) Police Department, interview with author.

399 Rice, interview.

400 Grimes, interview.

401 Ethel Diké, Columbia (SC) Police Department, interview with author.

402 Brian Coddington, "Memorial Planned for Slain ISP Officer," *Spokane (WA) Spokesman-Review*, June 21, 1998.

403 Michele McPhee, "Cop Left to Raise Daughter Coping with Loss," *Southern Illinoisian*, September 12, 2002, p. 3.

404 Al Baker, "911 Dispatchers Still Haunted by Voices of September 11th Attacks," *Indiana Gazette,* April 17, 2002, p. 9.

405 Phoenix Police Department, "Arizona Police Officer Jennifer Moore Inducted Into IACP/DuPont Kevlar Survivors' Club," press release, November 12, 2008.

406 Amy Westfeldt, "Female Police Officer Shot, Killed During Bank Robbery," *Indiana Gazette*, January 3, 1996, p. 3.

407 Jonelle Greear, Idaho State Highway Patrol, interview with author.

408 "Rookie Cop Fatally Shot Four Days After Graduation," *Arlington Heights (IL) Daily Herald*, February 24, 1994, p. 19.

409 Cheryl Sanders, Tennessee Highway Patrol, interview with author.

410 Tim Brooks and Earl Marsh, *The Complete Directory to Prime Time Network TV Shows, 1946–Present* (New York: Ballantine, 2007), p. 123.

411 Peter Horne, "Policewomen: Their First Century and the New Era," *Police Chief*, September 2006. http://www.policechiefmagazine.org/magazine/index.cfm?fuseaction=display_arch&article_id=1000&issue_id=92006.

412 David Simon, *Homicide: A Year on the Killing Streets* (New York: Ivy Books, 1991), p. 48.

413 Lisa Desimini, author/artist, interview with author.

414 Horne, "Policewomen."

415 "Topics: On the Street Police Story," *New York Times*, August 2, 1985.

416 Susan Reed, "Nicknamed 'Calamity Jane,' Rookie Cop Anita McKeown Gets Nothing but Bad Breaks," *People*, August 12, 1985.

417 Roxanne Arnold, "'Calamity Jane': Rotten Luck is Officer's Beat," *Los Angeles Times*, December 24, 1986, p. OC12.

418 "Suspended Policewoman Sues for $1 Million," *Galveston Daily News*, April 27, 1982, 5 B.

419 "Officer Is Awarded Back Pay," *New York Times*, November 10, 1985.

420 George James, "Police Officer in *Playboy*; This Time, Official Yawns," *New York Times*, June 27, 1994.

421 "Policewoman Fired After Posing in Nude," *Daily Sitka (AK) Sentinel*, March 8, 1995, p. 10.

422 Joseph P. Fried, "Following up: The 'N.Y.P.D. Nude' Enjoys Work Again," *New York Times*, August 8, 2004.

423 "Top Cop in Buff Huff, Wants Play Time Over," *New York Daily News*, March 9, 1995.

424 Laura Fahrenthold, Alice McQuillan, and Michael Lewittes, "Under Covers Cop Another Nudie Run for NYPD," *New York Daily News*, March 29, 1995.

425 Ibid.

426 "Cop Poses in *Playboy*," *Extra Spin*, May 30, 2001, http://telepixtvcgi. warnerbros.com/reframe.html?http://telepixtvcgi.warnerbros.com/daily-news/extraspin/05_01/05_30a.html.

427 David Pierson, "LAPD Officer Leaves Uniform Off for *Playboy*," *Los Angeles Times*, May 30, 2001, p. B-3.

428 Robert Reinhold, "Policewoman in Denim Is Betty Grable of Gulf," *New York Times*, February 15, 1991.

429 Ibid.

430 Katherine Martin, *Women of Courage: Inspiring Stories from the Women Who Lived Them* (Novato, CA: New World Library, 1999), p. 239.

431 Ibid.

432 Dorothy Moses Schulz, *Breaking the Brass Ceiling: Women Police Chiefs & Their Paths to the Top* (Westport, CT: Praeger, 2004), p. 150.

433 Penny Harrington, *Triumph of Spirit: An Autobiography* (Chicago: Brittany Publications Ltd., 1999).

434 Harrington, *Triumph of Spirit*.

435 Roberto Suro, "Houston Mayor Removes Female Police Chief," *New York Times*, February 18, 1992.

436 Wendy Cole, "To Each Her Own: Combining Talent and Drive, Ten Tough-Minded Women Create Individual Rules for Success," *Time*, November 8, 1990, p. 46.

437 Walter Shapiro, "Reforming Our Image of a Chief," *Time*, November 26, 1990, p. 80.

438 Suro, "Houston Mayor Removes."

439 Lisa Belkin, "Woman Named Police Chief of Houston," *New York Times*, January 20, 1990.

440 Suro, "Houston Mayor Removes."

441 Shapiro, "Reforming Our Image."

442 Belkin, "Woman Named Police Chief."

443 "Person of the Week: Ella Bully-Cummings," *ABC World News Tonight*, November 14, 2003, http://www.abcnews.go.com/WNT/personofweek/story?id=131845.

444 Ibid.

445 Ben Schmitt, "City Officials May Be Tried for Allegedly Slandering Police," *Detroit Free Press*, January 24, 2008.

446 Ibid.

447 "D.C.'s First Female Police Chief Not Afraid of a Challenge," *CNN: People You Should Know*, May 8, 2007, http://www.cnn.com/2007/US/05/08/pysk.lanier/index.html.

448 U.S. District Court for the District of Columbia, *Deposition of Sgt. Cathy Lynn Lanier*, Civil Action No. 95-1297 (SS), Washington, D.C., April 16, 1996.

449 Ibid.

450 Ibid.

451 Angela Valdez, "Feeling Blue," *Washington City Paper*, May 2, 2007, http://www.washingtoncitypaper.com/display.php?id=1397.

452 Jim Leusner, "Orlando's New Police Chief Brings Take-Charge Attitude to Job," *Orlando Sentinel*, November 28, 2007.

453 Ibid.

454 Ibid.

CHAPTER 7

455 Meghan Durbak, "Mom on the Force," *Kokomo (IN) Tribune*, May 11, 2008, p. A6.

456 Michelle Cotten, Virginia State Police, interview with author.

457 Peter Horne, "Policewomen: Their First Century and the New Era," *Police Chief*, September 2006.

458 United States Department of Labor, Women's Bureau, "Quick Stats 2007," http://www.dol.gov/wb/stats/main.htm.

459 Elizabeth Robinson, Indianapolis Police Department, interview with author.

460 Peggy Fox, Topeka (KS) Police Department, interview with author.

461 Lynda Castro, Los Angeles County Sheriff's Department, interview with author.

462 Donna Bacus, Iowa State Patrol, interview with author.

463 Horne, "Policewomen."

464 Joel Rubin, "SWAT to Get Female Trainee," *Los Angeles Times*, March 29, 2008, p. B-5.

465 Julie Myer, Wisconsin State Police, interview with author.

466 Cotten, interview.

467 Bacus, interview.

468 Shannon Spreckelmeyer, Indiana State Police, interview with author.

469 Lora Lee Fry, Madison (WI) Police Department, interview with author.

470 Bernadette Jaramillo, New Mexico State Patrol, interview with author.

471 Robinson, interview.

472 Jonelle Greear, Idaho State Highway Patrol, interview with author.

473 Adelaide Kerr, "Women at Their Work, Lady Cop Likes Job," *Council Bluffs (IA) Nonapreil*, June 11, 1946, p. 6.

INDEX

AUTHOR BIOGRAPHY

ALLAN T. DUFFIN writes books; magazine, newspaper and Web articles; and television and feature scripts. A recipient of the Bronze Star medal for outstanding leadership in a combat zone, he is a veteran of the U.S. Air Force who commanded three squadrons during his time in uniform. Allan has written and produced for the History and Discovery TV networks, taught college history courses, consulted on website design and marketing, and worked at the museum at the Massachusetts Institute of Technology and the film archive at the University of Southern California. He has a master's degree in history from Northeastern University in Boston and a bachelor's degree from the Massachusetts Institute of Technology. He lives in Los Angeles with his wife Michele. Visit Allan's Web site at www. aduffin.com.